WHEN BIG DATA WAS SMALL

WHEN BIG DATA WAS SMALL

My Life in Baseball Analytics and Drug Design

RICHARD D. CRAMER | *Foreword by John Thorn*

University of Nebraska Press | *Lincoln*

Library of Congress Control Number: 2018047749

Set in Chaparral Pro by Mikala R. Kolander.

Frontispiece. A page from my first baseball research project, showing who played each position for every American League team from 1941 to 1945. Starting by spacing the team names onto blank sheets of paper, five columns of league seasons to a page, I worked through Turkin and Thompson's *Official Encyclopedia* player list, entering any player season of one hundred or more games played into an appropriate empty position slot. I then tried to fill the remaining empty slots, wherever no one had played one hundred games, by repeated season-by-season passes through Turkin and Thompson. Courtesy of the author.

Contents

Foreword
JOHN THORN

Five or six years ago, Bill James and I were booked for a panel at the MIT Sloan Sports Analytics Conference. As we walked the long corridor toward the ballroom in which we were to appear, I remarked upon the hundreds if not thousands of fresh-faced young people who surrounded us on all sides, each hoping to make a career in sports analytics.

"Remember when the number of sports analysts was a relative handful?" I asked him.

"I remember," he replied, "when you could fit all of them in a hotel room."

Even in 1977, when James self-published his first *Baseball Abstract*, Dick Cramer would have been in the room. He was present at the creation, when the entirety of SABR's statistical analysis committee consisted of Dick and Pete Palmer.

But, you may be asking, who is Dick Cramer? Why would he write a memoir? I can answer the first, briefly, as I have known him for thirty-five years, and we have played now and then in the same baseball sandbox; he will tell you a great deal more soon enough. But it is the second question that truly commends this book to your attention.

Cramer has led a life of extraordinary accomplishment, fueled by curiosity coupled with persistence and a knack for making things work. *When Big Data Was Small* recalls a seemingly simpler time when information science was finding its feet and so was he. His interests as a boy might have predicted the future of many an aspiring nerd, myself included: list-making, model-airplane building, Gilbert chemistry sets (and Erector sets), baseball statistics and simulations, antiquarian music (in his case Dixieland, in mine country blues). Finding reality not altogether satisfying, he suspected that Pythagoras might have had it right—that in mathematics one might hear the music of the spheres.

A winner of lifetime achievement awards in baseball and in chemistry, both for information-based work, Cramer grew up near Wilmington, Delaware, where his father worked for DuPont. He tells the story of his formative years in an utterly charming way, describing offhand oddities as if they were the run of the mill. This portion of the book is to me sweet, sad, and splendidly ordinary: all of us experienced childhood as he did, seldom pausing to think that our experiences, or indeed ourselves, might be in the least unusual.

Young Dick turned to baseball early on. In 1958, when he was sixteen, he bought a baseball dice game called APBA (an acronym for American Professional Baseball Association), in which players performed as probability indicated, based upon their past performances. That his favorite team, the Philadelphia Phillies, managed to toss away the 1964 pennant with an epic slide in the season's final weeks may have confirmed for him that the mathematical realm of baseball might be less frustrating. Later in that decade, he moved beyond APBA to computer simulations, including OXS, or on-base times slugging, his invention of an early incarnation of OPS (on-base plus slugging).

With Pete Palmer, he was present at the creation of the baseball analytics movement—at first in a nascent baseball research society, later within Major League Baseball via the first computerized analytics system in the game for the Oakland A's in 1981. (It was in that year that I met Palmer.) Along the way, Cramer had earned an AB in Chemistry and Physics from Harvard and a PhD in Physical Organic Chemistry from MIT.

The implications of analyzing a team's assets (players) mathematically rather than intuitively led Bill James to label the analytical movement sabermetrics, in honor of SABR (the Society for American Baseball Research), where so many of us had cut our teeth; when Michael Lewis named it "moneyball" in his book of that title, the concept soon began to extend beyond baseball to the unrelated realms of microbiology, economic markets, and data mining research, with new avenues to understanding opened up by what has come to be termed big data.

Beginning with a baseball dice game and a boyhood chemistry set, Cramer has come up with discoveries that transformed both disciplines. He was a cofounder of STATS LLC, which after some corporate shakeout that included Dick's departure, continues as a force in sports information.

In a delightful confluence of Cramer's vocation and avocation, in 2013 he received the Herman Skolnik Award, presented by the American Chemical Society's Division of Chemical Information. This entitled him to chair a symposium at which University of Delaware emeritus professor of microbiology David W. Smith spoke. In the baseball community Smith is known as the founder of Retrosheet, which excavates play-by-play records of ancient major league games. Cramer has long provided Retrosheet with a significant percentage of such finds and at the time of this writing has turned his records-spelunking efforts to the nineteenth century.

For a memoir to be worth reading, it ought to sum up not only one's own accomplishments but also the people who were important in enabling or obstructing them. Even the most seemingly solitary life, populated largely with ideas and actions, is lived among others. Present at the creation and himself a creator, Dick was, like all of us, more than the workings of his own mind.

What makes this book more than a curriculum vitae, no matter how distinguished, is that it is about a life like any other: filled with great expectations and shattering disappointments, both personal and professional. Cramer pulls no punches, while acknowledging his share in whatever mischief may have befallen him. Has he loved his work too much and hewn to his own path in an uncompromising way? Perhaps. But from where I sit, his is a life worth emulating and his endeavor—in his eighth decade, making bold to write a memoir—may be worth emulating too.

Acknowledgments

This memoir owes its existence to John Thorn, Major League Baseball's official historian, who first convinced me that I should write a memoir and then, after some pointers about writing conversationally and candidly, and inspection of my first efforts, assured me that others might enjoy reading the result.

Introduction

The world we live in is mostly uncertain and unpredictable. Yet each and every one of our ancestors, all the way back to the primordial archaea, is one of the few organisms in each generation who survived and reproduced, in part because they better predicted (though far more often lucked into!) what would happen next and took appropriate action. A drive for better prediction has been baked into our genes.

Okay. But where do predictions come from? If you think about it a little, the only possible basis for any prediction is previous experience, by oneself or (especially for humans) as reported by others. Prediction then is a recognition, consciously or unconsciously, that some pattern among past experiences makes some future event more likely to occur. And such patterns are more likely to be recognized whenever experiences have been recorded and somehow organized. For example, recognizing that weather tends to repeat itself in 365-day patterns depended on someone counting sunrises and associating each day's weather with the pattern of the stars—over many years. Using that prediction to decide when to hunt animals or plant crops worked much better than simply sowing on the next warm moist day, because nice days occur as often in October as in April. And it worked almost as well before it was discovered that the earth actually went around the sun, rather than the other way around.

The term *big data* vaguely summarizes the immense collections of organized past experiences made possible by the latest information technologies. These collections are foundations for our expectations of personalized medicine or self-driving cars, and already, by empowering Facebook or Google, they quietly but significantly impact our lives. Within big data, searching for predictive patterns requires specialized and increasingly complex statistical methodologies, for which *analytics* has become something of a buzzword.

Even more of a big data buzzword is "moneyball," originally the title of an acclaimed book and movie that recounts how the Oakland Athletics baseball team succeeded, despite financial weakness, by embracing novel performance statistics as well as scouts' judgments when making player decisions.[1] Perhaps because of the dramatic tension between the cultures of statistical analysis and athletic competition, moneyball then became a general label for an emphasis on measurable quantities over subjective opinions when making organizational decisions. At least in baseball, where hundreds of millions of dollars can depend on the performance of one individual, the teams that most rapidly and effectively blended these two disparate cultures have indeed experienced the better records.

The success of moneyball is also my reason for deciding to write this memoir. For, as *Moneyball* and another noteworthy book, *The Numbers Game*, relate, I was heavily involved in the birth of baseball analytics, also called sabermetrics.[2] During the 1970s, before fantasy games, personal computers, and Bill James's incandescent writing triggered an explosion of interest in baseball analytics, almost its entire literature was letters and manuscripts I exchanged with Pete Palmer. One study in particular, on clutch hitting, became something of an enduring classic, among others summarized in John Thorn's *The Hidden Game of Baseball*.[3] These experiences primed me for a remarkable opportunity, to create and develop probably the first in-depth, pitch-by-pitch baseball information system while cofounding and then refounding STATS Inc., which today as STATS LLC is the worldwide leading provider of sports statistics, its little red logo appearing in the credits at the ends of many televised sporting events. There are a lot of origin stories yet to be told and a few details to be amplified and clarified.

Yet for me baseball was always a side interest, even if a very intense one for fifteen years. My real fifty-year career was founded on different big data activities, as a chemist who pioneered in the use and development of specialized analytics approaches, intended to guide the discovery of pharmaceutical drugs, collectively known as computer-aided drug discovery (CADD). Any international renown that I've enjoyed has resulted from that work, especially the creation of comparative molecular field analysis (CoMFA), whose popularity is attested by many thousands of publications citing its use and, I like to think, must somewhere have contributed to the all-too-rare discovery of a new medicine. And there is a second startup story of a company called Tripos, whose CADD software product, Sybyl, was the worldwide leader for twenty years, but which like most startups eventually stumbled and was absorbed, digested, and finally eliminated by a larger company, Certara. Therefore, with apologies in advance to any of you who are turned off by geeky scientific stuff (as opposed to geeky baseball stuff?), I must tell you something about drug discovery, computer-aided, with a few thoughts about how analytics and big data have become central to baseball and might be made more effective for drug discovery.

Receiving lifetime achievement awards in both baseball research and computational chemistry would seem to establish my credentials in these fields, but are these activities representative of big data? Admittedly, the quantities of their "recorded and organized experiences" (okay, from now on let's just say "data") were tiny compared to today's big data galaxies. But in their day, these were new systems that stretched the limits of the available hardware. Wikipedia endorses my position, declaring that "big data . . . seldom [refers] to a particular size of data set." Surely the pervasive effect of analytics on baseball is irreversible—just look at how the infielders are constantly repositioning themselves. And some association of big data with drug discovery also seems enduring because novel analytics tools are often thrown at the frustrating mysteries of drug discovery—though so far with only modest and scattered successes. However, it should be noted that it is not analytics but physics-based simulation, in which most CADD scientists have been trained, that underlies most of the popular chirping about "discovering drugs with computers."

In any case, this book is primarily a memoir of a very lucky man who did not pursue some vision of wealth or fame and is as surprised as anyone at how well things turned out. I have always been much more of a Wozniak than a Jobs, taking life one step at a time, hoping for nothing more than earning a respectable salary for doing things I mostly enjoyed. Yet at several key moments, I just happened to be in the right place at the right time with the right skills and motivations. Along the way, my half century of grappling with the waves of advances in the underlying information technologies may be of some historical or nostalgic interest. I've also enjoyed interesting pursuits and adventures having little to do with baseball, drug discovery, or the computer. Finally, I've crossed paths with many well-known names, especially in baseball, and worked closely with some should-be luminaries, like the guy who while a high school student was probably the first to discover a recognizable form of the now omnipresent baseball statistic known as OPS and has today taught more than three hundred different courses at Harvard, perhaps more than anyone else in its history, or a fellow Dixieland jazz trombonist who reported creating the world's first operating system.

WHEN BIG DATA WAS SMALL

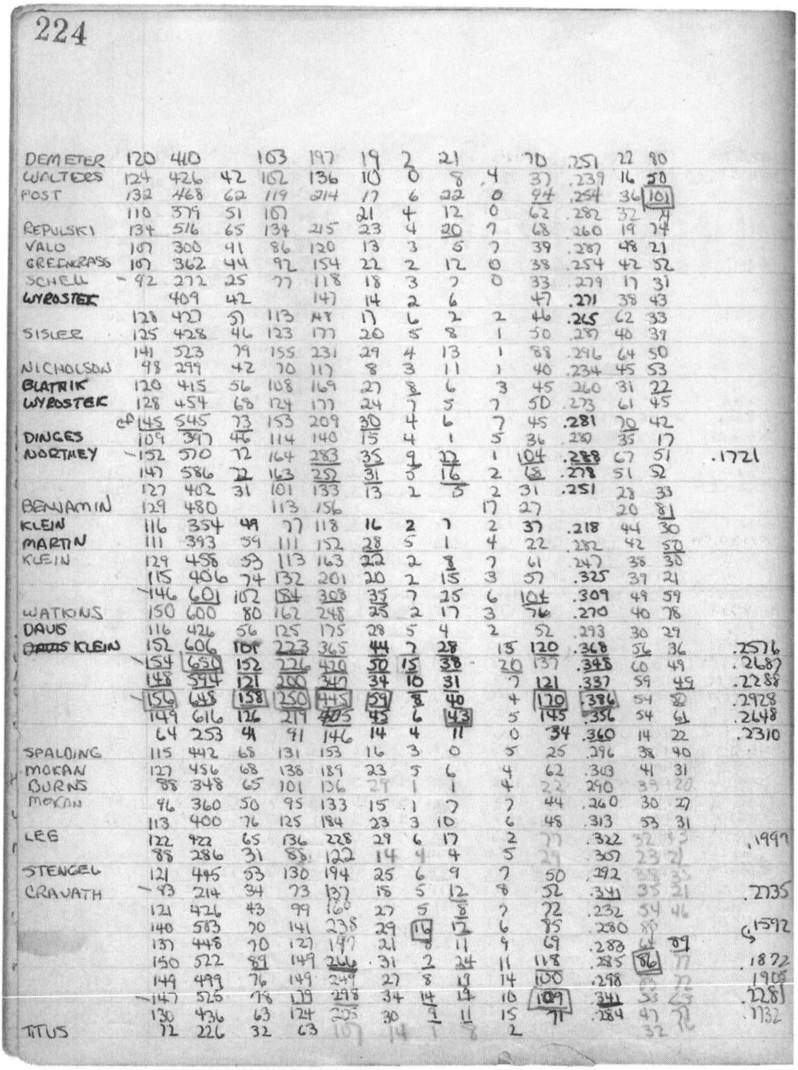

Fig. 1. A page listing every Phillies right fielder from 1911 to 1961 from my compilation of the most important statistics for the most important players. My motley sources were scattered contemporary newspapers and official baseball guides; I spent much of my first week ever in Los Angeles copying these values from guides in a sports library. The rightmost column contains a few slide-rule-generated values of on-base times slugging (OXS; effectively, runs contributed per plate appearance, as explained in chapter 6). Underlining marks team leaderships. Publication of the Macmillan *Baseball Encyclopedia* in 1969 ended this project (joyously!). Courtesy of the author.

1 Setting the Stage

My parents grew up in Norman Rockwell country, in two towns along the Juniata River in central Pennsylvania, linked by the Pennsylvania Railroad. Most of their predominantly Pennsylvania Dutch ancestry can be traced back to at least the early nineteenth century. My father's mother had wisdom and a warm spirit so compelling as to set the tone for the upbringing of all her fourteen grandchildren, and so lasting that half a century later those grandchildren and their grandchildren still faithfully attend an annual reunion. Education was her top priority, and despite Depression challenges her four children all finished college by commuting from home using free fares that her husband's administrative railroad career provided. My mother's father was a major figure in her town, as his youthful preference for automobiles over his mother's horse brokerage developed from a Model T Ford franchise into a garage that became the town's general store. But at her home there were tragedies—my mother's mother died of Spanish flu, and my mother's brother's crippling childhood polio, which he cheerfully overcame to become a world-traveling college history professor.

Both my parents were stand-out students in Juniata County, my mother reportedly being regarded as "smartest" and my father as "most likely to succeed." They met when the county included them both in a Washington field trip, and mutual attraction soon followed. After a 1937 public ceremony endorsed a year-old secret wedding, my mother followed my father to Harvard, where he had been accepted for PhD studies as a chemist. His thesis advisor was George Kistiakowsky, a genial Russian, then German, political émigré best known today as a key designer of the Fat Man nuclear weapon, and then as Eisenhower's

science advisor, the first to hold that position, before resigning to better challenge the military-industrial complex. (Considering the many
excellent books on various Los Alamos physicists, it is surprising that
no popular biography of such an interesting and accomplished chemist
exists.) "Kisti" was also a chemical da Vinci. My father's PhD thesis
described something completely different: the first use of a radioactive
atomic label in a biological experiment. This groundbreaking research
is still cited, which, because I was given my father's name, suggests
an implausibly long scientific career for Richard David Cramer in the
indices of scientific literature!

Marriage for a graduate student was then a somewhat risky endeavor,
undertaken only because, as my mother's classmates put it, "Gwen
knows how to marry without having children"—of course by means
that in Massachusetts were then legally banned. At Princeton, marriage
meant dismissal for a graduate student of either sex. But my mother
fondly recalled that her employment as secretary to a Baker Chocolate
executive allowed her to splurge on a home typewriter with special
chemical symbols so that she could proudly type my father's PhD thesis.

After the twelve lean years of Depression, in 1940 almost every American's priority was financial security and asset accumulation, so accepting an offer to leave an associate professorship at Carnegie Mellon in
grimy Pittsburgh to join a new research group at the DuPont Experimental Station in Wilmington, Delaware, was a no-brainer. The DuPont
four-thousand-dollar salary paid for a suburban house with an elegant
mansard roof and a 1937 Ford V8 and helped my father's younger siblings to finish their higher educations and become a high school district
supervisor, a radiologist, and a nurse turned wife to a DuPont engineer.
And, most important, it allowed my parents to start a family. I am the
oldest of four, who, reportedly as intended, was followed in two years
by a brother Marvin, after another three years by a sister, Mary, and in
two more years a second sister, Sara, whom we call Sally.

We four appreciate one another. Marv is a respected Long Island
cardiologist, married to Eva Cramer, a dean at State University New
York's Downstate College of Medicine, who now heads BioBAT, Brook-
lyn Navy Yard's new biotech center. They have two children, Jocelyn

and Jeff, and three grandchildren. Mary's marriage to David Dawson, a mathematician turned legacy IBM System/360 authority, produced two children, Richard and Megan. Sally administers the University of Massachusetts–Amherst's biochemistry department and farms in the Berkshires with her husband, Donald Ives. As children and as adults the four of us resemble each other (according to a midnight cabal of our spouses during one family reunion) in being conflict-averse, emotionally restrained, and responsible family members. We establish daily routines for ourselves that include personal health rituals, and we all read voraciously. Put differently, the four of us are perhaps light on charisma and even a bit dull at times, yet earnest, dependable, and reasonably accomplished.

When Pearl Harbor brought the United States into World War II, my father was old and DuPont-relevant enough to be exempt from the draft, and I was en route, to be born on February 26, 1942. I have vague memories of unexpectedly sitting in the dark one evening as my father walked the block looking for blackout violations that might silhouette an oil tanker for Nazi submarine attack, and of being carried to a victory garden that my father planted in a nearby vacant lot.

With everyone expecting the lean years to return when the war ended, my parents seemingly believed that financial security for their growing brood might depend on economic self-sufficiency, which implied acreage. In 1945 they chose a former farm owned and occupied by an eighty-year-old spinster, Mary Carlile, who had supported herself alone for many decades by selling off pieces of land originally granted to her ancestors by William Penn. Terms of her final hundred-acre sale to my parents included an agreement that she could stay in her house undisturbed as long as she was capable of doing so and required immediate payment in full, with an eight-thousand-dollar loan from my mother's father.

The house had been built during the farm's mid-nineteenth-century prosperity, achieved by meeting demands for milk from rapidly growing Philadelphia and for willow-tree charcoal to help make DuPont's black gunpowder. So it was a substantial three-story cube of double stone wall construction. But when refrigerator cars and smokeless powder appeared, these markets disappeared, so electricity or running water had never been added, and heating and cooking still required cutting wood. Not a satisfactory twentieth-century home, especially for a growing family. Moreover, mere habitability would not be sufficient for my father, and that reportedly provoked some private arguments, though ones acknowledged only after my father's death. For, perhaps remarkably, as children my siblings and I were absolutely never exposed to any parental disagreement. Furthermore, my father would have been embarrassed to express and was irritated even to be exposed to "gossipy" discussions of personal feelings or motivations. So it's not easy today to understand how such an exceptionally competent man convinced himself and my mother that he could almost singlehandedly remodel this worthy antique into a Frank Lloyd Wright–inspired showplace while, of course, earning his salary and paying appropriate attention to his children and the local community. It helped that he required little sleep; every evening he would commute the fifteen miles "out to the farm" to plan and work, seldom returning, I was told, before 1:00 a.m. On clement Saturdays and Sundays we would all pile into the Ford, drive to the farm, and picnic together. There were a few unsuccessful farming forays, such as the pasturing of a couple of steers on the least overgrown field, and the purchase and winter-long resuscitation of an antiquated Case 12-20 tractor to help clear the decades of brush, which after a week of noisy pushing and dragging expired while reportedly throwing a piece of crankcase just past my father's head.

But within a year or so Miss Mary suffered a stroke, and was admitted into an old folk's home where we would visit her every Christmas afternoon until her death. Serious remodeling began. Comprehensive architectural plans had already been drawn up, presumably with some professional assistance. Certainly professionals drove the bulldozer that carved the slope to position a garage and driveway. But my father brought in electricity and plumbing almost by himself, converting one of the two staircases into a tier of bathrooms and completely rerouting the other one, hiring only the occasional day laborer to help with heavier work like digging the septic tank. The farmhouse was ready for us in June 1950, with central heating added before winter set in.

Our new locale, a declining family farming community at the east-
ern end of the Mason–Dixon line near Landenberg, Pennsylvania,
was attracting other young DuPont professionals. The surroundings
included several ruined grain mills, a covered bridge then still very
much in use, scattered Indian arrowheads, and some reputed Under-
ground Railroad hiding holes. Elementary education was provided in
two one-room schools, each authentically equipped with hand pump
water and his-and-her privies, each schoolhouse respectively handling
around thirty pupils in grades one to three and four to six. Inadequate?
Well, two of my classmates and I would later attend Harvard!

For the most part, we newcomers blended smoothly with the existing community. There were community collaborations in the spirit of
traditional barn-raisings, one erecting a (prefabricated) community
building and another resuscitating a third vacant one-room school the
day after one of the other two burned down. There were only a few
awkward edges. In 1952 my father was elected to the local school board
as reportedly the only Democrat elected anywhere in Chester County,
thereby becoming a supervisor to our two teachers, one who, with the
veteran assurance of someone now teaching her previous students'
kids, had infused the classroom with her own politics, having us listen to MacArthur's now-notorious Korean recall speech to Congress.

Baseball? Not yet on my radar. Somehow the Phillies' 1950 pennant completely escaped my awareness. I didn't even know the basic
rules—in an informal Cub Scout game I was confused when a well-hit
ball was nullified for being foul. This is the more surprising as baseball
was integral to the culture of both my extended families. For example, my mother favored the Dodgers as a racially enlightened team,
though she preferred Roy Campanella to Jackie Robinson because he
didn't "make trouble." During visits to grandparents I was dragged to
the town's battered grandstands for baseball games, where a hat was
passed to pay something to the players and memories were shared of
big-leaguers such as Billy Cox. And eventually I went to my first major
league game, on September 27, 1953, when my father put aside a day
of remodeling for a family outing to watch the Dodgers edge the Phils
at Connie Mack Stadium.

I had been something of a wunderkind, reportedly reading by the age of two or three. Lists (or, might I offer, ur–big data?) were an early fascination. I spent hours copying and creating lists, charming my mother by using her beloved typewriter. At first these lists were of capital cities, but somehow by 1949 antique cars, and especially steam cars, had become my first major obsession. For example, if you wanted to know, say, what kinds of Fords preceded the Model T, I could (and perhaps still could!) enlighten you. At my mother's urging, I wrote an enthusiastic letter to the main provider of the antique car literature at the Wilmington Public Library, one Floyd Clymer, who confirmed that I was his youngest reader. (At that time, libraries were the only source of such specialized books because new books were so expensive that my mother satiated the family's general love of reading by haunting used book barns.)

However, with the family move to the farm, my privileged role in suburban classrooms as an indulged and unregulated "teacher's pet" prodigy was completely reversed in that one-room school to "know-it-all" pariah. The fourth-to-sixth-grade teacher disparaged my eager cleverness in favor of rote and disciplined order—unsurprisingly, considering her temperament and probable training as well as the educational demands inherent to a one-room school. Exceptionally thick glasses, deficiencies in empathy and ability to fit in (still extant, *sigh*), athletic ineptness, physical awkwardness, and pathologically picky eating didn't help. Surely suspect were my first appearance at the community Halloween event—my mother accentuated my Cinderella costume with grapefruit halves on my chest—and my preference during lunchtime recess for the playground swings with the girls, instead of the softball game with the boys. The beating my self-esteem took in those three years continued well into my twenties.

But weak self-esteem may have encouraged my development of other intense interests. In those days most boys collected stamps, which appealed to me perhaps because public library books included exhaustive stamp catalogs—in other words, more lists. Collecting stamps demanded more money than my monthly allowance provided, but the remodeling provided a lot of earning opportunities. One representative activity was stacking lumber. To provide the natural patina that Frank Lloyd Wright advocated, the architectural plans called for wood paneling, to be obtained by harvesting the farm's abundant hardwood regrowth. But between trees and paneled walls there's a lot of work; woodwork will warp and crack if the lumber is not first dried thoroughly, a process that takes years without kiln heating. So there were tons of lumber that had to be stacked and restacked, board by board, carefully spaced by shims between each layer so that the air could circulate. Once dried and milled, the lumber needed finishing, tedious and laborious work that we shared with our mother. Meanwhile there was year after year of dust and debris, in rooms sometimes demarcated only by two-by-fours and hanging canvas. Sally returned from her first visit to a neighboring farm to excitedly report that "they have doors on their bathrooms!" Nevertheless, in spirit we kids were completely on board and proudly anticipated a showplace, and with family meals and many family board game evenings, there was no reason for any of us to feel neglected.

However, in 1955 this remodeling campaign was interrupted. Our dog contracted rabies and bit my father. The Pasteur treatment induced an autoimmune response and a creeping neurological paralysis starting with his legs. The outlook for my parents must have been ominous. How far would the paralysis spread? Would my father lose his job? And what sort of financial asset was a half-finished remodeling project surrounded by stacks of lumber? Yet, as always, nothing of this sort was ever said aloud, so I doubt that any of us children ever sensed these threats. And as matters developed, for all the sorrow this illness brought for my parents, one of the results of my father's incapacitation was positive. His blunted passion for remodeling was constructively redirected to his research activities for DuPont, ultimately resulting in two prize-winning publications. He later commented that had this not happened, his previous indifference to his job would probably have cost him that job, just as would happen to many of our neighbors as DuPont began a long retrenchment. And remodeling activities were put into the hands of two expert carpenters, who made the work affordable for us because it was an especially gratifying project that they could fit into the gaps between their other jobs. Four years later the Frank Lloyd Wright inspiration had become a reality.

At about this time my mother was also succeeding at what was then something of a nationwide obsession, becoming a successful quiz show contestant. She succeeded twice in two attempts, on one show setting a record for longevity and on the other a record for total prize value. Both were daytime shows with contests that slowly revealed some common phrase, the winner of course being the first to decipher that phrase. One of the contests involved a rebus, a picture representing a word in the phrase; this might have been *The Jan Murray Show*. She would spend at least a year researching her target show, deciphering and recording any patterns in its phrases and pictures as she folded laundry. When she felt ready, she would travel to its New York studio, join the show's audience, and then, to encourage her selection as the latest challenger, sit near the aisle and behave very effervescently (not her usual persona). I was in the studio audience, at least as excited as she was, for what turned out to be the last of her appearances. Ironically the tax rates of that era made her winnings, mostly of whimsical products rather than cash, a mixed blessing for family finances, requiring further creativity. For example, there was the donation of a twelve-foot stuffed giraffe to a local high school for use in "street fairs," providing a deduction which allowed us to keep a relatively fungible but much more useful Oldsmobile 88 behemoth.

Her greatest accomplishment, though, was later: making possible the creation of the White Clay Creek State Park by her decades of solitary effort in ultimately blocking an ill-considered damming of the creek. But this story is not one that I know enough about to tell.

2 Baseball and Science Surface

My earliest notice of pennant races was in 1953, when a hot start by the Phillies prompted daily blackboard recording of the standings by my seventh-grade history teacher. Phillies hero Robin Roberts had been appearing live on our newly acquired TV as an off-season car salesman. I began perusing the baseball annuals and record books that my better-grounded brother had brought home and found—more lists! By 1955 my brother and I were inserting baseball into the family dinner conversations, and my father revealed his allegiance to the Pittsburgh Pirates. Maybe it was the Pirates' sorry performance in those years that fueled his uncharacteristic contempt for all things Phillies—the announcers were inarticulate homers, Ashburn didn't drive in runs, Willie Jones hogged popups to boost his fielding statistics. Another feasting on library books exposed me to baseball's well-recorded history, and a cousin introduced me to *The Sporting News*. During 1956 the daily pageantry of a baseball season became absorbing. More and more of my summer days were scheduled around a Phillies telecast or broadcast.

Model airplanes were then my biggest interest. These airplanes flew in a circle around an operator, who could make them climb or descend with a simple puppet-like control. I particularly enjoyed building models of World War I fighters from elaborate kits, constructed by gluing together bits of balsa and covering the resulting frame with doped silk. I also built a flying wing of my own (unsuccessful) design from sturdier wood. But controlling them was a problem. Repeatedly spending months building a model and then smashing it on a first flight was a depressing waste of time and money. So I recall a quite consciously economic decision to forsake model airplanes and enjoy more baseball.

Many fans memorialize the green-field panorama of their first Major League Baseball game, but what about their first in-depth baseball season? Especially if your team unexpectedly becomes involved in the pennant race? In the mid-1950s, major league standings had been rather constant year to year, with the Phillies finishing somewhere around .500 and fourth place. A big influx of newcomers suggested 1957 could be different. And indeed the Phillies battled four other teams in and out of first place, with a 56-44 record as late as August 1. But the Braves then pulled away, as the Phils fell back to another .500 season.

I was so impressed by an obscure contributor to the Phils' exciting July, Joe Lonnett, as he hit five of his six major league home runs, all in Phillie wins, that I even more improbably started ruminating about and projecting his lifetime totals. Then a classmate—female!—introduced me to the first baseball encyclopedia, compiled by Turkin and Thompson and published in 1951.[1] It provided only three statistics for every player season in major league history: fielding position, games played, and batting average (games won and lost for pitchers). Today, a website such as baseball-reference.com can display many hundreds of such statistics. Yet, if you imagine a single spreadsheet of every player's season-by-season statistics, the contents of this first encyclopedia would essentially complete its player season rows, with all other stats, old and new, simply being additional columns in such a conceptual spreadsheet. I was utterly captivated and persuaded her to let me borrow her copy, which, I'm ashamed to say, may be the one I still have.

Anyway, that winter, the Turkin-Thompson volume became the source for my first major baseball project, one that, though sabermetric in no more than spirit, clearly marked the onset of a serious baseball addiction. Baseball fans care much more about a favorite team than any individual player. Yet team wins and losses substantially depend on the performances of their most important players. Perhaps it was some such proto-sabermetric logic as well as my innate listing compulsion that persuaded me to reorganize Turkin-Thompson into a team-based compilation, listing regulars (those who most played at each position) for every major league team in history. The frontispiece contains a page that my mother preserved from this project. I absorbed lots of baseball history, and more to the point, of course, I thoroughly enjoyed the actual doing of the project.

Came next season. For its first half, the Phils struggled to break even, then collapsed in the second half, finishing last. This puzzled me, considering outstanding performances by some individual players, and indeed today's sabermetrical evaluation is that the 1958 Phillies should have been a sixth-place team. I took enormous solace from embracing the APBA baseball dice simulation game, a baptismal experience for so many baseball analysts. My parents had taken a rare vacation together, leaving me with some contingency funding. I don't remember why it seemed excusable, but I decided to use some of those funds to succumb to an alluring APBA advertisement. The cost of that 1957 (previous season's data) game was perhaps $200 in today's money, and surely I have never gotten a better return on an entertainment dollar! And my parents weren't all that upset on their return, when I of course agreed to work off the expense, maybe by distributing the chicken coop leavings onto the vegetable garden. (We still farmed whenever it wasn't too much trouble to do so.)

Some of my earliest APBA experiences could have been sabermetrically educational. Replaying an entire 154-game schedule was time-consuming at first because decoding each dice throw involved shuffling through two stacks of cardboard. So my first season replays were limited to the two New York teams. A few of the resulting season totals were painfully discordant with their actual values—the obscure Curt Barclay amassed a 4-20 won-lost record instead of his actual 9-9, and Gil McDougald's doubles total surpassed his actual 13 in the first month of the Yankee replay season. Was it really possible that random variation could produce such discrepancies? Or did they result from deficiencies in APBA as a model of real baseball play?

Anyway, it didn't take much insight to deduce that dividing a regular player's 600 seasonal plate appearances by APBA's 36 ordered dice roll possibilities would yield roughly 17 occurrences of each possibility, and then to observe how the APBA rules tuned this basic relationship to more precisely reproduce actual statistical counts by making the final event also dependent on the current baserunner situation. Ted Williams's card was especially provocative. Despite the .388 batting average it represented, it contained the same number of base-hit codes as Hal Smith's .303 batting average card. The reason of course was the great number of walk codes on Williams's card. In 1957 the actual frequency of base hits per plate appearance was indeed about the same for Smith as for Williams (though Williams's hits went farther!). But many of the die rolls that meant outs for Smith became walks for Williams, more chances for his teammates to hit, with an additional runner on base. That seemed like a good thing. Yet many fans and some professionals faulted Williams for accepting so many walks. (In fact, just as I am writing these words sixty years later, with the Phillies game webcast on, Mike Schmidt—whose acclamation as the greatest third baseman ever includes league-leading walk totals—is not sure that Odubel Herrera's unexpected [if transient] selectivity at the plate is benefiting the team!) And indeed there did seem something wrong with Williams's driving in only 87 runs with 38 home runs and a .388 batting average. So perhaps it was naïve to associate more runs and wins with more walks. Yet what was I overlooking?

The other focus of this memoir was also starting to take shape. Whenever vague thoughts of adulthood arose, I never imagined working at anything other than science. Even then I was completely convinced that technological progress is the primary engine of human progress— therefore it must be the right thing to do. And looking at my father's occupation and the others around our community, a PhD seemed a simple rite of passage, rather like a union card. I fortified these tenuous impressions with science fiction, again reading everything in the public library. Significantly, my heroes were inventors James Watt and Thomas Edison rather than "true" scientists Isaac Newton and Albert Einstein; I've always sought more to create new stuff than to discover new stuff. On the farm, my car interest became a hazard to any unused wheeled machinery, as I would unfasten pieces to see how they were constructed or visualize how they might be modified. Real science began with a Gilbert chemistry set and the observation that I could divert a bit of my father's attentions away from remodeling by asking him chemistry questions. The Gilbert inventory of reagents and equipment soon became somewhat professional because when my father had been in graduate school, students had to purchase for themselves and could therefore preserve everything they had used. So some dusty crates were opened and pillaged for usable chemicals and glassware. At that time attitudes toward chemical hazard were carelessly indifferent—my father had no objections to my bringing pound quantities of metallic mercury and uranium acetate back to the basement hand-me-down kitchen cabinet that my mother had donated to serve as my laboratory.

To provide education following the one-room schools, our township reimbursed the high school in Kennett Square, where I continued an undisciplined approach to studies that frustrated my parents. I'd work hard on the occasional subject or project that I liked, but usually after skimming the textbook, I daydreamed through classes and skimped on homework. Knowledge that was somehow structured was relatively engaging, so for example, within English classes, despite my addiction to reading, only diagramming sentences (a discipline that seems to have become an educational casualty) had any appeal. And my first science course, sophomore biology, with content then little beyond qualitative descriptions of cells and organisms, left me cold. But that autumn Sputnik went up, and my remaining science courses, chemistry and physics, also became patriotic priorities. With some coaching from my father, two prize-winning science projects followed—in my junior chemistry year, a collection of notionally pure elements mostly generated by electrolysis using a model train transformer, and in my senior physics year, a thermopile, which generates an electric current by heating alternate junctions along a circuit made from strands of regularly alternating metals.

3 College

In the fall of 1959, my mother and I set out for Harvard in her Oldsmobile trophy, thanks to the new highway network a mere one-day trip, marred only by the commonplace flat tire and the brown haze of air pollution over New York City. College had new distractions. Sputnik's challenge had helped to produce a freshman class whose majority envisioned a career in science, so I felt myself a bit less of the ugly duckling geek. But I'd never had a date, partially because the long school bus commute to Kennett Square had prevented any hanging out with high school classmates until I could drive, by which time the prevalent dating culture of going steady had limited the remaining possibilities. Having thus never learned any appropriate rituals and always being socially backward, my initial dating ventures in college were so mutually unsatisfactory that I abandoned most such embarrassing initiatives until graduate school.

It was rumored that someone named Paul Bamberg was the most promising among all of us aspiring freshmen scientists, and soon, courtesy of the Harvard Band, I crossed paths with this paragon. We quickly hit it off, beginning a lifelong friendship. For one important thing, we shared a strong proto-analytics interest in baseball. With a national-prize-winning high school science fair project, rewarded with a shake of President Eisenhower's hand, Paul had already discovered a variant of OPS, a fundamental sabermetric statistic that is today becoming more widely followed than batting average. Yet, and quite surprisingly and awkwardly considering our friendship, I was told of his discovery only some fifty years later, by an email from Paul after the moneyball phenomenon crested. Perhaps kindly, Paul will not offer any explanation of his reticence. Nevertheless, his discovery seems to have been the first rendition of a simple one-term OPS-like formula, to wit: $(H + W + TB) \div (2 \times (AB + W))$. These are the usual abbreviations, but for readers who are not baseball-jargon literate: H = hits of any type; W = walks; TB = total bases that the batter advanced on his own hit; AB = appearances at bat, excluding the walks. Because of its historical interest, various drawings from his original report, which a friend of his found somewhere online, obviously the work of a high school student, appear as figures 4 through 9, and the appendix reproduces his text.

The Harvard Band would also be the springboard for my third lifetime enthusiasm—playing Dixieland jazz, on either trombone or trumpet. In its spirit, this music seems almost the antithesis of organized big data, being mostly collective improvisation, and primitive and intuitive in its harmonies and emotional dynamics. Yet my hunger for the loosely controlled chaos of Dixieland jazz performance has been shared by an extraordinary proportion of the software pioneers I've met. My first exposure to what already was a declining musical genre had been from my father, who haunted jazz clubs while in graduate school and, as his illness curtailed remodeling activities, organized a monthly jazz-playing session of like-minded DuPonters at our home. We children were all taught to play piano from fake books, which provide melodies and chord progressions for popular tunes, and played various instruments in high school bands and orchestras. For me the music stuck, in part because I believed that it broadened my social image beyond "geek," hopefully with females. I began alleviating summer boredom by playing along with those of my father's records for which sheet music also existed, increasingly deviating from the printed page. When I returned to Harvard for my junior year, a note on the band's bulletin board sought a trumpet player for a newly forming Dixieland band, to be called the Seven Sons of Harvard. Sounded good to me, and I was deemed acceptable by its energetic organizer, Charles F. Goldfarb, who was secondarily (or so it seemed!) a law school student. Charles, being very much from New York, knew the promotional ropes and how to work them, so my next spring break saw my first plane flight with the band to Bermuda, and my next summer found the Seven in Germany at taxpayer expense, touring American army bases in underpowered VW microbuses as USO entertainers, mostly Ivy Leaguers playing dated jazz to GIs who hadn't gotten weekend leave. Not the most receptive of audiences, but there were also sit-ins in bomb shelters converted into jazz clubs, where crowds of German students uncritically admired the "authenticity" of any American jazz musician.

Charles took his Harvard Law School degree to IBM, where he would become the marketing pioneer for generalized markup languages as a lecturer and the lead author on the 1970 paper in which IBM first proclaimed this development.[1] Though you probably don't know it, you almost certainly speak a markup language—more exactly, your web browser, whether Explorer, Safari, or Chrome, speaks little else. More details of this event, the birth announcement of what might be dubbed the world's first truly universal language—reversing the curse of Babel?—can be found, appropriately, on the web.[2] And, if you're a veteran web programmer geek, you may own Charles's subsequent opus, *XML Handbook*, with more than one hundred thousand copies in print in six (conventional) languages.[3]

By the way, there was another Harvard Band trumpet player on European jazz tour that summer: Ken Houk, first chair as a freshman with an immaculate Miles Davis–like sound. Ken's subsequent research career, rooted in computational chemistry, is also of first-chair quality. Yet Ken tells me that a third member of that trumpet section is surely its best known alumnus: Ted Kaczynski, the Unabomber.

But what about that scientific education that my parents were shelling out almost two thousand dollars a year to obtain for me? Many scientists recall an intense moment-of-truth realization that they love scientific research. But with my background, becoming a scientist was more like becoming a physician or a lawyer—a suitable professional career that prescribed an orderly succession of courses to be continued with graduate education. Had my future profession instead been inspired by a teacher, I would have become an economist, even though at that time at Harvard many of the introductory science lectures were delivered by scientific icons. Organic chemistry professor Louis Fieser, an Alfred Hitchcock lookalike whose textbooks are still standards, shamelessly boasted of how his napalm invention had contributed to Japan's defeat, pointing out the parking lot site of its first trials, and also of his laboratory prowess, which he flaunted by competing with his students as they completed the year's final laboratory exercise. Kistiakowsky returned from Washington to teach introductory physical chemistry. (No, I hadn't the nerve to introduce myself!) A young astronomer whose lectures Paul Bamberg recommended turned out to be Carl Sagan. And I was listening to an introductory biochemistry lecture by James Watson (the DNA guy) on the morning his Nobel Prize was announced. No doubt a significant scientific discovery, I thought, but could anything useful ever be done with it?

Paul and I undertook a lot of science courses and lab exercises side by side, and his academic record might well have been the strongest in our class. Especially impressive to me was how, as I desperately scribbled away hoping I could later make sense of what I was hearing, Paul would settle for a one-line topic heading. I struggled, and seldom successfully, to earn an A. But only once did Paul reveal the imperfection of a B, an overall performance that helped to reward him with a Rhodes Scholarship for his graduate studies, which would of course take place at Oxford University. Yet that B did make my own best-in-class grade on the final in that same course, organic chemistry, seem significant. I also recall ruminating to Paul on one occasion, prophetically, that what seemed most scientifically appealing to me was trying to understand how differences in molecular structure produced differences in molecular properties.

With the Phillies out of radio range, I had to make do by following the Red Sox. At least visiting Fenway Park from Cambridge didn't burn a travel day, and good seats were always available at the gate. (Yes, things have changed!) On Opening Day attendance was even compulsory for me because as part of the preliminary ceremonies the Harvard Band would parade around the field. My first Red Sox game in 1960 was such a freebie, and my first impression was "Major league? Where's the upper deck?" (With the Phillies being a National League team, the only Fenway feature I recognized was the legendary "green monster," the left-field wall). And, with the lordly Yankees as the opponents, the crowd already seemed dispiritedly resigned to the beating that ensued, as the Yankees' newly acquired leadoff batter hit 2 home runs and a triple. A good start to what would become Roger Maris's first MVP season! But at least the transcendent Ted Williams, beginning the last season of his spectacular career, still the best hitter in the world, hit one out in the ninth. Although I would return that fall to watch the Orioles trounce the Red Sox in Williams's next-to-last game, by 1966 the Red Sox would displace the Orioles as my American League preference.

Perhaps oddly, though, in general my baseball addiction has seldom extended beyond more than a game or two each season of actual attendance. It's the unfolding of a pennant race, with the unexpected twists in its many individual story threads, rather like a TV serial combined with a reality show, that keeps me absorbed. (Not to mention the contemplation of all those lists!) I mostly like to read and to work with my computer, activities that a baseball broadcast will enrich but that game attendance will interrupt. It's the same way for me in music—I'll take a lot of trouble to play jazz with a good group but almost never leave home to watch other musicians perform. It seems that in general I'm a doer, not a watcher, though a doer very grateful that there are so many watchers to foot the bills.

Thus, during college, APBA remained the core of my baseball interest. By now I could myself generate card values that should represent any player's seasonal statistics. But where could those statistics be found? Sources were thin in the early 1960s. Most fans never saw any statistics beyond the current season's batting average, home runs, runs batted in, wins, losses, and earned-run average—delivered by newspaper, as daily batting top fives and on Sunday as batting average ranked tables including most regulars. (How would you like to see your own professional performance so frequently and prominently ranked and displayed?) A *Who's Who* newsstand pamphlet provided additional seasonal stats for the more prominent current players. With so little information available, most fans' historical perspectives could be remarkably shallow. For example, a roommate savvy enough to propose and win a bet with me that in 1962 Tommy Davis would drive in more runs than Vada Pinson was surprised to learn that Babe Ruth, then even more the legendarily dominant home run hitter, had also been a consistent .300 hitter.

Only *The Sporting News*'s annual official baseball guides contained the stats needed to completely define an APBA player card (such as doubles, walks, strikeouts, steals). I already owned a few guides, and Harvard's library included more. So I started a new statistical compilation, each page a year-by-year list of the regular for a particular team and position and each line recording the stats, including walks and strikeouts, for that season's regulars (fig. 1). There was another page for a team's most active substitute, and five more pages for the team's most active pitchers. With the save statistic not yet proposed, I didn't do anything special for relievers.

The 1894 season, the highest scoring in major league history and featuring the Phillies' all-.400 hitting and all Hall of Fame outfield (though not yet so recognized because Billy Hamilton's batting average was then recorded as .398), fascinated me, and in a Harvard library basement I discovered that the *Boston Globe* contained detailed box scores of every 1894 game, from which I could build APBA models of 1894 if I manually tallied all the players' doubles, triples, and walks. That proved easy and enjoyable enough that I extended these tallying activities into the twentieth century, approximating the batters' walks, which by then had disappeared from box scores, by mapping the opponent pitchers' walks backward into the discontinuities within a lineup's at-bats. (Whenever a batter walks, no at-bat is recorded.)

My feelings about all these APBA-motivated activities were much like those a drug addict supposedly has. Primarily I felt shame that these compulsions so enjoyably and repeatedly drew me away from the studies and other activities that everyone, and especially me, expected of an undergraduate, and also embarrassment, for as far as I could imagine, in contrast, say, to alcoholism, to my classmates this apparently unique compulsion would seem an inexplicable weirdness, as well as an addiction. A classmate acquaintance did once stumble upon me in the library sub-basement, and perhaps my red-faced explanation made some sense because when my baseball activities first hit the media decades later, he made the connection and wrote me with a question about whether pitchers with big leads eased up. (They don't, but in the absence of data, it's at least as reasonable a supposition as the tenacious belief in clutch hitting.)

Like many students, during my senior year I experienced doubts about the brightness of that light at the end of the educational tunnel. Rather to my surprise, considering grades I was not that proud of, I had been accepted as a prospective physical chemist by each of the three top graduate schools (and I was promised full financial support because educating more physical scientists was still a subsidized matter of national security—financially, it's a lot tougher today). But a summer's employment at DuPont had left me feeling about my expected career destination of plastics laboratory research much as Dustin Hoffman's character in *The Graduate* would later feel. An almost farcical low point was a night in the Cambridge jail, the result of my passive indifference to some unreasonably large fines associated with my accidentally unregistered and uninsured motorbike.

I spent the summer between college and graduate school on Cape Cod playing trombone at the Red Garter, a 1960s-innocent version of a singles bar, whose hopeful habitués sat at long tables covered with red-checked oilcloth, shelled peanuts, drank beer, and sang Tin Pan Alley songs to the accompaniment of banjos and brass. When that summer's events enticed me to remain in Cambridge, accomplished by successfully switching my pending graduate school enrollment from CalTech to MIT, my father sent me an unexpectedly stern letter, likening me to the legendary flake pitcher Rube Waddell in blowing off my talent. But, as he surely knew, I was not nearly good enough or interested enough to imagine making a profession of music. And surely MIT was CalTech's equivalent? Much later I learned that his ire was fueled by his close research collaboration with a CalTech professor. Perhaps another irritation for him was that my mother had spotted another quiz show opportunity, this time for me, as a baseball expert, on a planned revival of *The $64,000 Question*. I passed a couple of tests, a phone interview from a Cape Cod bar, and then a personal interview in New York and was scheduled to become a contestant during World Series week. But the show's (justifiably!) poor initial ratings led to its almost immediate cancellation. Yet no doubt fortunately with graduate school beginning, only my mother was disappointed that this distraction disappeared so quickly.

4 Graduate School and the 1960s Computer

In any case, while the specific objection of my father's stern letter was debatable, his unspoken underlying concern was timely and on target. The world expects responsible and responsive behavior of its college graduates, and I had been flippant and self-indulgent in switching my enrollment. As I think back over my life, he may have been even more concerned about his observations of two tendencies in my nature, tendencies that continue to exist, though less problematically once the computer became my central tool.

These conflicting tendencies represent the two sides of a figurative coin—I believe very strongly and uncritically in the reality and realizability of my own ideas. Or, put differently, I have been both blessed and cursed with an unconscious courage of my convictions. Blessed—whenever I have an idea that seems to me worth pursuing, I will persist in trying to make it work as tenaciously as resources permit. The cumulative record suggests that on balance those ideas have been successful. But cursed—I'm reluctant to be diverted by and often even oblivious to what to me seem irrelevant or superfluous and boring verification activities. That's not how scientists are expected to think! And in the laboratory such uncritical thinking is potentially costly and dangerous, as one of my early graduate school experiences would dramatize.

Earning a PhD, the objective of graduate school, requires an eventual thesis, prepared in association with a professorial advisor, and usually on a subject closely related to that professor's previous work. In the physical sciences, the advisor provides laboratory facilities for experimental work and often some financial support. After a first semester of coursework reconfirmed that my math chops weren't good enough for physical chemistry, I switched my specialty to physical organic chemistry. An unusually charming professor, Gardner Swain, had a project to work on that fit my unambitious expectations—just do some well-defined experiments that would inform the use of a generally accepted approach to answer a specific question and collect a PhD. Once I accepted, Swain thenceforth paid almost no attention to me or my activities during my years in his lab. Which never troubled me.

However, my project started (and might well have ended) with a bang. Its goal was to determine which, among several possible sequences of atomic rearrangement, effected the decomposition of an exotic molecule (triphenyloxonium cation). The published procedure for the first step, synthesis of the substance, was laborious, messy, and inefficient. Chemical theory suggested to me that a minor tweak to one of the ingredients (ClO_4^- for BF_4^-) might improve its yield, so, after unsuccessfully searching the indexed chemical literature back to 1915 for mention of such a tweak, I decided to try out my seemingly original idea. Continuing my search to 1907 or discussion of the idea with a co-worker might have alerted me to the danger. Instead, halfway through this reaction, while I was writing up this brainstorm at my desk ten feet away, there was an extremely loud crack, acrid smoke filled the room, and, ears ringing and half deafened, I turned around to see only granular rubble on the shattered lab bench where the apparatus had been. Luckily, it was spring break, so hardly anyone else was present. I had impatiently acted upon an appealing idea, beguiled by its apparent originality, without any possibility of accident occurring to me. Oddly, from today's much more safety-conscious perspective, and surely very fortunately for my future career, there was never any formal investigation or report of this thoughtless experiment, nor even much of a reprimand from anyone. Lesson learned, though; there would be no more fireworks from my subsequent laboratory activities.

Nevertheless, the heads-tails, yin-yang outcomes of my unconscious courage of convictions continued to affect my thesis research. I had some original and successful ideas for experiments and their interpretations, making my research results so interesting that Swain would choose them for his presentation at the prestigious annual Gordon Conference on Physical Organic Chemistry. But I ignored some confirmatory supporting experiments, contenting myself with the barest minimum in characterizing the side products implied by my interpretation of my experiments. I also became less conscientious about recording details in my laboratory notebook, especially those surrounding a final critical value generated by the MIT mass spectrometry lab. Several years later, questions arose, and these deficiencies reportedly made it impossible to reproduce my results. Quite appropriately under the circumstances, this research would never be published.[1] Not that I cared. As crucial as publication is for academic employment, it's almost irrelevant to the industrial research career that I anticipated and often even impossible because of the commercial demands for secrecy. I'd successfully served my PhD apprenticeship as hoped and planned, in a bit less than the usual four years. Mission accomplished!

Furthermore, MIT had also provided me with a first exposure to computers and their programs. Of course, although few of us—even at MIT—had seen an actual computer, everyone had seen them on TV—shipping container–sized boxes recognizable by their blinking lights, spinning tape drives, and subterranean locations, having the same societal significance but personal irrelevance as satellite launches or nuclear submarines. Most of the calculations in Swain's group were done with a slide rule or if more precision was needed, the group's Friden calculator, a cash register–like device that took several seconds to clunk mechanically through a single long division. However, for one important class of calculations, the iterative fitting of a differential equation to a series of experimental measurements, the Friden was too slow and error-prone to use. So the group also had an account on MIT's basement mainframe IBM. However, the frustrations of using this resource made its use, my first contact with computing, quite the opposite of love at first sight. Using an organ-like and jam-prone card punch, I would type each of my dozen experimental measurements onto its own IBM card. These cards were then appended to a binary deck headed by some especially mysterious JCL cards, producing the "job," whose critical card ordering was preserved with a rubber band. At a bank teller–like window, this deck would be entrusted to an IBM acolyte, and a day or so later, the deck would reappear in a mail cubby, wrapped by a scroll of paper onto which the numerical values obtained at various stages of the calculation were printed. If all had gone well, one or two of those values became the desired result. But sometimes (and for me, embarrassingly often), accidental misplacement of a character in one of the input data values would have distorted the experimentally obtained smooth sequence of values, 1.0,2.0,3.0 for example having been rendered as 1.0,20.0,3.0. Back in the lab, my colleagues' response to such a disappointment would be a condescending "garbage in, garbage out!," and there would then be another two days' wait for the corrected results. I must admit naïvely thinking to myself, "Why couldn't this stupid computer have inferred my mistake and corrected it immediately?"

Computing activities could go wrong in other ways. For example, any accidental disordering of a binary deck was a venial sin because the budgetary impact of its regeneration (compiling and linking) was not negligible. Today such an accidental disordering is impossible because a computer's file system takes responsibility for maintaining the structural integrity of all programs and data files. (Indeed, internet communication fundamentally relies on breaking a message into pieces for sending; these pieces often travel by different routes and are correctly reassembled wherever the file is being received.) So why didn't those IBM mainframes also store our information in files? Actually they could have done so, if requested, but at a prohibitive cost. This morning, for a dollar a month I added fifty megabytes of storage to my iCloud repository, but in 1965 fifty megabytes of data storage would have cost more than a million dollars to provide. Since that million dollars could instead buy fifty years of 1965 graduate student support, our computing mishaps and frustrations didn't bear notice!

Yet computers were becoming more evident, driven by such mainstream cultural events as the blockbuster movie *2001: A Space Odyssey* with its errant computer HAL. For me, even music was providing some tangential exposures to computing. I was still playing Dixieland jazz trumpet, sometimes as leader, but most memorably as a sideman in a predecessor of the New Black Eagles, who eventually became the largest fish in the rather small worldwide pond of Dixieland jazz. As a further example of this odd attraction between computer pioneers and Dixieland jazz performance, its piano player, Robin Verdier, was the first self-identified programmer I met. A strange incident involved one of my apartment mates during 1963–64, Austin "Larry" Lawrence, a teenage trombonist with jazz great Luis Russell who much later became an eminent Massachusetts mental health professional. Of course, Larry politely ignored my primitive jazz stumblings; he would listen only to Duke Ellington, about whom he later wrote an acclaimed biography.[2] Anyway, in his Duke-like urbane manner—soon after my laboratory explosion so perhaps as a hint—Larry introduced me to an MIT acquaintance of his who was experimenting with computer-generated 3D images of molecules. However, those images seemed uselessly crude to me, scientifically Larry's MIT friend was way above my league, and anyway I would never have considered leaving the assured career progression of my ongoing thesis project. Yet what I had seen would ironically turn out to be the first implementation of molecular modeling, today the technological foundation that is most essential for me and every other CADD practitioner. (Yes, fellow CADD specialists, Larry had fruitlessly introduced me to the fabled Cy Levinthal.)

Instead it was baseball that provided the critical impetus for my first attraction to computers. During graduate school, baseball had been front stage for me only during the Phillies' triumphant summer of 1964, which I spent at home, working another summer job for DuPont and missing the broadcast of only one game—Jim Bunning's perfecto. Yet by the time of their infamous September collapse, I was back in Cambridge, anesthetized to this disaster by showing off a newly acquired Austin-Healey Sprite to a long-forgotten Wellesley student. However, in 1966, I was surprised to discover MIT Press's second-edition release of the first book devoted to baseball analytics, Earnshaw Cook's *Percentage Baseball*.[3] Considering its relation to the phenomenon that baseball analytics has become, Cook's work might be metaphorically analogous to Leif Erikson's voyages or John the Baptist's prophecies. However, its egotistical tone and impenetrable prose have not endeared its few readers. Yet for me Cook's work was something of an inspiration, suggesting the possibility of a single algebraic expression that would summarize a batter's contribution to his team's run scoring (this, of course, is what OPS now does). His own Dx formulation had correctable deficiencies, for example a strange downweighting for the value of a double and, most seriously, the absence of any validation. That might be a project to keep in mind. But not one to execute with a slide rule.

The event that first lured me into my lifetime of computing activities was an unexpected bounty from my sister Sally—a baseball simulation program. She had spent her 1965 summer vacation at Penn participating in an educational experiment to teach programming to gifted high school students. A fellow student had written a baseball simulation program, she recognized that I might find it interesting, and she persuaded him to give her a copy that she sent to me. (Thank you again, Sally, for such a thoughtful and extraordinarily significant initiative!) What I received was a card deck representing the program itself, but this time in source code form rather than the binary, ready-to-run form that Swain's students used. (Source is the human readable and writeable form of a program, written in a language such as, in this case, FORTRAN. Such languages provide, among other benefits, portability—the baseball program had been developed on a UNIVAC, but I had access only to IBM computers.)

At least as important as the card deck itself, her shipment also contained a sheaf of computer printout paper, providing sample input and output along with a listing of the card deck's contents, the lines of text that the cards represented. Since most of the listing simply duplicated the cards, why was this printout so important? Two reasons. First, leafing line-by-line through individual cards is a poor way to absorb the overall logic of a program—and what if the cards get scrambled? Second, not so obviously from today's perspective, at that moment to me the card deck itself was unusable. My only computer access was by submission to that MIT IBM, where each job would record another entry on the Swain group account's monthly statement. There could be no justification for diverting such an expensive shared resource to satisfy even so minor a personal craving as a listing.

This tension between computing costs and personal resources would continue to be a major challenge for my next twenty years, until the reorganized STATS would buy its own MicroVAX. I am sometimes asked for my opinion on why sabermetric activities have so dramatically proliferated from my exchanges of letters with Pete Palmer during the 1970s to become a mainstream cultural phenomenon. To me the answer is obvious. It was the personal computer. Many kids and not a few adults have been fascinated with baseball statistics. But computer access was needed for anyone, other than a very few thoroughly addicted hobbyists like me, to do much more with statistics than compilation. It was our early professional access to computers that gave head starts to Pete Palmer and me. All the more credit to Bill James, then, because his earliest research and writings included an outspoken antipathy to "computers in the dugout."

Anyway, I bought an introductory FORTRAN manual and, reading the printout that Sally had sent me, began to work backward from the sample program output through the lines in the source code that had produced them to gain an understanding of the overall logic flow. Incidentally, there were only a few such books to choose from because until the personal computer appeared, most computer manuals were provided only by a computer's manufacturer, as the only supplier of any language software that would run on that computer. A long way from today's downloadable and instructionless apps!

5 Industrial Synthetic Chemist

In 1967, at least for a newly minted MIT PhD in the physical sciences, getting a job was not so much a matter of finding an opening as selecting an employer. Part of the reason, then as now, was the inclination of most graduate students to imitate the only scientific mentors they ever had and seek an academic career. Industrial science was only for losers. But my father had been winning some prizes for his latest research, so somewhat naïvely I assumed that high-quality research could be done within a company laboratory by anyone who had the talent and energy to successfully identify and tackle a company's problem. Indeed, for me something like that would eventually happen, but of course there were awkward interludes.

So which employer to select? Polaroid was an easy choice. Although subsequent events might suggest otherwise, by nature I'm strongly inclined to stay wherever I find myself, and I'd been in Cambridge for eight years. And there was Polaroid's history—the creation of one man, Edwin Land, that remarkably had become a glamorous company, publicly traded on the New York stock exchange. Remarkable because during the 1960s the technologically innovative industries were mostly capital-demanding colossi—plastics, aerospace, defense, petrochemicals, again unlike today, where the kaleidoscopic revolutions in biotech and information and communication technology can make "how many startups have you been in?" a cocktail party question. Polaroid sounded a lot more interesting than a DuPont or a Chevron.

So in April 1967 I signed up to "design photographic dyes and developers" in a rain-leaking lab housed by a masonry monolith that, remarkably, considering Cambridge's dynamism and Polaroid's fade, still stands at 730 Main Street. There was a good match between my skills and Polaroid's challenges, so during my two years there I had some substantive encounters with Dr. Edwin Land. ("Dr." was an honorific important to him, an undergraduate dropout, another interesting contrast with the self-stylings of today's high-tech titans!) The first was at the company Christmas party, where I sat in with the band. When the set was finished, Land, surrounded as usual by his court, emerged from the crowd to greet me. Apparently one of his minions had informed Land that I'd invented a variant of vitamin C that made it useful as a developer, which as it happened had been a pet belief of his, and indeed this variant made me a co-inventor in twelve patents that Polaroid received much later.[1] On another occasion, to help address a chemical challenge, Land recruited consultation from his very distinguished friend and neighbor, the self-consciously legendary Robert Woodward, whose Nobel Prize was an almost incidental distinction, since his work essentially defined much of the research scope of today's synthetic organic chemistry. One agenda item was a theoretically based concern I had raised about an important Polaroid chemical strategy, and Woodward agreed with my concern. Solid brownie points for me, but it seems that eventually the theory was found inadequate, and we were both wrong!

Of more lasting importance to me, again, I soon discovered that Polaroid had its own IBM 1130 computer, on hand to perform mysterious defense-related optical calculations, but mostly unused and presided over by a sardonic New Englander, Alan Ames, who was willing to grant me hands-on access and answer a few questions. This was my first face-to-face encounter with a computer. What I saw was a sterile windowless room with a raised white vinyl floor that surrounded a row of desk-sized boxes. One box was topped by a keyboard and a display screen; that, I was told, was the actual computer. Two others were a punch card reader and a printer.

So I finally brought out the cards that Sally had sent me. A bemused Alan added some JCL cards, put the deck into the reader, and started the computer. Soon there was an error message from the compiler. The program was too big. I had two very naïve questions. "Which box is the compiler?" and "Could we make the compiler bigger?" Alan ignored my first question—actually a compiler is itself a program, the major player in translating readable source into runnable binary, today called executable, code—and snorted, "You'll have to make your program smaller."

From studying its fraying listing, I already understood that to simulate a baseball game, this program, like all its many successors, compared random values between 0.000 and 1.000 with the batting statistics of the current batter. To explain how this works, here's an over-simplified example: assume the current batter's average is .300. If the next such random value is less than .300, that batter will hit safely; if higher, the batter will be out. Of course a baseball game is much more than hits and outs, and the program code included many of these other possibilities. Deleting some of those possibilities would make the program smaller. So I began cycles of removing cards, filling the resulting gaps in logical flow by punching and inserting new cards, running the changed deck through the computer, correcting any mispunched cards, and finally getting another program size complaint. I was learning to program by modifying an existing program, just as a lot of other programmers have done, especially when there was little formal training.

As I recall, the breakthrough came from my thoughts on improving Cook's batting summary Dx statistic. If the only thing I really cared about was how randomly generated sequences of hits, walks, and so on combined to produce runs, then all the code that created an actual game, with the nine innings and the two lineups, could be removed. What would remain would simply be one lineup that repeatedly played half innings of batting. This drastic surgery produced a much smaller code deck that successfully compiled and was soon running, and I started playing around with lineups.

It will probably surprise veteran baseball historians to learn that Lee Allen, the Baseball Hall of Fame's preeminent historian, became interested in this work and even posed a baseball analytics question for me to answer. I would occasionally drive to Cooperstown to add the contents of another season's official baseball guide to my statistical tabulation (fig. 1). This seemed curious to Allen, so I explained how the statistics powered my baseball simulation program and went on with my ideas about the underappreciated values of home runs and walks. Lee proposed an experiment. Based on the career records of Hall of Fame–caliber players, could I devise a lineup that would score more runs, in this baseball simulation, than a lineup composed of the players with the highest batting averages? Lee was pleased with the results. With the powerful Babe Ruth, Rogers Hornsby, and Ted Williams reserved for his highest batting average lineup, none of the lineups I could devise was better.

Paul Bamberg had returned from Oxford to become a junior Harvard faculty member. He told me that his career goal was to become a tenured Harvard professor of physics without doing any research. I kept my doubts to myself, wisely because today Paul is still a Harvard faculty member who has taught an extraordinary number and variety of subjects; he switched to the mathematics department twenty-five years ago, where he has created a large fraction of the ongoing courses. He may well have taught the largest number of different courses by anyone in Harvard's nearly five centuries of distinction. Paul modestly compares his own career to that of Rabbit Maranville, a baseball player whose Hall of Fame tenure owes more to the duration than the superiority of his play.

While at Oxford Paul married his high school sweetheart, Cherry Fletcher, who, after raising their two daughters Lisa and Amy, now edits for the Rhode Island Genealogical and the New England Historical Societies. The two of them brought Anglophilic tastes back from Oxford and had furthermore become vigorous travelers and foodies, featuring a then-exotic interest in wines and wineries. Paul would obtain choice vintages in return for his advice to Boston's leading wine importer and soon offered a Harvard extension course in enology. During my Polaroid tenure, I spent many weekend days at their home, playing Sancho Panza to Paul's Don Quixote as he created several intricate and absorbing board games that modeled the behaviors of a variety of systems, such as real estate, horse racing, and population growth. The tour de force game was a baseball simulation, one based on the batting, fielding, and pitching skills of the players rather than their statistics, much like today's electronic baseball games. I was always welcome, despite the persistence of my awkward eating neuroses, as memorably noted by Paul, "Dick, you are a true Renaissance man . . . for you believe tomatoes are poisonous." Paul and I also attended many baseball games together, at his suggestion and usually on the spur of the moment. The last of our Fenway excursions was Opening Day in 1971—no problem with tickets, and the van that left New England that afternoon had been packed very quickly! Sadly, my second and third wives, both midwestern scientists who seemed to me almost paranoid in perceiving hints of Ivy Leaguer condescension (even though they were married to an Ivy Leaguer?), could be embarrassingly unsociable around Paul and Cherry. Nevertheless, whenever events such as scientific conferences have taken me back East, I almost always visit them, and my friendship with Paul and Cherry has been the most memorable relationship of my life—much more durable than the marriages!

Meanwhile, during those after-hours sessions with Polaroid's 1130, I was discovering that for me the hourly rhythms and rewards of programming were far more satisfying than those of the organic chemistry laboratory. Chemical synthesis is a lot like cooking in that you mix stuff, often heat the mixture, and wait. (I don't care much for cooking either.) With the goal of synthesis a single pure substance rather than a tasty mixture, the most time-consuming synthetic activity is usually a final purification, which at that time comprised daylong cycles of dissolving and evaporating, trying different solvents and protocols, more or less at random, until success was indicated by the crystallization of a major product. I was finding the slow pace and uncertain outcome of this tinkering to be discouragingly tedious and felt little of the sense of accomplishment, when well-formed crystals finally appeared, that my colleagues joyously shared with one another. Belatedly it was becoming evident that within an organic chemistry laboratory I was an alien spirit. Of course computer programming is also dominated by cycles of debugging, some intensely frustrating, until the program works as intended. Yet these cycles are much shorter and faster, success is clearly defined, and a sufficiently mindful analysis of a debugging failure should soon pinpoint its cause and solution, in contrast to the meandering cut-and-try spirit of repeated recrystallizations.

Unfortunately, when compared to the salary and perks of a PhD chemist, computer programming hardly seemed a more realistic career alternative for me than playing jazz. Were there other jobs I could do for Polaroid? Many industrial scientists leave the laboratory to take on more business-related responsibilities elsewhere in their organization. But it was also becoming evident, probably even more to my management than to me, that my weakness in fitting in was another handicap, especially within the *Mad Men* business culture of 1969.

Reinforcing these concerns was a pending first marriage. I've been married and divorced three times, so perhaps a few generalizations associated with these repeated failures are in order here. As attractive and intelligent and accomplished as each of these women were and are, the pleasure I took in work and my hopes for additional achievement got most of my attention. Furthermore, I am highly self-reliant, which, it seems to me, made my marriages functionless to my wives and easier to abandon without much guilt or the feeling of a responsibility abandoned. Nevertheless, their professional goals were important to me, generally having far more influence than mine on our major family decisions. This was a somewhat self-serving approach on my part, though, because I did therefore hope for a greater acceptance of my inattentiveness. Being conflict averse, I've been on good, or at least courteous, terms with all my former wives, even throughout the divorces (which may not always have been a good thing). I could never have imagined proscribing any of their activities and was rarely judgmental. Finally, my own conduct has always been compulsively monogamous, in fact if not always in spirit. Nothing there to be suppressed!

My first wife, Melanie Gendron, had overcome an exceptionally challenging childhood to graduate from Boston's School of the Museum of Fine Arts, only to marry badly. Left on her own to support her five-year-old daughter, Cassandra, she had successfully turned to fashion design. My sister Sally, well trained by our mother, had taken a summer job as her seamstress (via my briefly dating Melanie's business partner), and Sally and Melanie became quite close, which made for immediate mutual trust when I began dating Melanie. We were soon living together and married at the MIT chapel in June 1969, a happy marriage until its ending. But my growing uncertainties about career directions at Polaroid added more stress to the adjustments of beginning a family life.

Then, suddenly—an opportunity! Many of the junior chemists at Polaroid were PhTs, working to "Put (their) Hubbies Through" PhD studies at local universities, and one of them told me of an ongoing research project at Harvard to "teach synthetic chemistry to a computer." Its champion was Professor EJ Corey, an emerging rival to the aforementioned Woodward. Woodward always likened his métier, the synthesis of a complex structure such as an antibiotic or a steroid, to artistic creation. Corey contended that a better mindset for designing such a synthetic route might be logical deduction. Today Corey's deductive process, retrosynthetic analysis, is how synthetic chemistry is universally taught, and it became the central justification for his eventual Nobel Prize. But in 1967 it was merely an intellectual concept, which, even if noticed, might only have been endlessly debated, to no practical effect. Wouldn't the power of retrosynthetic analysis be dramatically validated by embodying it in a computer program that produced acceptable synthetic routes? And then an ideal creator showed up, postdoctoral applicant Todd Wipke, whose Berkeley PhD in organic chemistry had been followed by two years of intensive programming experience with early guided missiles, fulfilling an ROTC commitment. Todd signed on and quickly discovered another key building block, the Harvard Research Computer, which fortuitously was already ideally accessorized for the project. His two years of brilliant toil had created OCSS (the organic chemistry synthesis simulator), which was about to be unveiled in *Science*, still the world's foremost platform for scientific publication.[2]

Might this project have use for another organic chemist with some enthusiasm, if minimal experience, for programming? In fact, I soon learned, very much so. Todd was about to transfer his uncommon capabilities to a faculty appointment at Princeton, leaving almost no one to continue the Harvard work. Corey's proffered postdoctoral salary even took generous consideration of my family responsibilities. A few weeks later, in April 1969, having formally been granted a leave by Polaroid, I took the leap.

6 Harvard's Research Computer

That leap plunged me into deep water. I felt that the future of my career and my new family's livelihood were at stake; returning to the laboratory was already unthinkable. Yet with my only actual experience being some tinkering with a preexisting FORTRAN deck, I really knew almost nothing about programming except that I enjoyed it. The Harvard Research Computer bestowed a programmer with an especially rich and demanding environment, and Wipke's OCSS creation had taken the fullest advantage of that environment. Before I could make any contribution to the further development of OCSS, I would have to acquire some competence within an unmapped morass of concepts, tools, and practices.

This Harvard Research Computer was a veteran PDP-1, the first in a line of computers that was launching Digital Equipment Corporation (DEC) into two decades of industry leadership, second only to IBM. In the 1960s, the PDP-1 had provided to programmers much the same kinds of improved accessibility that the Apple II would provide to many more programmers in the 1980s. For example, the cost of a PDP-1 was hundreds of thousands of dollars rather than millions. And PDP-1 program developers were not encumbered by the IBM legacies of punch cards and job submissions. Such accessibility had encouraged one hobbyist programmer, or "hacker," to create the first interactive video game, *Space War*, in which the two players' spaceships shot at one another while orbiting a central sun, by pressing switches on the PDP-1 console.

Harvard's PDP-1 had also been equipped with then unusual accessories that could support programs that were interactive in the same ways that all computers are today—a mouse for pointing, a cursor to track the mouse, and multiple interactive windows. (Here the mouse's role was played by a RAND Tablet, a flat panel that tracked the tip of an attached pen.) These accessories provided OCSS with a critical capability. Chemical structures are, of course, network-like diagrams of atoms connected by bonds, often forming hexagonal rings; chemical synthesis is then a matter of making and breaking the right bonds in the right order. Organic chemists can hardly communicate without drawing and discussing such structural diagrams. If a chemist were to view Corey's synthesis design program as relevant, he (or she, but not so much then) would expect to draw his query structure just as he would do on paper and would expect all the structures OCSS proposed to be represented by more such drawings.

These accessories have become universal only because today's computers are vastly more powerful than Harvard's Research Computer, with its six banks of 4,000 eighteen-bit words as memory and drum, rather than disk, for backup storage. Each of its 432,000 memory bits ($6 \times 4,000 \times 18$) was an individual entity, a ferrite core. The actual degree of this vast improvement is always hard to communicate and visualize, but here's another attempt. If computer efficiency is the product of speed, memory, and cost, then the laptop that I am writing on is something like 10^{10} times more effective than that PDP-1. That's a really big number. If you were to receive 10^{10} times more money than this laptop cost me, you could buy everything the entire United States produces in a year (i.e., a figure comparable in magnitude to the current U.S. gross national product)!

However, as a novice programmer, my immediate challenge was the PDP-1's software rather than its hardware. OCSS was written in DECAL, an obscure extension of PDP-1 assembly language. You've never heard of an assembly language? Neither had I. An assembly language works in intimate contact with computer hardware. I was about as well equipped to program in DECAL as a weekend hiker might be to scale the Matterhorn. The bits of DECAL documentation available assumed mysterious concepts and experiences that I could find no way to learn. Also, to better represent the complexities of chemical structure despite the PDP-1's limitations, Todd had further extended OCSS's DECAL tool set with linked lists, binary sets, and virtual memory management. On the other hand, just as had previously happened with the baseball program, the code of the working OCSS program did provide many of the intellectual hand- and footholds needed to begin my programming ascent.

Operation of this PDP-1 was also somewhat intricate. Instead of punch cards, to begin each hour-long session, a pleated paper tape punched with boot-up code was threaded into a reader, and a miniature magnetic tape containing the operating system was mounted onto its drive. Console toggles were flipped until their sequence correctly represented the memory address from which this PDP-1 should take its first instruction, and the chrome-plated (hey, it's a 1950s design!) start lever was pressed. If everything had been set up properly, the paper tape slithered through its reader (usually to fall onto the floor), and the tape drive then spun back and forth for about five minutes, until this Rube Goldberg skit terminated with a *ka-chunk* from a teletype. Programming, using this teletype to pound in commands, could begin. Yet although the mechanisms—paper tape for source input, magnetic tape for code storage, line printer for text output, teletype for commands and the debugger—were clunky and slow, the PDP-1's compile-link cycle of program construction would be conceptually familiar to any professional programmer today, if not yet to me. In contrast to the recurring revolutions in computer hardware technologies, the fundamentals of computer software development haven't changed much in fifty years.

The next couple of months were the most intellectually stressful and arduous of my life. Generally speaking, whenever I run into an obstacle to a goal, my instinct is to persist by seeking some easier path to that goal. As my brother once protested, "You won't do things that you're not good at." (He wasn't thinking of my softball struggles!) But achieving competency with this PDP-1's technology was the only conceivable route to the goal of contributing to OCSS and thereby hopefully becoming a PhD-compensated programmer. This barrier could not be bypassed or avoided but had to be surmounted, no matter how long or difficult the battle. Mostly on my own, because Todd was a conservative and taciturn show-me Missourian, hardly one for newbie handholding. (For example, before Todd left, Corey asked me to copy any nuggets within Todd's stack of publications, so I did, displaying my selections on his desk for his observation. When I arrived the next morning, his publication stack had been replaced by a locked file cabinet.) I struggled toward what felt like an endless series of dead ends, trying to identify and grasp some basic concepts onto which I might hope to graft some competence, repeatedly paging back and forth among obscure books and pamphlets until the accumulating frustration and tension would start me to pacing the room.

Nevertheless, after a month or so of this self-flagellation, I could begin contributing to OCSS's development by addressing one of its major scientific weaknesses. OCSS already fulfilled its original goal, a convincing embodiment of the retrosynthetic principle. Sketch your target structure of interest and OCSS would respond with precursor structures, those that could be converted to your target in one reaction step. By then repeatedly selecting one of these precursors as a new target and asking OCSS for its precursors, a synthetic tree could be generated. Whenever the user recognized that such a precursor was already accessible, the sequence of structures connecting it to the original target would constitute a complete synthetic route. However, for such a synthetic route to be useful to an actual chemist, each of its reaction steps must work in the lab, which for OCSS routes was unlikely because its representation of reactions was too simplistic. I had an idea that I never doubted (as usual!) would fix this problem, and, despite Todd's mild skepticism, I began coding. Some months later, I had implemented a chemist-friendly general language to describe synthetic retro-reactions, by representing those features within a target structure that would affect the outcome of a particular reaction that could produce it. Indeed, this language would be the only migrant when OCSS was ported to a new PDP-10, becoming LHASA (Logic and Heuristics Applied to Synthetic Analysis—my coinage, archly hinting of ivory-tower chemistry). By the way, this new PDP-10 was also the one later used by Bill Gates and Paul Allen to illicitly develop Microsoft's famous first program, a BASIC language interpreter for the Altair. My new language also became the backbone of my first publication, the last of a trio published in the *Journal of the American Chemical Society*, then as now the world's leading journal for chemical research, detailing OCSS's functions and components.[1]

Feeling reassured by the satisfaction Corey took from this advance and no longer inhibited by Todd's oversight, I yielded to the temptation to renew sabermetric research. The first step was rewriting the baseball simulation program because although the PDP-1 didn't speak FORTRAN, it had more memory than Polaroid's IBM, permitting a more detailed and realistic simulation. With my research goal now explicitly being discovery of something like Earnshaw's D_x, a simple season-long stream of half innings, without the complications of whole game simulations, would continue to be a satisfactory architecture. And an extraordinary new publication, the famous Macmillan *Baseball Encyclopedia*, now provided all the baseball statistics. To validate my new program's results, I selected teams whose regulars had played most of their team's games and compared the runs the team had actually scored with those that the simulation generated, varying parameters such as error and double play frequency, base-running aggressiveness and stolen base attempts, and the degree of variability in the opposing pitchers' quality. I stopped tweaking this simulation when these deviations between such teams' simulated and actual runs scored met three criteria: their average was close to 0.0; especially high-scoring and low-scoring team averages were also close to 0.0; and their standard deviation was a bit over 20.0 runs. The simulator seemed ready for research.

My approach would be to compare the runs (per plate appearance) as calculated by trial algebraic expressions with those generated by the simulation for various lineups. The more extreme the lineups, the more likely that any relationship found would be general. So, with the batting statistics of individual players obviously varying much more than those of teams, I tried lineups of nine identical players having extreme seasonal statistics. For example, as variants of high-walk players, I submitted lineups of nine 1956 Eddie Yost, nine 1894 Billy Hamiltons (to add high batting average), and nine 1920 Babe Ruths (to add high batting average and high power). Also, to put an upper bound on the effects of batting order variation in real lineups, I constructed two lineups of best and worst hitters (five 1920 Ruths and four 1963 Sandy Koufaxes), one with the Ruths batting consecutively and the other with Ruths evenly distributed. The most bunched Ruths outscored the most evenly spaced Ruths by fewer than 100 runs. (Other Ruth and Koufax sequencings yielded smaller differences.)

With a few dozen of these player-season simulations in hand, I quickly found an algebraic expression that could express the runs their simulation scored. If runs per plate appearance is graphed against the simple algebraic expression on-base average times slugging percentage (OXS), the result is a remarkably clean straight line. (On-base average (OBA) is essentially (H + W) ÷ (AB + W); slugging percentage is TB ÷ AB.) This was the first discovery of such a surprisingly simple and general algebraic formula to be extensively validated, as far as I knew then, and I was excited. But did anyone else exist, anywhere, who would be interested?

Of course, it's on-base average plus slugging percentage (OPS) that has instead become a foundational batting statistic, and indeed the points in a graph of runs per plate appearance versus OPS form just as straight a line. But here are some fine distinctions of OXS, included mainly for the possible interest of fellow sabermetricians. If the grounded-into-double-play count is subtracted from the numerator of OBA (representing the loss of a base runner from the double play), the straight line of on-base average times slugging then also has a slope of 1.0 and an intercept of 0.0, a finding that confers two desirable properties. First, OXS is a very good estimate of the average number of runs that a batter contributes in each plate appearance. Thus, for example, the OXS for a player who has an on-base average of 0.400 and a slugging percentage of 0.500 would be 0.400 × 0.500, or 0.200, indicating that in the five plate appearances such an all-star-caliber batter might have in a game, he would typically contribute a run to his team's total scoring. Second, because batters faced by pitcher (BFP) is also the denominator of on-base average, canceling the two BFPs allows a player's runs contributed to be calculated directly, as his on-base occurrences (H + W + hit by pitch) times his slugging percentage.

If you try this yourself, you'll probably be expecting that the runs a team actually scored will be roughly equal to the sum of the runs contributed by all its individual batters. However, in general the sum of products is greater than the product of sums, so this runs-contributed sum will tend to be a bit higher than the actual runs. Yet with some more effort, the expected equality can be obtained by expressing a player's runs as his effect on his league's runs (league runs minus the league runs excluding that player's batting statistics). However, it may then be a surprise that, with this formulation, poor hitters will contribute negative runs. For example, in 2017 Pirate pitcher Ivan Nova batted fifty-one times with only one hit. Subtracting these values from the appropriate elements of the 2017 collective major league OXS yields a runs contributed total of -7. Seven more Pirate runs if Nova never batted? Nonsensical? No, this result is meaningful because each out recorded denies an opportunity for some later batter to contribute. As an illustrative, if artificial, example, consider game 1 of the 1988 World Series, when with two outs in the last half of the ninth inning, his team a run down, and a runner onbase, the limping Kirk Gibson pinch-hit a home run, reversing the pending Dodger loss into an immediate victory. However, in the scoreless third inning, a Dodger batter had walked. If that Dodger had instead been out, all the twenty-seven outs that complete a nine-inning game would have already occurred, before Gibson could bat.

So do I then believe that OPS's dominance is an unfortunate historical accident? Hardly! As OPS's inventor Pete Palmer observes, addition is a lot easier than multiplication—especially when multiplication required slide rules or pencil and paper! Such practicality matters. Even if OPS didn't exist, the clumsiness of multiplication makes it unlikely that OXS could ever have been as popular as OPS has become. Far better an OPS that today is accepted and used by almost everyone than an arguably superior OXS that would generally be ignored!

7 Computer-Aided Drug Discovery

Although both these pioneering accomplishments with the PDP-1 in chemical computing and baseball seemed worthy, I wondered how I would next support my new family. I was a PhD organic chemist, now with some programming credentials but with little skill or interest in teaching or the laboratory. The OCSS project fascinated most chemists who saw it demoed, but no one said they thought it useful. As a pharmaceutical recruiter explained, "We seldom need to ask *how* to make something; instead we want to know *what* to make." That want did sound like something a computer might help with, something I might contribute to. But Corey was dismissive of the few relevant publications.

Meanwhile, there were other possibilities. One was an outgrowth of environmental politics, an activity that from time to time I've greatly cared about. I found convincing the arguments in books like Paul R. Ehrlich's *Population Bomb* (Borlaug's "green revolution" not being foreseeable—and not necessarily repeatable), and I became heavily involved in a zero population growth movement, serving as its Massachusetts chapter's first president. Two regular meeting attendees were Dennis and Donella Meadows from MIT, who were building computer models of how the world's future state might evolve from present world trends, and there was some discussion of another postdoctoral position for me to help improve their models. I was interested but couldn't convince myself that anyone's understandings of these trends and their complex interrelationships could ever become strong enough to guide human responses. Nonetheless, their core conclusion—the high likelihood that continuation of current exponential growth trends would produce a catastrophic crash and a very unhappy future world, soon to become the central message of their seminal book *Limits to Growth*—has always seemed self-evident to me. (The opposing mantra, "no worries, emerging societal needs will inevitably stimulate timely technological solutions," always strikes me as far more of a hope than a prediction.)

Anyway, then came another lucky break—a laboratory-free job opportunity for a PhD organic chemist! It came from Smith, Kline and French (SK&F, now the SK in GlaxoSmithKline's GSK), whose Philadelphia location would also put me near my parents, the Phillies, and an opportunity to continue playing Dixieland jazz. Another no-brainer. Even more fortunate, though I didn't yet know of it, was SK&F's existing interest and experience in seeking ways to use computers in drug discovery research.

Instead, my new duties would primarily be in compound acquisition. Then as now, drug discovery is primarily a process of testing compounds until satisfactory activity is found, in some biological assay that is believed or hoped to be predictive of therapeutic efficacy in humans. A lot of needle-in-the-haystack testing is usually needed, and testing protocols of the 1970s typically consumed a lot of each tested compound. Compounds are expensive to make, especially with 1971's tedious purification techniques. So I was to seek additional compound freebies by visiting North American universities, offering to lecture on LHASA, and promising modest support or royalties if any leftovers in professors' desk drawers actually turned out to be promising when tested. One memorable visit included the first minor league game I ever saw, played by the Eugene Emeralds, who coincidentally, were the Phillies' AAA affiliate. My host professor was an Emeralds fan, specifically of then first baseman Greg Luzinski, and after a few drinks in the gathering following my lecture, he persuaded many of his University of Oregon chemistry department colleagues that an Emeralds doubleheader was the right place to spend the rest of their evening.

A committee of SK&F chemists then assigned each of these compound acquisitions to the biological assays for which it seemed most promising. This rather intuitive decision-making, it soon occurred to me, might benefit from a computer program, one that I might create.

Moreover, SK&F already had the two requirements for developing such a program, an accessible computer and, less obviously, a list of available compounds in some computer-readable form. In 1971 that form couldn't be the structures themselves, because even with something like OCSS's capabilities for manipulating structures, drawing in a structure would have required something like the PDP-1's special accessories, and entering SK&F's forty-thousand-compound inventory would have taken thousands of man-hours. However, SK&F had already been providing research chemists with a bit of structural guidance when selecting from this inventory. Chemical structures can be considered assemblies of substructures, so an individual structure can be distinguished by recording those among these substructures that might interest a chemist. Representing these substructures in computer records as present or absent had already been done, by visual inspection, for each of those forty thousand structures.

The accessible computer was another IBM 1130, this the one used by the biostatistics department to support clinical trials for FDA submissions. Fortunately, the head of biostatistics, Mike Free, himself a former analytical chemist, was interested in my idea. Indeed, he had already developed and published his Free-Wilson analysis, a CADD approach that still has its proponents.[1] Of course, clinical trials had priority, but SK&F's half dozen biostatisticians usually went home at 5:00 p.m., leaving the computer free during the evenings for my project. From the perspectives of me and my family, I would simply be continuing to work the same hours I had recently been doing at Harvard.

Some months of moonlighting later, I had written a program and performed two studies. As hoped (well, expected!), there existed a statistically significant and unbiased tendency for structures to be active more often if their substructures had been more frequently found in other active structures, though this tendency was not strong enough to encourage its actual use in assigning compounds to biological tests. When published (my first paper as the senior author), this substructural analysis method became perhaps the first example of an approach that today, associated with labels such as 2D fingerprints and Tanimoto coefficients, is one of those most often used in CADD.[2]

Yet I've never been fond of it, because biological targets surely do not perceive substructures in the same ways that synthetic chemists do. A computational method that more directly represents the behaviors of biological targets should provide better guidance. I wanted to try to create such a method.

Here are a few historical asides, for the possible interest of younger CADD specialists. First, today's widespread use of substructural analysis as fingerprints, began almost automatically once OCSS's technology became commercially available by means of Todd Wipke's founding role with Molecular Design Limited (MDL). Second, to help chemists take fuller advantage of those forty thousand structures, SK&F had also been outputting chemical structural diagrams on the only available graphics device, a line printer, by using additional characters and a special typewriter for structural input. Finally, the Wilson of Free-Wilson, though a respected chemist and courtly Virginian, never had the slightest interest in or even awareness of chemical computation. As Mike Free confided, he had added Wilson as a coauthor to expedite his publication—Wilson had been a student of the founder and editor of the *Journal of Medicinal Chemistry*.

This was an ironic contrast for me, though, because the two coauthors on my substructural analysis publication were unwelcome, one being my boss and the other a colleague whom my boss had charged with CADD responsibilities. When the colleague, who certainly fit in much better than I did, was then promoted and I was not, my ill-considered complaints nearly got me fired. Instead, the entire department, whose compound acquisition activities had not been highly valued by the rest of the organization, was dismantled and its staff dispersed. To my surprise and delight, I found myself reassigned to the chemistry department, with my only responsibility to provide CADD support, presumably computer-based, for any of SK&F's discovery projects. Today there are perhaps a thousand such CADD specialists; I had just become one of the first two or three.

So what does a CADD specialist do? The first big event in a drug discovery project is when an interesting compound shows promising activity in a biological test and becomes a "lead." A chemist then begins making variations on this lead structure, hoping to improve both its primary biological activity and also its transport to the site of that activity. The CADD specialist's purpose is to suggest structural variations to the chemists, drawing on her expertise with analytics or physical chemical simulation. At that time, the only CADD methodology practiced was QSAR (pronounced *cue-sar*), an acronym for "quantitative structure-activity relationships." A QSAR model should, with sufficient accuracy, express the differences in biological potencies among the previously tested structures as a linear function of one or more "structural descriptors," properties that could be calculated for each of these tested structures. From the implausible platform of professorship at undergraduate Pomona College, Corwin Hansch had created and somewhat dogmatically led this QSAR field, naming it; adding a new logP descriptor, strongly related to biological transport, to a sigma parameter inherited from physical organic chemistry; and applying these descriptors, in combination, to previously published data sets, using multiple linear regression, to formulate and publish dozens of QSARs. Because biological tests then were mostly performed on animals and tissues rather than on cells and their components as they are today, transport processes strongly influenced observed biological potencies, frequently making this logP a powerful structural descriptor.

With big data analytics today a part of every MBA's toolkit, it may be a surprise that in the 1970s, even for most scientists, equations including more than one such structural descriptor were something of a novelty. The only tool for exploring cause-and-effect relationships had been graph paper, which of course is limited to two dimensions, one effect associated with one cause. When an effect might have multiple causes, scientists would usually try to combine those causes into an algebraic expression that yielded a single number, from which a graph could then be drawn, exactly as Earnshaw Cook and I had done to uncover Dx and OXS. But new computer programs that performed multiple linear regression were starting to make the derivation of multivariate linear equations a rather trivial exercise. Unfortunately, this simplicity also encourages a behavior that a colleague once described as "turning on the computer and turning off the brain."

I didn't yet have access to this QSAR methodology when my first CADD opportunity arrived. Nevertheless, there's always graph paper, and by imagining biological activity as a third dimension, I spied a rather crude pattern involving two descriptors and proposed a structure that would be more active—if the pattern worked. Indeed, when synthesized and tested, the proposed compound was the best that the project had yet found. So I was asked to propose an even better one, and a structurally unorthodox suggestion turned out to provide extraordinarily high potency, greater by two orders of magnitude (though accompanied by a decisive deficiency—very poor solubility).[3] Management of course was pleased and impressed. Neither of us could yet guess how rare such an unambiguous predictive success from QSAR would prove to be.

Meanwhile I had obtained those CADD essentials, a multiple regression program and access to a computer that could be run during normal working hours from my office. That access was provided by an acoustic coupler modem and telephone line to another PDP-10, a prized possession of the University of Pennsylvania Medical School. An acoustic modem consisted of two rubber sockets into which the earpiece and mouthpiece of Bell's standard telephone handset could be squeezed. (Bell, then a monopoly, would not permit anything other than representations of sound to be transmitted on its lines.) With the acoustic modem, which transmitted data at a rate of 1,200 bauds, it would have taken years to download a movie. But computing from an office desk was vastly more productive for me than camping out at the PDP-1 or IBM 1130s had been.

8 Sabermetrics' Infancy

Baseball is a game whose stately pace facilitates discussion, with "Who's better?" a major topic. My OXS discovery seemed to me the best tool that anyone had ever had to answer this type of question for batters and especially convenient to apply using a revolutionary new device—the four-function calculator, replacing the nudgy slide rule for only $125! So I set about using OXS to rank the greatest batters. Not that anyone seemed likely to be impressed, or even to listen, if the puzzled skepticisms of my father and brother were any indication! I did send the Phillies a letter recommending more playing time for their young outfielder John Briggs because he walked so frequently. A week after I received their polite reply, they traded him for one Pete Koegel, who would bat .174 in his ninety-two MLB plate appearances (while Bill James recently ranked Briggs as the 113th-best left fielder, among the thousands of left fielders in major league history). Nevertheless, the dawning of sabermetrics was imminent.

It was probably early 1972 when I noticed a classified advertisement in *The Sporting News* for a "Society for American Baseball Research." Whatever this society might be or do, surely I should belong! In answer to my letter of enquiry, SABR founder Bob Davids referred me to a Pete Palmer, the other SABR member with interests similar to mine. Pete then lived in Lexington, Massachusetts, ironically a few miles from where I had just been living, but only because of SABR would the two of us learn of each other's common research activities. (Today with the internet, such a mutual ignorance presumably would be very unlikely.) Over the years, Pete and I have been able to meet now and then, on one occasion at Paul Bamberg's home, thereby unknowingly assembling the threesome of OPS pioneers.

While it was Bill James with his volumes of provocative ideas so eloquently expressed who brought sabermetrics out of the closet, Pete Palmer was its intellectual creator, the Newton or the Darwin of sabermetrics. Yes, there were earlier voices in the wilderness. But Pete, by combining some of that earlier work with insights of his own, assembled a coherent overview that became the foundation—or at least the departure point—for almost everyone else's subsequent sabermetric work. Pete is also a model correspondent and an unselfish collaborator, one who initiated contact with all of his sabermetric contemporaries and predecessors and often wrote letters many pages long in response to their work.

Pete seems to me a sort of modern-day version of a colonial Yankee artisan, unassuming in manner and with a deafness in one ear from a softball accident that sometimes makes his New England twang hesitant. Therefore, as is true for many of us sabermetric pioneers, his merits can be slow to appreciate in personal meetings, which for me happened to be on Nixon's second inaugural day. Politically a bleaker day for me than for him, as philosophically Pete seems a libertarian who, oddly, it seems to me, for a Yale-educated engineer, is a human-caused-global-warming skeptic, arguing that the glacial ages speak to the magnitude of non-human-caused climate changes. (But, Pete, please consider the much greater speed and acceleration of global warming.) As a self-described sabermetrics "hired gun," he turned down my offer for him to join STATS during its most halcyon days, instead proudly raising his late-arriving children with Social Security benefits. Yet, while we are no longer close, there are few people in whose energetic and unselfish character I have more confidence. In a recent email exchange among several veteran sabermetricians, he even volunteered how comparatively little recognition I had received (to which I responded that I thought none of us had much reason to feel neglected!).

Pete replied to my introductory description of OXS with several pages summarizing his own work. It was clear that there was much he could teach me. I had yet to think about the most fundamental sabermetric relationship, between run differential and won-lost record, so I was immediately and irreversibly converted to his version of what Bill James later popularized as the Pythagorean theorem. Pete's version is a simple linear proportionality using a season-specific runs-per-win constant, with a value around ten, to express the decreasing value that each run has whenever there is a higher overall frequency of run scoring. Its virtue, compared to the Pythagorean alternatives, is linearity. Everything balances—the run-differential-derived win total in a league season exactly equals the loss total, just as do a season's actual wins and losses.

His letter also introduced me to linear weights, Pete's best known contribution to sabermetrics, as his solution to another primal challenge—expressing how a team's performance is related to the performances of its individual players. The central idea in linear weights is to compare, as differences between the runs each player contributes (hitting) or yields (pitching, fielding), and the runs a league-average player would contribute or yield in the same number of opportunities. Add up these run differences (appropriately signed!) over all of a team's players, multiply this sum by Pete's above-mentioned season-specific runs-per-win constant, and you will have the expected difference in wins between this team and a league-average team. To conveniently visualize this sort of calculation in a contemporary setting, go to the "2016 Chicago Cubs Statistics" page at baseball-reference.com and scroll down to the WAA (wins above average) columns in the "Team Player Value" tables. The totals in the WAA columns are 19.2 for Cubs batters and 8.4 for Cubs pitchers, or 27.6 together. A break-even team wins and loses 81 games, so the Cubs' mostly likely win total was 81 + 27.6, or 108. They actually won 103 games (one game was not played).

Hmm—103 is a lot of wins, but it's not 108. Why the discrepancy? Why had the 2016 Cubs tended, in their close games, to score a few runs less and yield a few more runs, while doing the opposite in one-sided games? Is there a missing signal—something consistently affecting team performance that the context-blind linear weights approach does not capture—such as weak clutch hitting (more on this later), or pitchers pitching to the score? In Bill James's version of linear weights, win shares, this overall five-win deficiency becomes a penalty, to be proportionately applied to the 2016 ratings of each individual Cub. Or, instead, is this sort of discrepancy instead simply random noise—such as at 'em balls, hanging curves in crucial moments, or gusts of the famous Wrigley Field wind?

To get some idea of how large the effect of such random noise on a baseball pennant race must be, consider a coin flip. If you flip a coin 162 times, and record 90 heads versus 72 tails, should you think the coin biased? The answer: probably not because the likelihood of a fair coin yielding an outcome at least this unbalanced is 9 percent. Then, moving back to baseball, how about 90 wins versus 72 losses? The same calculations apply. So even if all major league teams were evenly matched, there is a likelihood greater than 95 percent $(1-.09^{30})$ that at least one of those thirty teams will win 90 games. And 90 wins has been enough for postseason play in the vast majority of recent seasons. Of course, teams are not evenly matched, and the likelihood of a league-average team achieving the Cubs' 103 wins is a meager .01 percent. Yet, overall, Pete reports that the differences among the final standings of major league teams are as influenced by differences in this unavoidable luck—"noise"—as by differences among players' skills—"signal."

How do you feel about this mathematically incontrovertible finding? I'm guessing that you'll blow it off. Remember our genetically baked drive to predict and constructively respond to future events? There's no place for chance. Deep in our psyches, everything that happens should have a deterministic cause, and therefore any trends that we observe should continue indefinitely. Probabilistic thought has only existed for a few hundred years and is still uncommon. Even Einstein wrongly insisted that "God does not play dice with the universe." Speaking only for myself, despite having been steeped for decades in probability considerations and thus certainly knowing better intellectually, I admit that as I watch a baseball season unfold, I will have feelings that this or that team is hot. More perversely yet, those feelings exist for me even when the season I'm watching is being simulated by a computer! It is then especially admirable to me that Pete has been so relentless in reminding the sabermetrics community about the unavoidable uncertainties that random chance brings to all analytics activities.

Also, to my mind, Pete's linear weights is still the simplest and cleanest solution to that fundamental sabermetrics challenge of relating individual player performances to team performances. And it was the first to appear in *Total Baseball*.[1] Yet today an alternative wins above replacement (WAR) formulation has clearly won the mind-share battle. Same idea, but instead of being compared to the league average, a player's batting or pitching runs are compared to those of a "replacement player," a conjectural minor league player whose unremarkable skills should be freely available (although fielding runs, perforce, are still compared to the league average). Here are some observations on this interesting evolution.

As I tried to convince Pete some four decades ago, and as Bill James has forcefully declaimed, Pete's treatment of fielding runs has deficiencies so serious that they may have raised unreasonable doubts about linear weights generally. Its fundamental weakness is an implicit assumption that the effects of pitching and fielding on team defense are completely independent of one another, which creates two problems. It is obvious that strong fielding will improve a team's pitchers' statistics, but Pete's treatment ignores this interaction and therefore tends to double count the effect of strong (or weak) fielding on a team's overall defensive performance. Also, the individual styles of a team's pitchers have enormous effects on the distributions of the batted balls and fielding chances. Here are two then-contemporary examples I remember citing to him. First, two pitchers compared: Bob Gibson, who won nine straight Golden Gloves, averaged .125 assists per inning pitched (IP), while Frank Linzy, sinker ball reliever, averaged .289 assists per IP. Second, consider my first love, the 1957 Phillies, who happened to set a modern team record for fewest assists while featuring fly-ball pitchers. In *Total Baseball* Pete reports that its center fielder's 27 fielding runs led the league but its double-play combo, who nevertheless enjoyed many seasons of regular play, cost that team a calamitous -58 runs—six games in the standings. Pete's numbers seem entirely inconsistent with on-field reality. And then even his numbers themselves disagree. Despite a total over all the 1957 Phillies of -43 fielding runs, *Total Baseball's* tabulations of team fielding wins instead reports a value of zero. For such a discrepancy to be completely ignored is troubling. Granted, achieving a reasonable balance between pitchers' and fielders' contributions to team defense while using only traditional fielding stats has been a puzzle so enormous that I would nominate the solution described in Michael Humphreys's *Wizardry* book to be the greatest single intellectual accomplishment in the history of sabermetrics. Yet failing to recognize or acknowledge some important deficiencies within linear weights, a methodology proposed to have universal applicability, may have damaged its overall credibility.

As just stated, the only difference between linear weights and WAR is a different baseline—league average for linear weights as opposed to the vaguely and variably defined replacement player for WAR. The objection to league average that Bill James and others put forth is that using league average isn't fair to players, especially at the beginning and ends of their careers. Consider a player whose season statistics are below league average. He's still a major-leaguer, therefore performing at an outstanding level and presumably better than anyone else his team might play out there. But when players are compared using their lifetime linear weight totals, a major league quality but below-league-average season will make a negative contribution to the sum of that player's seasonal statistics, the usual measure of his overall greatness. For example, while Ron Santo had three such inferior seasons at the beginning and end of his career, the iconic Joe DiMaggio quit while he was still ahead. Simply erasing Santo's deficient trio makes Santo's linear weights total equal to Joe's. Advocates of WAR quite reasonably argue that every respectable major league season should positively contribute to a player's rating.

Here is how I interpret this conundrum. It seems to me that these fundamentally similar approaches (with linear weight and WAR differing only in their baselines) are being asked to answer two quite different questions. I agree that league average is inappropriate and unfair if the objective is to rank individual players against one another—"Who is better?" But Pete and I (and, one might think, Baseball Prospectus, WAR's champion!) are usually more interested in "Why is this team better?" For that purpose, negative linear weight values are more informative. For example, improving a team by finding an average player to replace a poor player is much more easily done than by finding an (obviously much rarer) superior player to replace an average one.

Anyway, back to 1972. Pete and I found that we had independently discovered OXS. And thanks to the devotion and diligence of SABR founder Bob Davids, there also now existed an annual *Baseball Research Journal*. A joint publication made sense to everyone, so I composed an article that appeared in the 1974 issue.[2] Together with a mini-review of on-base average that Pete had contributed to the 1973 issue,[3] you might reasonably suppose that SABR had begun its embrace of analytics, which today finds even its name semi-embedded within the "sabermetrics" cognomen for baseball analytics, and is strongly experienced during its annual Baseball Analytics conference in Phoenix during spring training, where professional and amateur sabermetricians freely congregate and mingle.

However, that embrace would be substantially delayed. Bob made it clear that he, as the journal editor, was not enthusiastic about articles involving statistical analysis. He believed that the research that most *Baseball Research Journal* readers enjoyed was historical rather than statistical and therefore that statistical researchers (he proposed "statistorians" as a neologism) should collect and tabulate baseball statistics but not analyze them. To me, thinking as a scientist, what should matter for publication in a "research journal" is whether the research significantly advances knowledge or understanding; readership appeal is only a nice-to-have. In response to my remonstrations, Bob asked me to carry out a survey of SABR members, asking how much they liked articles falling into various categories that he enumerated. When I did so, the results strongly confirmed that Bob knew his readership. The statistical analysis category, though the favorite for a few, was the most disliked by a large majority of the responders. The upshot was that Bob agreed to publish a quota of statistical analysis articles, one every other year, and that Pete and I would form a statistical analysis committee that would advise Bob on the merits of such submissions. Neither Bob nor I could have imagined how statistical analysis has become part and parcel of daily baseball broadcasts everywhere today.

Geography prodded my other SABR activities. An energetic Brown undergraduate, Ben Weiser (today a *New York Times* reporter), and I organized its 1974 national convention in downtown Philadelphia. Forty attendees listened to Fred Lieb, formerly the dean of baseball reporters, detail how eccentric scoring had contributed to a batting race, a .400 season, and a no-hitter. (Nevertheless, while I drove Fred to that meeting, he disappointed me by objecting to my Hall of Fame nomination for baseball's World War I home run king, Gavvy Cravath, by saying, erroneously in fact though actually not in effect, that he was a left-handed hitter, making his home runs an artifact of his home park's dimensions.) The attendees also participated in the first SABR trivia contest, twenty questions on Philadelphia second basemen that I had assembled. Its reception was chilly—trivia quizzes were an unprofessional activity, and the questions were too hard. (Sample: What Philadelphia second baseman had also had the most wins in a season by any Philadelphia pitcher? Kid Gleason won thirty-eight in 1890.) Another irony: today the annual trivia tournament takes center stage on the Thursday and Saturday evenings of every SABR National Convention.

Ben also launched a second annual SABR publication, which had the same name, *National Pastime*, as a current SABR annual. A second opening for statistical analysis publications. I remember contributing two short historical articles to its few issues, one on the emergence of relief pitching, and the other on nineteenth-century scoring criteria for stolen bases. However, Bob Davids was uncomfortable with this unchartered enterprise by an undergraduate, and it soon shriveled away.

My suburban Philadelphia home, located midway among the homes of SABR's leaders, also became the site for several executive meetings. The SABR website reports that I served one year as SABR vice president and five years as a board member but with no purpose and to no effect that I can recall. My only recollection of these SABR organizational activities and appointments is my brash prediction as a SABR executive meeting was gathering that Mike Schmidt, in spring training about to start his third season, would someday be recognized as the game's greatest third baseman.

I have a few impressions of SABR's early leaders. Bob Davids was of course The Man, as SABR's instigator, organizer, shepherd, the author of its newsletter, and the editor of its research journal. His manner was somewhat reserved, much as would be expected from his professional career at the highest levels of the Atomic Energy Commission and its successors, especially during Republican administrations. Which doubled my surprise and pleasure when he and his wife, Yvonne, appeared at a Dixieland jazz appearance in Washington that I had casually mentioned that I was making. Such intersections among my science, baseball, and jazz passions have been very rare. Bob McConnell was Bob Davids's alter ego. His skepticism when I first described OXS to him even awakened me to one of its useful properties, for as a power plant engineer he was generally alert to cancellation of units and specifically to the above-mentioned cancellation of BFP. I was glad to report back soon that my further calculations confirmed the correctness of his observation, which, though he had framed it as an objection, had really been an enlightening deduction. Cliff Kachline, then the Hall of Fame's historian, found some kinship with me in the both of us being Pennsylvania Dutch. Subsequent SABR president Kit Crissey was an occasional dinner guest at my home.

However, for me, SABR mostly continued to be about doing and publishing my own individual research. Judging from the vigor of its continuing discussion, the most significant of my biennially allotted baseball research publications was "Do Clutch Hitters Exist?," the first study to ask this question (though evidently not to conclusively answer it!). There even existed a website devoted to making all the subsequent debate available. A clutch hitter is someone who hits at a level superior to his normal performance whenever the outcome of the game is in greatest doubt. *Star Trek*'s Vulcan Spock would be surprised to hear that a clutch hitter is a hero. What's so admirable about a professional hitter who doesn't perform at his best in every game situation? But we humans all feel pressure when called upon in some crucial situation and believe that this pressure is likely to degrade our performance. A clutch hitter would thus be a hero whose batting skills are unaffected by the greater pressure of a close game. Many players are certain that clutch hitters exist and regard success in such situations as a hallmark of superior personal character.

Why did I start investigating these universal impressions of clutch hitting, apparently posing the title question for the first time? First, Pete and I were increasingly confident in the ability of the OXS and his Pythagorean-like formulation to reproduce team run and win totals. Could there remain any run-scoring anomalies left for clutch hitting to explain? More importantly, there now existed the two ingredients that would make this study possible. OXS provided one key ingredient, a single measure of game-situation-independent batting skill. The other key ingredient was a single measure of clutch hitting performances, one that had recently been published for the 1969 season, derived from an analysis of its play-by-play game records. Today anyone can download a play-by-play account for almost any game as far back as 1929 from retrosheet.org. But in the 1970s it seemed incredible that the play-by-play information for any major league's full season of games had ever been assembled. Nevertheless, this had somehow happened, and a player win average (PWA) statistic, which its proponents Eldon and Harlan Mills had elegantly derived from those play-by-play records, seemed to me and to most subsequent writers a unique and irrefutable measure of clutch hitting—the extent to which the results of each of every batter's 1969 plate appearances had cumulatively contributed to the probability of his team's win or loss.[4]

My results, once again, came from a graph, this time of PWA compared with OXS for every 1969 batter. It was no surprise that these batter-points formed a fuzzy straight line—whatever the situation, good (high OXS) hitters should contribute more than bad hitters to their team's probabilities of victory (high PWA). The relevant information in this graph was not so obvious. Clutch hitters—those whose hits, however frequent or not, were more frequent when they would be most decisive—were those whose batter-points were located above this straight line and whose PWAs were higher than their OPSs would suggest. The question, then, is what is the cause of such deviations?

Was it the batter's superior character or some other matter of personal skill, or did the opposing pitchers just happen to hang a few more curves in his few key situations, or experience some other matter of luck? The small magnitude of the variance of such deviations among all batters was at least consistent with the idea that clutch hitting is random, not much, if at all, a skill.

Not the most convincing of arguments, but when I shared these results with Pete, he recalled that PWAs had also been recorded for 1970, and he sent me a copy. Today any sabermetrician would know what to do next. If clutch hitting is a skill, there should be a tendency for good clutch hitters in 1969 to show up again in 1970. When I applied this test (apparently for the first time by a sabermetrician), there was almost no such tendency. More specifically, an r^2 of 0.038 between 1969 and 1970 for the National League (NL) deviations and 0.055 for the American League (AL), where r^2 has the value 1.000 for a perfect agreement and 0.000 for a complete disagreement. So clutch hitting seemed mostly a matter of luck. For example, consider Carl Yastrzemski, whose extraordinary batting in September 1967 had dragged his Red Sox to the AL pennant, but who was the most un-clutch hitter in the majors in 1969–70 (though surely then the best hitter by far in non-clutch situations!). Had Yaz's character really cratered? The guy who would eventually come to bat the most times in American League history?

Thinking that additional play-by-play data was unlikely to ever appear again, I believed that this study would be the last word on clutch hitting. Not so! Nevertheless, now that the same approaches can be applied to play-by-play accounts for every game of the last sixty years, the same sort of results are obtained. For example, the legendary clutch hitter David Ortiz indeed had the two most clutchy seasons in those sixty years, yet Ortiz's lifetime clutchyness was slightly chokey (below average)! However, because we all feel pressure when asked to perform in critical situations, the belief that clutch hitting is a player skill seems likely to persist.

A different question. How do today's batters compare with those of the past? Which league is the stronger? How much does expansion dilute quality? These are some of the questions addressed by the most laborious of my baseball research projects, an attempt to place the average batting skill of each major league season onto a common scale.[5] Again, the general approach of this study would today be familiar to any sabermetrician—to compare season A with season B, somehow compare the performances of batters who played in both seasons. In this project, to generate as many comparisons as possible and thereby improve their (still rather insufficient) collective accuracy, such season-to-season comparisons were done for all year separations up to five, with these comparisons in all of their possible pairings then weighted, summed, and merged. It is embarrassing to recall that I had been slowly generating these comparisons by hand for years, before my second wife, Libby, observed that, really, it would be okay by her if I were to use our family funds to establish a private account on the PDP-10 that I was already using at work. (Although computer activities had been too expensive to conceivably be funded by ordinary individuals, its costs were coming down.) In general, my findings were as follows: When the seasons being compared were within, say, a decade of one another, the combined comparisons that I obtained made sense. For example, the averaged quality of major league competitiveness dropped substantially during World War II. Nevertheless, if there also exists a small but systematic bias in these combined differences, for example from how batters leave or enter these combinations, the effect of such a bias would accumulate over the decades and either contract or expand any true batting skill differences. Yet the results from one relevant if meager validation were positive; the magnitudes of the post-1961 (inter-league trading begins) AL-NL comparisons were consistent with those of the 1901–4 (AL founding) AL-NL comparisons. So I proceeded to the highly speculative but more entertaining topic of "how well would a young Babe Ruth hit today?" Not a good idea, because of an understandable skepticism (though with some misreading) that my answers to this question generated. Maybe that's one reason why this study seems never to have been repeated or updated, as relatively easy as it would be today.

This study of course depended on my having calculated values of OXS for every player season in major league history, which I had done with an HP-65, a pocket calculator for which an assembly code program could be written and saved onto a chewing-gum-sized plastic strip. While doing so, I had also tried to overcome the deficiencies in fielding runs that I saw in Pete's treatment, including most of the now well-understood effects of a team's pitchers' repertoire on the chances offered to its fielders. It seemed obvious that knowing the type, direction, distance, and velocity of each batted ball would further improve the measurement of fielding performance, but such an idea then seemed another useless fantasy. To the baseball establishment, especially to the press, the keepers of its intellectual keys, proposals for any sort of change in its recordkeeping practices, especially coming from outsiders, would have seemed as sacrilegious as marijuana or homosexuality then did. Pete, who was providing programming support for the Boston-based Howe Service, custodian of the official American League statistics, had to lobby for years before triumphantly reporting to me, maybe around 1979, that on-base average would be added to their annual batting stats.

Therefore, since there would never be any additional data to be analyzed, I felt that for (still-to-be-named) sabermetrics, the golden age of discovery had ended. Further massaging of the traditional baseball statistics would no longer reveal any new and deep understandings. For the most part this impression has held up through the decades. But one remarkable discovery, by then unknown Voros McCracken, would completely astonish all us sabermetricians (both baseball outsiders and any baseball insiders who noticed).[6] He considered the following question. What sorts of play-by-play outcome frequencies distinguish those baseball pitchers who are consistently superior? Fewer walks, more strikeouts, fewer home runs allowed? Yes, yes, and yes. Fewer hits allowed? No! Once all plate appearances that resulted in walks, strikeouts, or home runs are deleted from a pitcher's statistics, any consistency among differences in what remains, the BABIP, or batting average on balls in play, is hardly detectable. Yes, BABIPs differ, but except for differences in the skills of the fielders behind them or the few active pitchers who rely on knuckle balls, these differences seem entirely random, chance, luck. McCracken reported that just as I had found earlier with respect to clutch hitting, the BABIP differences between two consecutive seasons' work by the same pitcher are almost entirely uncorrelated.

9 Scientific Recognition

The 1970s were especially satisfying and productive in my real world also, where I was SK&F's only CADD specialist. These feelings began a significant and permanent transformation in how I thought about myself. Until then, as do most men, I believed that the most important rewards that life might bring were various forms of organizational appreciation, such as a promotion or a bigger salary or a prestigious award. Now I came to believe that, with my current share of these rewards already being sufficient, for me it should be far better to take pleasure only from my work itself and to take pride only in doing it effectively. Not that more money or a spiffier title would be unwelcome! Nevertheless, along the rest of the way my relative indifference to conventional career opportunities and honors have probably confused some managers and colleagues. That might have been good news for my managers, in that although I might quietly sulk after an organizational rebuff, I almost never again rocked the boat or pressed for bigger rewards. To me life has seemed too short and other opportunities too numerous to waste my time and energies in personal squabbles or concerns.

Since no one yet had much idea what a CADD specialist should be expected to do, I was mostly free to invent my own job. My only specific charge was to provide QSAR support to the dozen active discovery projects. This support would not necessarily be welcome, though. One issue is that being named as the inventor of an important patented drug guarantees a prestigious career. This raised a critical question; if a structure that CADD analysis had recommended was claimed in a patent application, would the CADD analyst then be among its inventors?

Such a policy would have made me a pariah, but fortunately SK&F's patent lawyers did not think so. Only the chemist who first made the magic compound could be its inventor. Still, CADD suggestions could become useful only if and when a synthetic chemist would make the compound, and there always exist many more promising structures than project chemists can make. When committing his own time and trouble to a synthesis, a project chemist usually has some freedom to choose between the CADD guy's suggestion or his own idea. Some degree of bias seems inevitable.

That said, the scorecard for my seven years of applying this QSAR approach to SK&F's discovery projects was as follows. I analyzed around forty different series (sets of similar structures), thirty of which yielded a recommendation. Project chemists responded with synthesis in fifteen occasions; in some of the other cases the project was discontinued. The test results for the fifteen syntheses were evenly divided into categories of "better," "same," and "worse." There was a second predictive success, fenoldopam (a specialized antihypertensive, recently reported to be highly effective for acute renal failure), though the compound would probably have been made without the QSAR. There was also a modest contribution to the Ridaura project (an orally active gold formulation used for treating rheumatoid arthritis). These contributions were regarded as adequate and somewhat encouraging, though far from game-changing. I would reassure myself that as one of around forty PhD chemists, my activities were adding sufficient value if they improved chemistry's overall productivity by at least 5 percent. And a particularly influential evaluation was positive—SK&F's head of research and development concluded one general review of our current discovery projects by singling out QSAR as the most significant recent advance in SK&F's discovery practices.

Most of my time was free to spend on trying to improve on the QSAR methodology, and there was a swelling ripple of scientific fashion for CADD, which seemingly buttressed the glamor of novelty with an expectation of substantial social relevance. Hansch was its only established thought leader. Many other academics welcomed CADD-inspired industrial contacts, thinking perhaps of funded collaborations. And

CADD methodology has always been an exception to the constraints and delays that intellectual property considerations place on most pharma research publications. I received increasing numbers of invitations to attend and speak at conferences. There were no complaints about my travel costs, so these activities must have pleased my management. With drug discovery so rare, it is hard to evaluate performances of both individuals and entire discovery organizations, including managers. Perhaps they believed that the prestige of an entire pharmaceutical organization would be boosted by a few well-regarded publications.

My research mostly explored the physical chemistry implicit in many of Hansch's ideas, starting with some relevant yet unconsidered data sets. Although they've never attracted much attention, I'm still especially proud of two purely scientific publications that resulted. Both were findings, using analytics approaches, of unexpected and arguably fundamental truths in physical chemistry. The first study showed that the relative solubilities in water of the rare gases (such as helium, argon, and neon) are inconsistent with hydrophobicity, then the dominant hypothesis about why, at the molecular level, oil and water won't mix.[1] The second reported that although a conventional 2D graph shows only a crude relationship between pairs of such fundamental compound properties as boiling point and solubility in water, when such properties are graphed into 3D as property triplets rather than pairs, there exists a very tight relationship, potentially visible by a flat plane rather than a straight line, just as Saturn's elliptical rings almost disappear when viewed exactly edge-on.[2] Of course with today's computer graphics, this finding would have been easy to display and become recognized, but the article's punch line, that subjecting these property values to factor analysis (then completely unknown to most scientists) yielded only two major eigenvalues, doubtless prompted most readers to skip to the next article. Hansch's response to this work, delivered in front of my conference poster, was that I must have somehow sinned—if true, he coldly asserted, such a fundamental relationship would surely have been discovered long ago.

One of these academic contacts would become a game-changer for me. In SK&F's UK laboratories, the project that would discover

Tagamet (also known as cimetidine), the world's first effective anti-ulcer medicine, was going very well. Wondering if SK&F's lone CADD specialist might be helpful, its eventually ennobled leader, physical organic chemist Robin Ganellin, asked his Oxford consultant, quantum chemist Graham Richards, to visit Philadelphia and have a look at me. Some nice words in the *New Scientist* followed about the unexpectedly "high quality of American industrial research." The lasting import of his visit for me, though, was his lecture in Philadelphia on quantum calculations he had done for a few cimetidine-related structures. He had drawn cross sections of the fields that surrounded a few of these flat structures and, while dramatically flinging his drawings to the stage floor, declared that the differences among the biological activities of these structures were caused by the differences in their surrounding fields. That pronouncement inspired fifteen years of off-and-on tinkering that would yield comparative molecular field analysis (CoMFA), and perhaps helped, eventually, to discover a drug or two.

Graham had called my attention to a physicochemical truth that should have been self-evident. Although chemical processes usually involve bonds being made and broken, most biological processes employ subtler interactions. Much as planets influence each other by their gravitational fields, adjacent molecules interact with one another primarily by two fields, steric and electrostatic. Because a planet is uniformly round, its gravitational field varies only with distance. But molecules are bumpy and also wiggly, rather like Tinkertoys, which means that the shapes of their steric and electrostatic fields are irregular and constantly fluctuating.

I was immediately convinced that a QSAR approach should be able to usefully relate differences in the biological activities of sufficiently similar molecules to their differences in these fields. Although implementing this conviction would be a long and tangled journey, the general approach (fig. 3) was clear to me from the start. Each of the descriptor columns in what would come to be called a 3D-QSAR table should contain the intensities of a particular type of field at a particular 3D location. For convenience these 3D locations might as well be evenly spaced and at right angles to each other. Two fundamental challenges remained. Because a 3D-QSAR table would have many times more explanatory columns (3D locations) than rows (structures), the only model-building technique then recognized by CADD, multiple regression, would be helpless. But my experience with factor analysis suggested there might be other techniques that would work, and I eventually learned of the one that afforded CoMFA. The other alignment challenge, that of systematically generating 3D molecular structures in meaningfully related poses, has persisted, though I am encouraged by results from a template CoMFA approach that I recently developed.

The greater physicochemical realism that this 3D-QSAR idea embodied, compared to substructural analysis or Hansch QSAR, was irresistible, and I began investigating some immediate obstacles to its implementation. Obviously needed was a practical method of generating 3D molecular structures. The only approach then generally accepted, quantum mechanics, the one Richards had used in generating his fields, was far too slow and expensive. Fortunately, today's customary approach, molecular mechanics, was being meticulously introduced by Lou Allinger. (Allinger also took pride in his earlier tenure as Detroit's leading Dixieland jazz piano player—another example of this strange association—and delighted in the few chances for the two of us to play together, such as the first Gordon Conference on Computational Chemistry.) It was easier, though, to work with a different academic, Tony Hopfinger, who welcomed the financial support of an industrial collaboration, and I became perhaps the earliest user of his 3D structure generating program CAMSEQ. Tony was also working on his own quite different 3D-QSAR approach, which would become probably the first to be published.[3]

Another of these obstacles was the limitations of 1970s display technologies. As already emphasized, chemical structures need graphics for communication, but affordable graphics technology was still woefully inadequate for rendering 3D. Only lines could be drawn, not surfaces, and a change to any single line required the entire screen to be redrawn. The dominant Tektronix technology began such a screen redraw with a green flash. (Amusingly, for a *Fortune* magazine photo that showed SK&F's president's hand on my shoulder as the two of us boldly peered into the Tektronix—of course the only contact we ever had—the entire room was bathed with green light!) Anyway, these static line drawings made determining whether one atom was in front or in back of another a very cumbersome and error-prone process. The underlying model would have to be rotated a few degrees, by keyboard command, while, before and after the green flash, carefully observing the shifts in the projected locations of the atoms of interest.

To wrestle with these and other obstinate challenges, Margaret "Merrie" Wise, a chemical information specialist (another 1970s rarity), was a fortunate hire. She pieced together a primitive molecular modeling system, awkwardly named DYLOMMS (dynamic lattice-oriented molecular modeling system).[4] DYLOMMS was first applied to a project that sought stronger GABA uptake inhibitors, because there was an appealing hypothesis for how the 3D structures of its candidate inhibitors should be superimposed, and Hansch QSAR was inapplicable. Nevertheless, generating appropriate 3D structures for a mere few dozens of those inhibitors was slow painstaking work; with program development the project took a matter of years for Merrie. Factor analysis of the resulting 3D fields did suggest a statistically significant correlation, but extracting a chemically informative interpretation from that correlation was a challenge. At the 1981 Gordon Conference on QSAR, Merrie and I heard about partial least squares (PLS), a new statistical tool that would eventually enable CoMFA, from its champion Svante Wold. But between the cumbersome graphics, the end of the GABA project, and a new management inclined to routinely reject its predecessors' projects, the writing was on the wall for DYLOMMS.

My other scientific projects were also tapering off, with the flat Saturn-like plane that factor analysis had revealed becoming far more fuzzy when extended to drug-like structures, which are more complex. I learned of PROPHET, an NIH initiative to promote the nationwide use of computers in drug discovery, based on remote access via modem from a Tektronix terminal, and I persuaded SK&F to sign up. Soon, programming in the languages I had been using until now, BASIC, FORTRAN, and PDP-1's DECAL, with their limited constructs and grammars, began feeling like conversation with a toddler. The PROPHET programming environment was one for grown-ups, even including a first-generation 3D molecular modeling capability, though one too expensive and Tektronix-bound to be of use to Merrie. However, while filling some hours by writing a PROPHET program, one that extracted a count of the binding sites on a target from the overall kinetic data, I imbibed important concepts for my future programming in both baseball and drug discovery, particularly for interface design.

In these years, with the enthusiastic support of Melanie, my first wife, music got far more of my extramural energies than baseball. Locally, at various times, I was the regular trombone or trumpet player in five different Dixieland jazz groups, and when I traveled I would carry a horn with me and seek sit-ins. Gigs took priority even over Phillies' postseason games. Yet one of the local groups, probably because its maestro had some Rocky-flavored political pull in Philadelphia's City Hall, realized my classic childhood fantasy of playing for the Phillies in a postseason game (on trombone in the stands, of course!), and we later performed on Veteran Stadium's steamy Astroturf during a pre-game photo op. Much the best among these bands was the Bix Beider-becke Memorial Jazz Band, a New Jersey–centric all-star band that played only at festivals and the like, most notably at a trans-European jazz festival in Breda (my second trip abroad). The band's favorite venue was the Goldenrod, an authentic showboat relic, which then was docked on the Saint Louis riverfront below the arch, and hosted an annual ragtime festival that attracted most of the best American bands. Saint Louis impressed me with its enthusiasms for both Dixieland jazz and baseball.

Alas, early in 1978 my marriage with Melanie fell apart. I had been a contented husband and, as my behavior in later marriages should confirm, would never myself have initiated divorce. I felt only fond amusement as Melanie evolved from puzzlement at feminism by a woman as stunning as Gloria Steinem to consciousness-raising feminist activism. However, Melanie, never well accepted by suburban Philadelphia or, sadly, my own family, was charmed by a California vacation and a guy who was returning there and, having unfounded concerns about my fidelity, volunteered some confessions that forced a break. Although the divorce process was distressing, then being alien to everyone in my extended family, there were no second thoughts, and the asset division was uneventful. Most of my related memories involve the struggles of a daily fifty-mile car-and-train commute during a historically severe winter from my parents' home, where I temporarily roosted, to SK&F in downtown Philadelphia. However, the distraction provided by these weather challenges was probably therapeutic.

The absence of any children of my own surely helped to minimize the emotional and financial upheavals. For some reason, the charm of infants has always escaped me, though my interest in kids increases as they mature. I would have been happy if any of my wives had wanted children, but none did. Two wives came with a stepchild, though, and I gladly continued to provide significant financial support for each of them after the marriages to their mothers ended, particularly for their best possible educations, their weddings, and, unfortunately, a funeral, because two years ago Melanie's daughter, Cassandra, succumbed to myelofibrosis. My third wife's son, Alex Chrisope, and I stay more or less in touch, usually discussing baseball or politics and, though we mostly talk past each other, music. He was even slower to develop a serious baseball interest than I had been, unexpectedly returning from college with a newfound enthusiasm for baseball analytics that had been ignited by a Vanderbilt roommate who had even dared to offer advice to David Price and Pedro Alvarez, both nearly major-league-ready players. I supposed Alex would then become interested in learning more about what I had done, but, as far as I know, not really. It's an amusing irony! I jokingly speculate that anything pre-internet was ipso facto obsolete for him, while during most of the time that he and I lived together, the STATS story was a sad one for me.

Alex had a demanding childhood, with his every week split between the custodies of his mother, a militant biologist, and his father, a Rush Limbaugh devotee. My own views on religion are what you would probably expect from a scientist who never saw his parents attend a service, buttressed by some amusing childhood experiences. On my fourth Christmas I was given books on both Winnie the Pooh and the New Testament, stories whose credibility seemed to have blended in my mind. Then, to get a schooling head start, for first grade I was dispatched to a Catholic school, where I dismayed my teacher, a nun, by mentioning that my parents never went to Mass. Her confident objection, "They must go before you awaken—otherwise they would be heathens," evoked only my silent disdain. So eventually Alex would also be exposed to my skepticism, as I would jokingly say, "I'm just like your father—he believes that all religions but one are dangerous nonsense, and I would merely add one more to his list," and more seriously, "Successful challengers of scientific authority are praised, but challengers of religious authority are ostracized—or worse." Alex has politely ignored these ripostes. Politically Alex and I are both passionate centrists, these days an endangered species.

Anyway, Alex would be two wives later. Back in 1978, to people with more capacity for passion and empathy within a relationship than I ever seemed to have, it may seem somewhat strange or even misguided that it was only a month or so after my divorce before I began seeking a new relationship. However, with marriage having been so comfortable for me until its end, it was a state I was eager to recreate. And then, as good fortune again would have it, an attractive young female biochemist, Dr. Libby Yunger, newly recruited by SK&F, appeared at a project meeting. (This was hardly an everyday experience then, when societal expectations and more robust glass ceilings deflected most women from obtaining PhDs.) The opening dinner-and-movie ritual was followed by a day trip to Washington. She and I very quickly felt comfortable with one another, both of us being outspoken, direct, and pragmatic rather than romantic. She could adjust a car's engine timing and even knew that star pitcher Tom Seaver was having a bad year. Impressive! Soon we were reversing the usual roles in a classic male-female dialog—I wanted marriage and she to maintain her independence—and she capitulated, to the congratulations of our SK&F colleagues. My enthusiastic parents were the only witnesses of our city hall wedding in the spring of 1979.

Libby is the heroine of this memoir. Indeed, married to almost anyone else, I would never have had occasion to write a memoir. For a woman who never wanted marriage to anyone, she was a lot better at it than I was, unselfishly supporting me at challenging or frustrating moments and also ready with an apt quip whenever egoism threatened to overcome my judgment. Amply supported by our dual PhD paychecks, she insisted on introducing me to some activities that became lasting favorites for me. One was travel, with usually a major and minor trip each year, some highlights being a cruise around Turkey on the illustrious yacht *Sea Cloud* and a raft trip of the entire length of the Grand Canyon. Another was frequent restaurant meals, as neither of us cared much for cooking.

10 Twists of Fate

Until that spring of 1979, nothing had yet occurred to greatly distinguish me from the thousands of other PhD chemists who attended an annual American Chemical Society meeting, this one in Hawaii. Certainly nothing memoir-worthy. But it is often said that the true value in a scientific conference is less in the talks themselves than in the occasion that it provides for its attendees to interact. Accordingly, two events before and after that meeting would combine to upend my life, provoking a cascade of activities that first created the company that would become my employer and subsequently provided its successful business model. And perhaps even influenced a major strategic choice by my then current employer.

The opening twist of fate was a chance encounter with an acquaintance, Garland Marshall, as we together endured a two-hour wait for baggage when we arrived in Honolulu. Garland was (and is still) a highly regarded professor of peptide and protein chemistry at Washington University in Saint Louis. There he was collaborating with a group of pioneering computer scientists to develop an interactive 3D graphics display technology that would be suitable for displaying molecules. I hadn't been that interested; I'd never even taken a look inside the van that carted their display apparatus to the Gordon QSAR conference in New Hampshire. To me, only data—numbers, not pictures—seemed truly scientific. Nor had I or SK&F much interest in peptides. Yet uncovering new opportunities is a potential benefit in any industrial travel, I had rented a car, and Garland offered knowledgeable company for a Hawaii newbie like me, so we did the Oahu 101 tour together, filling an otherwise eventless Sunday and becoming better acquainted. For his part, Garland was surely aware that with Tagamet's introduction, SK&F had opened a gold mine. (Quite rightly so, because until then stomach ulcers had been a life-threatening misery.) In its first year, 1980, Tagamet sales alone exceeded SK&F's total revenue in 1977, and in another few years Tagamet became the world's first billion-dollar drug. Cultivating SK&F's only CADD scientist must have seemed to him a worthwhile endeavor.

During the meeting, there were several harbingers of more significant roles for computers in chemistry. The moniker computer-aided drug discovery (or design) appeared, perhaps for the first time, as the title of a major symposium, and there was a computer on the exposition floor, demonstrating MDL's first commercial offering of a chemical database system. But for this story, it is what followed the meeting that mattered. To fill in its last few hours, I had approached a peptide chemist from Beckman who had described some biological results that might interest someone more knowledgeable back home. Probably neither of us expected our exchange of pleasantries and business cards to go any further.

And then the other twist of fate—a wildcat United Airlines strike suddenly canceled almost all flights back to the mainland. We chemists were stuck in Hawaii at least through the next weekend (poor us!), so I agreed to a sudden dinner invitation from the Beckman guy's bosses. Who, it turned out, had a proposition, motivated, as they candidly emphasized, by SK&F's burgeoning Tagamet revenues. Peptides, which are simply short proteins, often have therapeutically reluctant effects. However, just like every other protein, they do not survive digestion, so they do not themselves make good drugs. Yet they may offer structural clues for the design of non-peptide molecules, a possibility that was being highlighted by the introduction of captopril, an exciting cardiovascular drug. Peptide synthesis also requires special techniques, ones with which SK&F had no experience. Surely the Beckman results that I'd noticed could be greatly improved upon, particularly as Beckman also had the exclusive services of an academic expert in peptide CADD. Wouldn't an SK&F-funded collaboration with Beckman be a win-win?

Their proposition was way above my paygrade. Yet back in Phila-delphia, there was a peptide groundswell as people became cognizant of the captopril success inspired by the angiotensin peptide and of a similar story developing around somatastatin. Technical evaluation of Beckman's proposal by an independent peptide expert seemed a good idea, and—fortunately—I now knew one. When I described the Beckman overture to Garland Marshall, he quickly responded with a proposition of his own. If peptide chemistry were to be of lasting interest to SK&F, as it should become, then rather than rent someone else's capabilities (and both Garland and I had reservations about Beckman's CADD consultant), SK&F should build its own. True, build-ing a new research capability from a standing start is slow. But, as it happened, Garland was starting his own peptide consulting service. Perhaps SK&F would take this opportunity to help fund his company and become its first client?

The two competing offers were sent up SK&F's chain of command, and it wasn't very long before my own recommendation to accept Garland's offer was decided on. Nevertheless, SK&F's research and development management had also been made aware of Beckman. A few years later, presumably while selecting one from among dozens if not hundreds of technology businesses, SK&F chose to invest some of its Tagamet bounty into the purchase of the entire Beckman corpora-tion. Admittedly this could have been coincidence. Nevertheless, even though Beckman has generally been known only as a manufacturer of scientific instruments, the news stories announcing the acquisition made prominent mention of its peptide chemistry credentials.

Be that as it may, with Garland's mentorship and SK&F's hiring of his student as the nucleus, SK&F began developing a peptide-inspired research program. Unfortunately, although as a business matter I had greatly preferred Garland's proposal over Beckman's, scientifically and personally I wasn't very interested or confident in the effectiveness of any of several peptide-based drug discovery approaches. Peptides are (mostly still!) too big and floppy to be modeled reliably. Neverthe-less, computational activities were a centerpiece in the vision for this peptide project, which meant additional staffing while hopefully raising the company's female headcount, a newly fashionable corporate goal. Both these boxes were checked by the hiring of Judy Hempel, a quantum chemist teaching at nearby Swarthmore, who in combination with Merrie also made me into a department manager. A normal career progression, you might think. But for me, not a good fit. My personal inclinations are poorly suited for administrative responsibilities. I feel no sense of accomplishment from making other people's activities more constructive, only from my own creative activities. Furthermore, because I had been productive without much managerial support beyond resources and a bit of direction, to me it also seemed reasonable to expect similarly self-directed behavior from my staff. However, perhaps understandably for a quantum chemist turning peptide chemist, Judy wanted some intellectual handholding. I must also confess to occasional joking but boorishly sexist references to my female staff as "my harem."

Then it suddenly emerged that the real mission of Tripos, Garland's new company and SK&F's seed investment, was to develop and commercialize the Trigraph, a complete hardware and software system for 3D molecular modeling. The $250,000 that Garland had received from SK&F, with my advocacy, represented half of Tripos's capitalization, the rest coming from a federally backed Small Business Administration loan. (It would still be several years until venture capital in anything like today's form would become available.) I felt an acute sense of betrayal, since Garland had not said a word about hardware or software commercialization in his pitch to me or apparently to anyone else at SK&F.

Fortunately, this revelation didn't seem to upset anyone else at SK&F. The relevance of an improved 3D graphics technology was obvious, if only to overcome the "what is in front of what?" obstacle that Merrie had been laboring over. With the Trigraph, a stick-image display of a molecule could be flown and twirled simply by twisting a joystick. However, the Trigraph hardware architecture linked its display screen, whose dimensions were so minute that they would have embarrassed a 1952 TV manufacturer, to a computer with impressive performance claims but a fiscally uncertain manufacturer, by means of a custom Tripos-designed board, produced somewhere in Florida.

Office chatter at Tripos suggested that these custom boards were flaky and unreliable. Still, an earlier pioneering crystallography software project at Washington University had equipped the Trigraph with a rich assortment of molecular modeling functionalities. This software assortment was named Sybyl.

On the other hand, an attractive alternative hardware for 3D display was being jointly offered by the high-end graphics hardware market leader, Evans and Sutherland (E&S), which combined its multi-picture system (MPS) display with two of DEC's hot new VAX minicomputers. One of the VAXes was dedicated to the most demanding computation, the effectively instantaneous update of the E&S line drawings. Furthermore, Tagamet's abundance had already bewitched SK&F R&D's fledgling IT department into purchasing this hardware configuration—but prematurely because hardly any molecular modeling software existed for an MPS-VAX. So although this new assemblage did allow me to at last show my colleagues the Saturn-like molecular properties that factor analysis had revealed, otherwise it was uselessly filling a room.

That was not my embarrassment, though. My own responsibilities were to chemistry, where, on the one hand, my staff very much wanted the bird-in-hand Trigraph, while on the other, I had become intensely suspicious of anything Tripos. Fortunately (again!), the groundwork for a resolution of this conundrum had already been laid, during an early trip to Garland's facilities, when I was introduced to his computer science collaborator, Rich Dammkoehler. Rich and I were pleasantly startled to recognize one another as trombone players at that Goldenrod showboat jazz festival, he the leader of its perennial host band. Despite our quite different personal styles, these musical and professional affiliations triggered a lifelong friendship. Like many other natives of establishment Saint Louis, Rich could have stepped out of a 1920s novel, being unflappably courteous, affable, methodical, and respectful of traditions—including social class, to my surprise, for it happened that his cousin was leading one of my Philadelphia bands; the cousin worshiped Rich, but Rich felt compelled to apologize to me for his cousin's somewhat plebeian job and manners. Central to Rich's life was Washington University, where he had been an offensive linesman good enough to be invited to a Detroit Lions training camp before becoming the university's first professor of computer science. He was also a true computing pioneer, reporting that he played a major role in developing the first operating system, during a mid-1950s position at IBM. Upon being introduced to the challenges of drug discovery, he had transformed Garland's active analog approach, the conceptual foundation of peptide-based molecular design at Washington University, into a powerful combinatorial algorithm in geometry. Alas, to his disappointment, I would always be doubtful that this approach's mathematically elegant dependence on geometrical precision would be compatible with the messy buzzing realities of biomolecular interactions.

Rich Dammkoehler was also the second largest (though still a very minor) Tripos stockholder and perhaps shared some of my concerns about the various instabilities and uncertainties of the Trigraph. When I mentioned the SK&F hardware orphans, he responded with another proposal, a beautifully engineered win-win-win. There would be two key agreements. In return for something like two hundred thousand dollars and the use of SK&F's dormant hardware, Washington University would develop the software core of a 3D molecular modeling system for this E&S MPS-VAX-VAX configuration. Into that core, Tripos would then install all of the Trigraph's modeling functionalities—the Sybyl apps—in return for the exclusive rights to commercially distribute the entire final package. Since agreements don't write programs, Rich could also provide convincing programming capabilities. He would himself design the system core, and its coding would be done by students who had already proven their excellence on a perennial national champion programming team that Rich coached.

Yet again, SK&F R&D management unquestioningly agreed to my enthusiastic endorsement of this proposal. Garland was far less receptive. He vehemently doubted whether anyone would buy a Trigraph today if there might be something much better in a few years. It might have seemed, though, that Trigraph competition was inevitable, and Tripos was being offered a second-generation product—for free. Yet I doubt that anyone who knows Garland—especially his pride in his own fixity of purpose—would be surprised by his reluctance to write down the Trigraph's sunk cost. Garland had also probably been informed of an even better technology that E&S was then secretly developing, which when introduced would displace the MPS-VAX-VAX configuration and make an orphan of the software core that Rich proposed to create for it.

Then, as SK&F's senior computer chemist, I was asked to consider a third source for a 3D molecular modeling capability. SK&F UK, the Tagamet creator, was funding Oxford don Keith Prout to develop such a system. Surely we in Philadelphia would prefer to share this expense rather than embark on the Tripos voyage? High tea at Oxford's Oriel College was a memorable experience, but the Tripos ship had already weighed anchor, the MPS-VAX-VAX configuration was unquestionably dominating the hardware market, and at that moment budgetary constraints were almost irrelevant within SK&F.

All considered, the implementation of Rich's three-cornered plan went smoothly. The command-line syntax that Rich designed would endure as Sybyl's now mostly hidden underpinnings. The two students who did the programming then became Tripos's best programmers, especially Greg Smith, still an employee of Tripos's successor Certara, whose career highlights include creation of a Python-like programming environment for Sybyl users in the 1980s and a product inventory system that tracked every step in the semiautomated syntheses and purifications of five hundred thousand compounds in the 1990s. However, my only vivid memory from the plan's execution is of a Saint Louis meeting that Garland strode into bellowing, "Dick, I'm going to sue the shit out of you!" Word of a pending Trigraph alternative had leaked, I was indeed probably culpable, and perhaps a Trigraph sale had evaporated or an SBA repayment loomed. At that moment, the future that would materialize a few years later would have seemed unimaginable. I would become Tripos's lead scientist. The Prout technology would, as Chemical Design, become Tripos's earliest competitor. Judy Hempel's favorite SK&F consultant, Arnie Hagler, after failing while on the Tripos board to convince Garland of the merits of molecular dynamics or venture capital investment, would organize Tripos's most important competitor, BioSym.

```
A FIRST LOOK AT THE 1981 OAKLAND ATHLETICS WITH 102:

        Dick Cramer  -  October 25, 1981


    The analysis of baseball player performance and baseball strategies
is on the verge of a great advance. Over the last two decades, analysts
such as Pete Palmer, Bill James, and myself have developed tools which
are extremely effective in explaining overall team performance as the
effects of good and bad statistical performances, offensively and to
some extent defensively, by its individual players. Further progress
depends on more and better statistics. With the data-gathering
capabilities of a BASE system and the data-compiling capabilities of
the 1022 data base management system, it is for the first time possible
to answer easily questions which team management and baseball fans have
been asking since the game began to be played.

    The following examples are questions that I posed and answered in
about six hours of working with the 1981 Oakland playing data. They
give only a flavor of the versatility of the tools. A creative baseball
executive is going to have many better ideas.

        THE NATURE OF THE 1981 OAKLAND ATHLETICS DATA

    For the studies described below, the 1981 Oakland season is converted
to a list of the 8992 on-the-field events. An event is any happening that
would go into a box score - some specific thing that a batter does or
that a baserunner does. An event consists of:

            the date, the opposing team, which team was batting;
            the "offensive player" (batter or runner) and the pitcher;
            the event itself;
            the inning, # outs, score, and on-base situation before and
                after the event occurs;
            when appropriate, the fielding play, type of batted ball,
                and the direction and distance of its flight;
            the sequence of pitches and the resulting count, pitch-by-pitch.

    (The As' operator began reporting the last two types of information
during the second season, so a number of the following analyses could be
applied only during the second season.)

    With 1022 one can retrieve and tabulate any combination of these events
that can be described in terms of these components. The retr
    s is extremely simple, making use of about half a dozen
    readily be taught to the team's operator.
```

Fig. 2. The first page of probably the first report that made use of batted ball direction and distance to try to allocate defensive performance between the contributions of fielding and pitching. This report was proffered to the Oakland Athletics shortly after the end of the 1981 season, the first season for STATS. Courtesy of the author.

This future was unimaginable also because in Philadelphia everything seemed to be going so much my way. SK&F management had decided that Philadelphia's R&D activities needed youthful new leadership, and indeed their hires, George Poste as head of U.S. Research, and Stan Crooke as head of U.S. R&D and Poste's boss, are still major figures in drug discovery circles. One of their key management innovations now looks like an early instance of a policy that eventually afflicted many

American businesses—to stiffen its cooperative if laidback culture with an ethic of individual competitiveness. A major dimension of this competitiveness would be high-quality science. I had happened to accumulate one of the strongest publication records in SK&F Philadelphia and so was named an associate director of chemistry and one of SK&F's first two research fellows. But this honeymoon soon ended, with baseball probably a major cause.

11 Birth of STATS Inc.

In 1980 Pete Palmer introduced me to Steve Mann, another Philadelphian, who had become the Houston Astros' statistician. Within a few months, Steve had arranged for me, when the Astros next visited Philadelphia, to, as he put it, educate his employers in sabermetrics. It would be my first face-to-face encounter with Major League Baseball professionals, yet perhaps because the meeting was in a hotel room, a more familiar milieu for me than a stadium office, I don't recall feeling nervous. Tal Smith (general manager), Bill Virdon (field manager), Bob Lillis (coach), and of course Steve Mann (statistician) comprised, I believe, the entire gathering. I remember a few fragments from that July 30 afternoon. The big one was a phone call reporting that Houston's star pitcher J. R. Richard, already on the disabled list, had collapsed while exercising. I was mutely shocked by the unconcerned, even disrespectful tone of the Houston management responses, and our discussions continued with no further interruption. (It turned out that J. R. had had a stroke and would never throw another major league pitch.) I also recall Bob Lillis's raising a question of why batters are weaker against pitchers who threw from the same side of the plate, to which I speculated that with the pitch trajectory usually moving away from rather than toward the batter, the split second when bat can productively meet ball might become milliseconds smaller. (Almost forty years later, it seems we still aren't certain of the cause.)

Although Steve's Astros tenure soon ended, he hoped to continue a baseball career, and I was interested enough to listen. He envisioned an elaborate information system, following the ball and each fielder on every play, much as MLB is doing today, though in 1980 that was obviously a complete fantasy, technically and financially. He did persuade me to seek business advice from an SK&F senior manager, but that phone call ended soon after my "new business to discuss" was revealed to be in baseball rather than drug discovery. Steve then reported a tangible opportunity that Tal Smith had found for him. Matt Levine, the head of Pacific Select, a sports team marketing company in San Francisco, had a project that needed the creation of a baseball information system. That sounded to me like a real opportunity, and we discussed the possibilities at my townhouse (now downtown so Libby and I could walk to work together) on October 19, 1980, while enjoying perhaps the most glorious day in the history of Philadelphia sports—a victory over the archrival Cowboys, positioning the Eagles for their first Super Bowl appearance, and the Phils' victory in a pivotal and tense fifth game of the World Series, on the way to their first and only twentieth-century world championship.

Steve and I agreed that he would go meet with Matt, and I would do some preliminary proof-of-principle programming. To be as error-resistant as possible, I thought there should be only one data entry operation in a baseball information system, recording each play as it occurred, much as a fan might score a game though in much more detail. The resulting data file would then be processed automatically to generate whatever statistical information might be deemed interesting or useful. Pete advised me that this wouldn't be feasible, though I never asked him why he thought so, and I couldn't see any difficulty. The only play-by-play sample I had was a compendium of World Series games, and, by writing a BASIC script that successfully captured a complicated half-inning, the first in World Series history, I confirmed to my own satisfaction that this approach would work. However, Steve came back reporting that Matt didn't believe that we could meet his needs. Too bad, I thought, because without such an ongoing business to associate with, there was no point in my further tinkering.

And then there was a second fortuitous flight cancellation, after an early January scientific meeting at Asilomar, that left me in San Francisco with a day to kill. Maybe contacting Matt Levine myself could be productive, and after a phone call I found my way to his elegant

Mount Parnassus home. After a short discussion, he suggested that we visit a "computer store" together. A retail computer store? Hard to imagine, because almost the only computers I had seen were those refrigerator-sized boxes adorned with rows of blinking lights and that cost considerably more than a car. This curiosity had to be experienced.

On the way, Matt described his project. As I already knew, the once glorious Oakland A's baseball team had lately been almost scandalously neglected by its owner, to the extent that a college radio station was the current broadcaster for its games. But the A's were about to be sold to new owners encouraged by a marketing study that Pacific Select had done for them. Pacific Select was now being awarded a follow-up contract, with one of its tasks being restoration of the A's public profile by rejuvenating its radio and TV presence. Something new and hot was needed.

In the 1981 Bay Area, nothing was newer and hotter than the personal computer. Furthermore, it happened that a marketing office for Apple was just down the hall from Pacific Select's office, and these two great minds had converged—conceptually—on a synergistic marketing jackpot for both Apple and the Oakland A's. The vision was to support the new A's broadcasters with a display of statistical nuggets that they might pass on to listeners. For example, Rickey Henderson is batting .350 with runners in scoring position, or Tony Armas had already hit a home run this year against the incoming pitcher, or Wayne Gross's next run batted in would be the two hundredth of his career. Apple would supply the hardware. But how would the programming be done? There wouldn't be much money. (My understanding is that the seventy-five thousand dollars Pacific Select received from the A's mainly financed an innovative redesign of their ticket purchasing processes.)

The computer store was a fantasy come to life. I had already noticed a personal computer in a stock trader friend's hands, an Apple II running a clunky-looking VisiCalc, the original killer app. But seeing them in the incongruous environment of familiar retail display shelves, attended by knowledgeable sales staff, was consciousness expanding (in 1970s lingo). I was feted with Apple II's displaying normal-looking text, eighty characters per line in lower case, and its ability to connect to floppy disk drives, modems, and printers. I was shown how to connect such peripherals to an Apple II by snapping open its case and thrusting a printed circuit board into one of the designated slots. Sounded a bit fragile, though, so it was reassuring to hear that very soon there would be a more conventionally configured Apple III.

Perhaps it surprises you that I would never have a second thought about taking on this A's-Apple programming project. For me, it was a once in a lifetime opportunity to assume a meaningful role within the sanctum of Major League Baseball as a professional expert doing something I greatly enjoyed and at no apparent hazard to my existing commitments. And almost as important to me, Pacific Select's sponsorship minimized a risk faced by any would-be innovator, that technological success would be negated by weak organizational support or follow-up.

Before my plane had landed back in Philadelphia, I had handwritten a brief technical proposal. Two aspects of this proposal seem worth mention. First, during a game, the Apple would display statistical information about the current batter at the top of the screen, for use by the broadcasters, and accept an operator's entry of the current game at the bottom of the screen. Among other things, this simultaneity would ensure that the broadcaster's top-of-screen information indeed referenced the current batter! Second, the PDP-10 that I was using for my SK&F work would also do the heavy lifting for the A's Apple, mainly because of my confidence in the PDP-10's muscle but also to provide me with easier control over the software and its results. This architecture would be employed as follows. Before the start of the next A's game, the Apple operator would call up the PDP-10, download the account of the previous game, wait for the PDP-10 to process all its accumulated game accounts, then upload the resulting files of statistics for each of the A's players, ready for the top-of-screen display in the next game. Most of the contents of these files would be splits, eighty-character lines of batting statistics that dissected a batter's performance by situation, an example being whether the opposing pitcher was left- or right-handed. Boring trivial stuff today, but in 1981 the only other way to get such breakdowns, even for someone in the media and at best approximately, would be to do them yourself. Bill James's first self-publications contained little more than tables of such splits that he generated himself.

I snail-mailed Matt this retyped plan, and it was quickly approved. However, my preference for the Apple III was a concern, and a week or so later I was back in the Bay Area to talk with the Apple people. Matt had assigned one of his veteran marketing specialists, Tom Black, as the point person for all work with the A's. Tom drove the two of us to a white stucco building, apparently a remodeled full-service gas station, on a side street in suburban Cupertino. There we joined six Apple staff, crowding into a small unpainted conference room. Two of the Apple guys, I was told, were product managers for the Apple II and the Apple III, and the body language of these two immediately indicated, even to me, that the A's Apple would not be a III. I listened to hints of production problems with the III, and to a cornucopia of glamorous peripherals that could equip a II. We quickly agreed that an A's Apple (the II, of course) would include the UCSD Pascal language software, a monitor (a tiny cubical TV display) connected through a Smarterm board that provided the eighty-character lines of lowercase text, two floppy disk drives (eventually four), a Hayes Micromodem for communicating with the PDP-10, a Symtec light pen for graphical input, and a Silentype thermal printer for hard copy (to be used, for example, as backup for an ongoing game entry). The three such systems needed for the project would together have retailed for about $7,500. Programming could begin once I received one of them, and spring training was not far off.

Meanwhile there were organizational issues. For me the most troubling was Steve Mann's role. Matt was adamant about excluding Steve, as he had not been comfortable with Steve's professionalism, and he was already paying experienced staff to do anything Steve might have done. Steve had also made an unfortunate impression on my wife Libby. Maybe a truly loyal partner would have joined Steve and walked away from this extraordinary opportunity, but "collaboration" would be a better description than "partnership" of how I had viewed my relationship with Steve. In the end, I asked Matt to transfer to Steve the compensation allocated for me as programmer, maybe eight thousand dollars, and Steve welcomed the cash.

Anyway, with the two PhD paychecks and mostly frugal spending habits, Libby and I hardly needed the money. Instead, I thought a more appropriate form of compensation would be some sort of equity. So, as a fiscally sophisticated McKinsey alumnus, Matt proposed a corporate entity that would be financially separate from Pacific Select. That was fine with me, and for some reason Libby and I also agreed to invest fifteen thousand dollars of seed money. I've forgotten how much ownership I was then allocated in this entity, but it eventually became immaterial when the whole thing was dumped in my lap. Tom Black conjured its name, STATS (Sports Team Analysis and Tracking System). This first edition of STATS Inc. included all the accoutrements, even a corporate seal imprinter.

However, STATS would be a hollow shell until programming could begin. The Apple-prescribed language, Pascal, would probably have won a popularity contest among 1981's programmers, and I soon recognized how handy its advanced data-handling features, such as sets, structures, and records, would be for my work, compared to FORTRAN or BASIC. The Apple II's implementation of UCSD Pascal behaved much like Python or Java does today, as a two-staged translation of Pascal source into machine-specific instructions, with the second stage occurring only while the program was running. The relatively low memory requirements of UCSD's intermediate P-code were probably critical to the project's success. However, there were some performance downsides in the P-code's generation from Pascal as well as in its execution. The rate of P-code compilation was no more than two lines per second. I would usually have time to read a page or two of something else while waiting for a beep signaling the next coding mistake.

But where was the Apple? I did some preliminary programming without it, such as translating the proof-of-principle PDP-10 BASIC into Pascal's richer syntax. Pete Palmer agreed to write the FORTRAN that the PDP-10 would run to generate those splits for the broadcasters. I'd already decided that the A's Apple would capture far more than the minimal information needed to create conventional statistics or box scores, items such as the weather and, using the light pen, the direction and distance of batted balls. The most impactful of these additions would be the pitch sequences themselves. Pitch counts and ball-strike ratios are such fundamental information today that it may be surprising that, as of 1981, no one seemed ever to have considered pitch sequences to be worth recording. (Reportedly some pitching coaches did record pitch counts, occasionally by assigning this job to the next day's starting pitcher, ostensibly to encourage his attention to the opposing batters.) It's possible, maybe likely, that the A's Apple was not the first computer system that interactively recorded play-by-play accounts, but I'd be very surprised to learn that its pitch sequence records were not a first. Pickoff throws were also recorded, surely a first, considering the ridicule this idea initially received!

Finally, on the same day that *The Sporting News*'s spring training edition appeared, late in February, the cartons of Apple equipment arrived. A month later, on March 28, I was at Hohokam Park in Mesa, Arizona, trying out the code that would be the foundation for the prospective system's game entry operation under ballpark conditions. The biggest challenge turned out to be how sluggishly the Apple responded whenever anything happened that needed quick entry. Every reading from an Apple II's floppy disk drive of crucial information, such as the splits for the next batter or the next segment of P-code to be run, usually began with a rattling sound as the starting point was located and then a few seconds of hiss as information was being transferred. Even replacing one line of screen text with another included a perceptible delay. The washing out of the computer screen by Arizona sun glare was another problem, though it might be a smaller one in major league press boxes.

Finally, using the light pen to enter the direction and distance of batted balls would be impossible, not only because of the glare but also because of a seconds-long delay whenever the Apple II shifted between its text and graphics display modes. However, no way would I abandon the possibility of better evaluating fielders by recording batted ball information. In the middle of that night I woke up thinking of polar coordinates as another means for recording direction and distance and had the idea programmed into its final form for a successful test at that Sunday afternoon's game. Reportedly STATS still uses this notation, with direction labeled A–Z and distance from home plate in feet, to wherever a batted ball is first fielded or otherwise lands. For example, a ground-ball single past the pitcher into center field might have its direction and distance code recorded as M180. However, I'd had to blow off a planned breakfast in Phoenix with my closest friend back in that one-room school, John "Joe" Alcock, who was on the way to becoming a Regents' Professor of biology, specifically animal behavior, at Arizona State. And I wouldn't again visit Phoenix long enough to see Joe until SABR began holding its analytics conferences there.

Shortly before Opening Day, Matt and Tom tried out game entry themselves, and Matt called to express concern with how clumsy the entry of player substitutions had been. Fortunately, I was already aware of this problem. Because a substitution was being treated as just another event, any wrong or omitted substitution would hopelessly jumble any further data entry, and no facility yet existed for editing a game account. But I'd already designed a fix; whenever a substitution occurred, the user was given the entire lineup to edit. Substitution errors thereby became much rarer, and their effects were easily and immediately correctable. Matt later confided that it was this preemptive correction that first convinced him that the A's Apple would become a reality.

His was an important conviction because achieving that reality would require more than hardware and a computer program. A trained operator was needed, and for this post Tom Black recruited an aspiring broadcaster, Jay Alves. For Jay this would be the first step of a thirty-year major league career in public relations with the A's and Rockies. Road trips were another challenge for the A's Apple II, a relatively fragile addition to a baseball team's baggage. Tom found that shipping containers for medical equipment could be customized to cradle an A's Apple and all of its peripherals within a spongy form-fitting padding. However, those containers were brutally bulky to handle. Whenever I encounter a former A's Apple operator, his first reminiscence is of lugging them up to the press box on a hot summer day. Tom Black must also have had introductory discussions with the A's newly hired broadcasters, respected Bay Area veterans Lon Simmons and Bill King. Finally, in anticipation of postseason marketing to other clubs, product names were coined: Edge 1.000 for the entire system, and Playball for the only program so far.

With game entry now working, my next step was to get the PDP-10 involved. Pete Palmer visited, bringing his tabulating program as a deck of cards. (He observed how easy program editing was with such a deck, simply by exchanging cards. "Compared to what?" I thought.) Its installation and integration with Playball's event codes went smoothly. The final piece was the communication process itself—the Apple program that would guide the Micromodem through the above-mentioned protocol: dialing up the PDP-10; sending the Apple's textual encoding of the latest game; the PDP-10 running Pete's program to process the accumulated game files and generate the splits for each A's player; and retrieving the statistical splits that the broadcasters would see, as a separate text file for each A's player. The Micromodem's built-in capabilities made this one of the easier pieces of the first Playball to code, but for the next fifteen years, until internet browsers appeared, mission-critical adaptations of Playball to the succession of improvements in communications hardware would present the most onerous programming challenges of my life.

On May 2–3, I was back in the Bay Area, helping to unveil Playball to the announcers. I'd been sent scorebook pages and had entered all the previous games. Two monitors showing the same display were attached to the Apple, one in front of the data entry operator, me on this occasion, and the other in front of the broadcasters. The A's had been following up a surprisingly strong 1980 with a record-breaking 19-3 start. In the press box, the sunshine did not overpower the displays' legibility; Playball's performance was fault free; the announcers found the invasion of their territory by a display monitor to be at least tolerable; and the A's beat the Yankees. An exciting start for Playball on a splendid East Bay afternoon!

Alas, a few more days of ballpark usage uncovered all sorts of problems. The most frustrating were mysterious midgame crashes, whose causes usually turned out to be hardware failures rather than software bugs. The numerous peripherals (display, disk drives, and so on) that Edge 1.000 depended on, occupying all but one of the Apple II's six slots, demanded power and generated heat, making endemic the failure of its motherboard (the computer itself) until the Apple IIe was introduced in 1983. Then, whenever Edge 1.000 traveled, the Apple II's thrust-card-into-slot method for connecting its peripherals presented another dilemma; leave the cards in and vibration would weaken the slot and perhaps fracture the motherboard; take them out and reconnection could fail or be botched. (My demo to White Sox owner Jerry Reinsdorf of his personal Edge 1.000 would flop when I nervously misaligned a disk-to-board slot and fried his board.) Another common type of hardware failure, though seldom mysterious and not limited to the Apple, was the fragility of floppy disks. Personal computer software documentation then always began with, "make a working copy of this program disk" on the disk drive where that program copy was to be run. And despite the recommended insertion of a piece of cardboard into each floppy slot before packing up, a disk drive head could slip out of alignment while traveling.

But, yes, of course, there were software failings too. I'd settled into a work rhythm that yielded almost forty hours per week of baseball work, starting most evenings around 7:00 p.m. and quitting at 11:00 to unwind—although whenever a coding problem was still unresolved, sleep might be evasive. If my fix to a newly discovered bug was critical, an evening might finish with a drive to the airport to FedEx a floppy or two. More hours on weekends. Yet I don't remember Libby expressing much irritation or disappointment at my new fixation beyond her sardonic observation that complaining about my jazz and baseball hobbies would be unreasonable because they were income-producing.

Although Playball was now supporting accurate game entry, the intended outcome, reliable delivery of correct statistics, was still to be achieved. There remained a few conventional bugs. For example, at first a bunt flyout did not bring up the next batter, invalidating the game state and thus making subsequent game entry impossible. And the safeguards against input mistakes were inadequate. When I showed Playball to a visiting Paul Bamberg, he immediately embarrassed me by successfully sending two runners to the same base with no out being recorded, though one of the runners disappeared. Unfortunately, there are only two means of detecting such bugs, either hours of systematic testing, for which I had neither the time nor the patience, or stumbling over them during actual operations. So Matt delegated as much testing as possible to a new Pacific Select recruit, Don Leopold, a Harvard graduate who had been teaching transcendental meditation, notably to the 1973 Phillies starting pitcher rotation, though not to good effect judging from the 1973 performances of these pitching veterans. (No slur intended; under Melanie's influence I too once regularly practiced transcendental meditation.)

Design shortcomings were also showing up. Playball's accuracy of course depended on every game having been correctly entered. But, except from the play-by-play record on the Silentype as a game was entered, there was no way to confirm a game account's accuracy. One check might be its comparison to a published box score, so I quickly added box score creation to Playball's functions. Nevertheless, a mistake in data entry could then be corrected only by reentering the entire game. Although Playball would never have the now-conventional undo, a Ctrl+Z, back-up-and-reenter-the-last-play capability, I did start work on a postgame editing capability. But this would not be finished until after the 1981 season.

Meanwhile, the collective effect of these teething problems was that Playball's statistical results were becoming more and more uncertain. If the statistics it produced were unreliable, how could the system be providing any benefit to the broadcasters? With no benefit, did the cost of Jay Alves's travel make sense? My long-distance impression was that West Coast frustrations were getting so high that the whole project might be suspended.

But instead—yet another break—a player strike suspended the entire 1981 season! When play resumed two months later, most of the worst software failings had been overcome, and Dave Stoddard, the tuba player in one of my jazz bands, had used my precious Apple, free while I was at work, to correctly reenter all the previous sixty games, working from copies of the scorebook kept by A's manager Billy Martin's factotum, Mickey Morabito. For the rest of the 1981 season, Playball's performance seemed quite satisfactory, so with everything finally working reliably, full speed ahead for the 1982 season!

12 White Sox and Yankees

A whole new dimension had already been added to Edge 1.000 at the initiative of Tony Stracciolini, my main contact among the PDP-10's staff and a sports enthusiast. I must have mentioned to him a remarkable SK&F memo that, with the goal of minimizing taxation of the ballooning Tagamet profits, urged the 1981 prepayment, wherever practical, of 1982 expenses. Tony proposed that if SK&F were to thus prepay my SK&F-related usage of the PDP-10, in return the PDP-10 facility would license a database management system, which would be useful to me when wearing my STATS hat. Although database management systems (DBMS) such as Oracle and MySQL are ubiquitous today, for example, underlying most web-browser-based applications, in 1981 DBMS technology was mostly limited to specialized custom-built applications, such as airline reservations, running on IBM mainframes. But I could visualize the possibilities and relayed this offer to SK&F management, sans mention of baseball. System 1022 was quickly installed, and before long Tony had loaded the A's 1981 games into a simple schema of games, innings, events, pitches, and comments.

Therefore, on October 25, a week and a half after the A's last postseason game, I sent the A's "A First Look at the 1981 Oakland Athletics with 1022." (Its first page appears as Fig. 2) Notably, the report included "a measure of the performance of their outfielders, bearing in mind that the A's pitching staff may give up more fly balls than does the 'average' AL outfield." This result was obtained by considering all fly balls that had landed more than 160 feet from home as potentially catchable and comparing the batting lines for those events that occurred when the A's opponents batted with those when the A's batted. By these criteria, the A's outfield turned an additional "65 hits, 9 being doubles and 8 triples, into outs," thereby improving an otherwise projected A's team ERA of 5.21 to the A's actual second place ERA of 3.30. Despite its limitations (maybe the A's batters' outfield flies were harder to catch), this was surely the first sabermetric-type analysis that included fielding beyond the traditional counting stats—a baby step toward today's world of defensive shifts and 4-5-3 double plays. However, I was never told whether Oakland made any use of this report.

Toward spring I began hearing that the Chicago White Sox were hot prospects. They wanted two new things. Could I expand Edge 1.000 to track the types and locations of each pitch? And would I also write an entirely separate program, a searchable repository for summaries of players' scouting report? These sounded like enjoyable projects, so I agreed.

Indeed, I agreed with a feeling of relief because my first off-season had been plagued with the first adaptation of Playball to new communication hardware. The Micromodem's 300-baud transmission rate, in principle thirty characters per second, but in practice, over noisy and erratic ballpark phone lines, much slower than reading speed, had meant, for example, that the Apple-PDP-10 session of game preparation might not finish between games of a double header. And the cost of lengthy long-distance phone calls was then more than incidental. There were two new products, the Apple SuperSerial card and the Hayes SmartModem, that could be combined to make possible 1,200-baud transmission, four times as fast. But controlling the interface between the dependability of a computer's internal environment and the vagaries of its external telephone connection was tormenting to program, especially for someone as ignorant of communication technology and protocols as I was. The SuperSerial card manual provided little beyond a listing of the card's assembly code.

The biggest obstacle was the last step of an Apple-PDP-10 session, during which the Apple was retrieving the statistical information, the text that the broadcasters were to see. Reading down its list of A's players, via the SuperSerial card, the Apple would ask the PDP-10 to "send me the latest Rickey Henderson splits," then would store the characters that the SuperSerial card received until it received a special "finished" character sequence, whereupon the Apple would tell the SuperSerial card to stop listening and instead transmit a request for the splits for the next player. No problem so far. But what if line noise prevented that special "finished" character sequence from being received? My understanding of the assembly code listing suggested that the SuperSerial card was then still in charge and thus would just keep waiting for more characters, which would never arrive because the PDP-10 had finished sending that player file. Gridlock! With Pacific Select's intercession, I sought privileged advice from Apple and eventually spoke to an engineer who had designed the card. From his suppressed sigh as he confirmed my interpretation of the assembly code listing, I naïvely fancied that I'd revealed this bug to Apple, though I later would learn that this problem was intrinsically unavoidable for an Apple II. Anyway, this conversation confirmed the cause and the unavoidability of this problem, so I settled for the kludgy workaround of also writing the incoming characters to the screen. Any halt in this flow of characters would alert the operator of the need to restart the splits retrieval. And, at least on noise-free telephone lines, the 1,200-baud project did make the Apple-PDP-10 sessions run four times faster in 1982. Later versions of the SuperSerial card, if I recall correctly, included a listing of some Apple assembly code whose inclusion within Edge 1.000 overcame most data transmission problems, except the few characters that were occasionally lost due to line noise.

In February of 1982 the White Sox officially became the second major league team to sign up for Playball. Years later I learned the financial parameters of this deal. Playball, including specified enhancements, and a Scout program, both yet for me to write, along with some training, totaled $45,000. Hardware (three Apples with lots of peripherals and a twenty-megabyte Corvus hard drive for Scout) probably cost at least $20,000. Their running costs would be a quarterly $2,500 maintenance fee from Pacific Select and about $2,500 a year in PDP-10 usage fees. (Multiply by 2.5 for the current cost, and consider that today's vastly superior functionally equivalent hardware would cost less than $500.)

The computer champion for the White Sox was Jack Gould, a senior vice president and shareholder who had close personal relationships with the White Sox owner, Jerry Reinsdorf. Jack's shrewd no-nonsense style had surely been honed by his thirty-five missions as a Distinguished Flying Cross bomber pilot in World War II. His own purpose in acquiring Edge 1.000 was to strengthen the White Sox's position in player salary arbitration hearings. Yet the money wrangles he would also get into with Pacific Select never dampened the hospitable receptions that he and the other White Sox staff always gave to me.

The new code promised to the White Sox for accommodating the additional information about pitches was not hard for me to provide. The White Sox endorsed my proposals of a five-by-five grid for recording pitch location, the central three-by-three portion for strikes, and six pitch types, fast, slider, curve, change, sinker/forkball, and knuckler. (No cutters or four-seamers yet.) Playball allowed this information to be entered either during or after the game. The White Sox internally debated the best location for making these visual observations, which, to everyone's surprise, was decided to be the home plate TV camera.

The Scout program was to be a searchable repository for reports on players by White Sox scouts. Today such a program would be built from an SQL DBMS (structured query language data base management system) like Oracle or MySQL, but no such DBMS ever existed for the Apple II. However, UCSD Pascal's support for files of records provided a workable alternative. The White Sox would be asking only one type of query, "find the players who fulfill some combination of criteria," so any cross-indexing of these records would have been overkill. But because much of a scouting report is free text, storing those reports would need what was then a lot of disk space. So the White Sox laid out at least ten thousand dollars for a twenty-megabyte Corvus hard disk, a box with the general dimensions of a microwave, shipped directly to me so I could write the Scout code.

Edge 1.000's White Sox operator would be a recent college graduate, Danny Evans, forming a brilliant partnership between man and mission. The Apple was Danny's first responsibility in a remarkably diverse baseball management career, including stints as player representative, league commissioner, broadcaster, and Twitter correspondent (@DanEvans108), and highlighted by an underappreciated two years as the Dodgers' general manager. Danny's energetic inquisitiveness extracted new insights from Edge 1.000's accumulated data and his relentless enthusiasm sold those insights to White Sox management. The first widely publicized baseball computing success story was Danny's discovery that during the 1982 season the White Sox at home had hit many more fly balls that were almost home runs than had their opponents. Suppose the White Sox moved home plate a few feet toward the fences? Management was convinced and did so, and the White Sox won the 1983 divisional title going away, as veteran White Sox slugger Greg Luzinski's home run total went from 18 to 32, and Danny reveled in Luzinski's boisterous appreciation. (As a responsible scientist with baseball-reference.com in front of me, I have checked some details, finding that the White Sox home park indeed increased net home runs by 12 [adding roughly two wins], but that Luzinski's increase of 14 home runs mainly occurred on the road. So perhaps the fence change was not as great a help as was then believed, but this story would become a minor legend.)

Just a few more clips from my half dozen visits to Comiskey Park:

In 1985 or 1986, hearing from general manager Rollie Hemond that the White Sox trade of LaMarr Hoyt (a Cy Young winner in 1983) for (future White Sox icon) Ozzie Guillen was inspired by Scout's stored scouting reports, which identified him as the only minor league shortstop who was above average in both hitting and fielding.

In September 1983, during pregame on the field with Danny Evans, dodging batted balls and sitting in an otherwise empty dugout, discussing Edge 1.000 with soon-to-be-celebrated pitching coach Dave Duncan, as he demonstrated his prowess with chewing tobacco by spitting just next to my feet (which I ignored). Duncan understood the computer's potential and during the first winter took an Apple to his Florida home. With mixed satisfaction, though, as Duncan then responded to my "how's it going with the computer?" with a thought that was so on point that I've often repeated it: "It's great when it works, but when it doesn't, you want to bang your head against the wall!"

Finishing an evening in the White Sox postgame Bard's Room, hanging out with announcers Don Drysdale and Hawk Harrelson, who boasted how hungover he had been in a 1968 game where Paul Bamberg and I, while gathering stopwatch timings for the design of his baseball table game, had seen him drive home all 7 Red Sox runs with 3 home runs.

Libby enjoying the press-box experience—though unmoved by the display of her name, as an honored attendee, on the new DiamondVision scoreboard.

On April 27, 1985, again in the press box with Libby, who unabashedly commiserated with Phil Rizzuto and Tony Kubek on their shock in learning that Yogi Berra had just been fired as the Yankees manager. Kubek also had lots of questions about Edge 1.000.

In September 1982, during a general review of the White Sox's first Edge 1.000 season, at the top of an empty Comiskey Park, listening to Jack Gould's soliloquy on how they'd like to renovate but there was no way to add enough of the critical high-revenue corporate boxes.

Accompanying Jerry Reinsdorf on a limousine ride to his north suburban home and having my naïve question about California real estate politely brushed off—on arrival, blowing the Edge 1.000 demo by shorting out his new Apple II.

Agreeing with Rollie Hemond that maybe my aging Phils could sneak into the postseason and meet the White Sox in the 1983 World Series (ultimately, it would be the Phils and not the White Sox in that World Series).

In the 1983 season, the Yankees became the third Edge 1.000 installation. As usual I had no part in the sales negotiations, and I heard only that the response to Pacific Select's first quote was "sharpen your pencil." My impression was that to George Steinbrenner a computer seemed a good thing to have but that the Yankee staff might therefore keep it at arm's length. Anyway, once the deal was done, with Yankee Stadium only a few hours' train ride from Philadelphia, I spent several weekend afternoons in a closet-sized appendage to the stadium press box watching a game being entered. The operator, Doug Melvin, made Edge 1.000 a career springboard, one that helped him advance from the Yankees' left-handed batting practice pitcher and a daily railroad commute all the way from family-affordable Rhode Island into an especially successful front office career. His twenty-plus years as general manager of the Texas Rangers and Milwaukee Brewers yielded five postseason appearances, of the twelve in those team's collective histories.

The first anecdote I tell to any baseball fan interested in my moneyball experiences involves Doug as something of a foil and takes the form of a "Who was this guy?" trivia question. Early in the 1984 season I was sitting with Doug as he entered a game against Kansas City, discussing the Yankee's prospects. I mentioned a left-handed hitting sophomore outfielder and first baseman who in the last half of 1983 had hit .283 with 4 home runs. Doug was dismissive. "He doesn't pull the ball—he can't even hit home runs off me" in batting practice! In the sixth inning this mystery player hit his first home run of 1984, off respected left-handed pitcher Bud Black. "Looks to me like he pulled that one pretty well, Doug!" So who was this player? Sorry—you could give baseball-reference.com a trial. A hint, though: if you are any kind of a fan, you surely know his name.

By the start of 1983, the interest that magazines and other periodicals were taking in Edge 1.000's novelty had become a mania. Here are some examples of articles about Edge 1.000, taken from the Wikipedia entry on Steve Boros, who as Oakland's new manager was the most publicly associated with computer usage: *Newsweek*, May 23, 1983; *Sports Illustrated*, June 6, 1983; *InfoWorld*, December 12, 1983, and August 13, 1984; *Digital Deli*, 1984; *Popular Mechanics*, May 1984; *Psychology Today*. A scientific colleague told me that he'd even seen a description of Edge 1.000 in an airline seat-pocket magazine. At first the media attention was fun. *Discover* did an early interview and even sent a photographer to take pictures of me awkwardly winding up on a neighborhood pitcher's mound. However, after the first half dozen telephone interviews, answering the same thoughtless questions again and again became boring, even irritating. For example, "How are the teams using the computer during games?" "I really don't know." "Do you like baseball?" "Yes." "Did you play baseball?" "No." Still, most of what appeared in print was simply excerpted from earlier articles so didn't directly burden me. But this flood of media coverage may have been a major cause in what happened next.

13 Scientific Career Transition

Left to my own devices, I would probably have continued as an employee of SK&F and its successors until retirement. Fortunately for me, as it turned out, SK&F R&D vice president Stan Crooke had different ideas.

Crooke was full of strong ideas. For example, there was the day he convened us research chemists to hear him pronounce that we should start measuring the redox potentials (tendencies to take up or lose electrons) of drug candidates because of the unrecognized impact of this parameter on biological effectiveness. His strange view reminded me of Trofim Lysenko, whose Marxist-based dogma had destroyed Soviet biology. Perhaps it was Crooke's previous career in cancer chemotherapeutics, whose drugs often do include multivalent metallic atoms, that had prompted this biochemically absurd generalization (which was of course quietly ignored by his audience).

However, the Crooke ideas that did affect me were new administrative policies. One was an ideal that drug discovery research should not be simply a lifetime nine-to-five vocation but also a calling that should, for example, often find the truly committed and valued scientist in the lab on weekends. Not that this expectation will seem unreasonably burdensome to many of today's scientists, especially those working in hopeful startups. But it was 1982, and SK&F was hardly a startup, so achieving this ideal would imply some major reshaping of the existing SK&F R&D culture. Therefore, it was widely believed that another of our new bosses' policies was to encourage turnover among their reluctant scientific veterans.

There are many means of encouraging staff turnover, and Libby was among the first to experience one. A management decision to end

SK&F's historic commitment to antipsychotic discovery put Libby, a neurobiologist, squarely in the crosshairs. Libby was given a hopelessly discordant reassignment, to develop an antibody for a leukotriene, something that even antibody experts had reportedly failed to do. My foolish protests irritated Libby as well as management. Then when she unexpectedly succeeded, her reward was a career choice—either immediate termination or be transferred to the clerical task of tabulating clinical test results, specifically, in a sort of sardonic symbolism, the observations of diarrheal side effects from a new drug candidate. She was expected to seek a new job. Yet my job and general aversion to relocation obviously limited her geographic flexibility.

However, management soon resolved our conundrum. Another of its novel policies was open scientific reviews of its active research programs, often attended by as many as a hundred colleagues. In this show trial atmosphere, though, it was widely assumed that most of the questions were actually staged by management. Early in 1983, CADD activities were suddenly scheduled for such a review, and while CADD's formal reporting relationships had become tangled, this review would focus on me, as the initiator and continuing champion of most of its ongoing activities. And although my CADD staff was optimistically proud of our group's accomplishments, I was not at all surprised when its outcome was my public humiliation—most likely its intention. My specific "scientific" failings included: some delay in completion of the Saint Louis Sybyl redesign project that I was still responsible for; the inconclusive results of the 3D-QSAR project; and having put too many of my own hours into nonprofessional, therefore implicitly shoddy, PROPHET programming, instead of focusing my personal scientific attentions on the support of the new peptide projects. Although these charges were factually unchallengeable, future events might suggest that management's interpretations were unduly pessimistic.

Libby helped me overcome my inclination to take the next few days off, and I feigned an indifference to the review's outcome. I was assigned sessions with a human relations consultant, another special Crooke hire, to help me overcome a "bad attitude." Although this HR guy allegedly reported that I was "redeemable," at a one-on-one meeting that I requested to clear the air, Crooke directly confirmed my impression that at SK&F I had become one of the irretrievably fallen.

The British discoverers of Tagamet were dismayed, and there were even hints of places for the two of us at SK&F's expanding UK labs. However, to me it seemed that it was only a matter of time before top management extended the Crooke-Poste restructuring of R&D across the Atlantic and that my UK friends would then themselves be seeking different pastures, as indeed happened. Yet why had SK&F R&D management selected Libby and me for early dispatch? Perhaps those *Newsweek* and *Sports Illustrated* articles on Edge 1.000 were embarrassing management by exposing a continuing allegiance to forty-hour weeks from one of its leading scientists? Or was there an element of "it is good to kill an admiral from time to time, in order to encourage the others"? My occasionally naïve or arrogant mouthiness surely didn't help. All pointless speculation, though, especially considering the happy results.

Libby and I now could easily agree on our course of action. Libby would be free to seek a new job anywhere, ensuring at least one PhD income for the two of us, and I would somehow adapt. One of my activities would of course still be baseball, as Matt had recently yielded to my insistence on half-time compensation, for tax purposes represented as a royalty to me on the exclusive use of Edge 1.000, which I was thereby implied to own. Otherwise, though, I never had the slightest thought of abandoning science or relegating it to a secondary status. Baseball still felt to me like a charmingly persistent fantasy, while drug discovery was a solidly promising reality. All across the pharmaceutical industry, the new 3D display technologies were feeding a growing swell of interest in the potential value of CADD. Particularly inspirational had been the cover image on the February 13, 1981, issue of *Science*, a strand of DNA viewed end-on, perpendicularly to DNA's familiar corkscrew image. My own CADD achievements had been widely recognized, for example by election to the chairmanship of the 1985 Gordon Conference on QSAR. Surely some sort of CADD activity could be resumed, maybe with whomever became Libby's new employer.

While waiting for Libby's shoe to drop, I thought of becoming a tool builder instead of a tool user by working for a software vendor rather than a drug company. It would be a more enjoyable activity for me, and the benefits of any new CADD methodology (which I never doubted I would myself create!) would not be limited to a single drug discovery organization. There were two vendor possibilities. One was Tripos, an organization lurching from one crisis to the next, including the delays that had contributed to my SK&F downfall, headed by an unsympathetic Garland Marshall, and probably a long and expensive distance away from Libby's future employer. So I approached the other vendor, MDL, whose Wipke-inspired MACCS chemical database system was rapidly gaining market acceptability, and explained my situation. MDL had responded to the swell of interest in 3D modeling by becoming the exclusive commercial vendor for the two leading and functionally complementary 3D structure building codes, Lou Allinger's MM2 and Tony Hopfinger's CAMSEQ. But without 3D display their customers were not finding much value in 3D model building. Perhaps an expert in 3D modeling could bridge this gap. And, as mentioned, I had already had unusually strong scientific and personal experiences with these codes and with their creators. Finally, like Pacific Select, MDL was based in the Bay Area—no telling yet what my travel expenses there might turn out to be, but at least they might be shared. A terrific fit, a no-brainer. I agreed with MDL president Steve Goldby to become the first CADD application scientist as soon as Libby's new position materialized.

I agreed despite some stealthy misgivings, though, because I really wanted to develop new, or at least improve on existing, CADD software myself. Working with MDL's development team at long distance was unlikely to be practical. Perhaps I could collaborate with Lou or Tony, but their responses to my feelers were lukewarm at best. On the other hand, Tripos had started getting its act together, and the occasion of a scientific talk during one of my visits reminded me that Tripos could provide a more scientifically oriented business environment that I would prefer. Not that these misgivings would have been relevant— except that Libby's new job turned out to be in Terre Haute, Indiana, a three-hour drive from Tripos.

Another happy windfall, and a game-changer, for Garland, Tripos, and especially me. At that summer's Gordon Conference, I had presented the Hansch-condemned poster that depicted how 3D graphics revealed the Saturn-like flattening of that cloud of data points. Garland was interested. Probably he envisioned a possible second major market, data analysis, for the 3D graphics technology that Tripos was commercializing. He also knew of my 3D-QSAR efforts at SK&F. And there would be some name value if I were to join Tripos. So he made me an offer. I forget the details, but Tripos would supply a desktop computer that I could use from home with dial-up (1,200 baud) access to a DEC VAX 750 computer that Tripos had acquired to fulfill its Sybyl commitment to SK&F. There must have been expense reimbursement and maybe a modest hourly wage. Most importantly, Tripos would, by supplying the appropriate organizational foundation, allow me to apply for one of the new SBIR grants, which earmarked federal funding for small businesses to perform innovation and research. To get paid, get funded—a familiar challenge for so many scientists!

Garland's proposition was compelling. What I would be expected to do, create CADD software, was what I most wanted to do. Frequent face-to-face contact with my coworkers would be geographically workable. A smaller and less certain income wouldn't matter, considering Libby's salary, the Edge 1.000 royalties, and Terre Haute itself, then a quintessential Rust Belt town where the only house on offer for more than our modest Philadelphia townhouse had a tennis court. (True, Terre Haute wasn't Philadelphia; we would be slightly alien there as the couple with no kids and different last names, and Dan Quayle would be our congressman. Yet an NPR radio show this August 2016 morning prophetically featured Terre Haute with its county as the most politically representative of all American cities.) Anyway, if this Tripos thing didn't work out, perhaps MDL would still be interested. I accepted the offer.

That turned out to be a fortunate and timely decision. That dominant supplier of interactive 3D graphics hardware, Evans and Sutherland, was about to announce a revolutionary new product, the PS300, with greatly improved performance. The vectors that the PS300 still drew with could now be brightly colored, no longer requiring a darkened room for their visibility, and could also vary in their intensity, providing a hint of depth perception. Furthermore, the PS 300 did not require a satellite VAX to rotate its 3D image, greatly reducing the cost of an installation. Together these advances would make it possible to include the 3D display of a candidate drug structure within its (much larger) biological target, hopefully providing key mechanistic details of how a successful drug might work.

Fundamentally new hardware usually demands fundamentally new software. To lead this Tripos-vital development project, Tripos hired John McAlister, and he was soon reinforced by Dammkoehler's SK&F-supported graduate students, Perry Simeroth and Greg Smith. John, Greg, and I would become the most significant of Tripos's lasting employees. John's admirable credentials included a PhD in crystallography, extensive formal training in computer science, and experience of system design with the Washington University ancestor of Tripos's Sybyl. Tripos and John would flourish together, with John eventually becoming Tripos's effective CEO and finally its president and sole decision-maker. Somewhere along the line John had developed a mild disdain for scientists as programmers and as managers which somewhat colored our relationship. Also, as the only Tripos employee who had substantial independent professional status, I would tend to feel a bit detached from its business challenges. Yet there was always a high degree of professional respect between us, especially, I suppose, as it became clear to John that I had neither the interest nor the ability to compete with him for managerial leadership at Tripos. Greg became the manager of software development when John first moved up. But just as I did, Greg found greater satisfaction in his own programming activities, adapting them to the changing business needs of Tripos and its successors. Greg and I have greatly admired one another's creations, making enjoyable our occasional red-blue counterpoint discussions on religion and politics. Perry would create Sybyl's robust force field methodologies before leaving to pursue other software opportunities in Saint Louis.

Whenever major software such as Sybyl is to be completely rewritten, the first issue is the language. Unfortunate language choice makes software orphans, just as the obsolescence of the MPS-VAX-VAX ensemble was already making an orphan of the SK&F version of Sybyl. Should Sybyl be rewritten in FORTRAN or Pascal or C? Today, C would be a no-brainer, but not in 1983. FORTRAN had persisted for decades, so it would have been the safe choice, but the clumsiness of its legacy syntax made that persistence a liability as well as an asset. Pascal was then the programmer's favorite, vigorously championed by DEC for the Tripos-all-important VAX, and the lingua franca for microcomputers. C was then relatively obscure, and its association with a Unix operating system, whose various flavors and shaky support, by warring academics, made its survival uncertain. Nevertheless, a minor DEC marketing division, education, had responded to the Unix academic ferment by offering a C compiler for VAXes. With respect to the creation of Tripos's new Sybyl, the decisive factor was the ability (and responsibility!) that C afforded to a programmer to manage the recycling of the computer's memory as a program carries out a user's commands. With the other languages, memory ordinarily had to be pre-allocated in chunks whose fixed nature would preclude the new Sybyl from displaying an unspecified multiplicity of independently maneuverable molecules, each having its own unspecified multitude of atoms needing computer representation. Our choice of the C language proved more than durable, and the fundamental molecular data structures and operations that John designed were of course extended over the decades but were never supplanted.

Mention might be made here of the symbolism in Garland's christenings of Sybyl and Tripos. In Greek and Roman times (and as also depicted, to my surprise, in the floor mosaic of the Siena Cathedral), sibyls were priestesses who, when suitably rewarded, foretold the future. However, their prophecies were ambiguously worded, requiring further interpretation. A notorious sibyl prediction was the answer to a Lydian king's query about what would happen if he attacked Persia: "he would destroy a great kingdom." The prophecy was indeed correct, but the destroyed kingdom was his own. Metaphorically, then, as a molecular modeling tool for drug discovery, Sybyl should be expected to provide hints, whose interpretation would be left to the CADD scientist. And a tripos (Greek for a three-legged stool) was where a classical sibyl sat, therefore also the seat for the Sybyl software. (*Tripos* has also been said to be French for a second-rate bordello, but the *Larousse* dictionary does not confirm this scurrilous rumor.)

My first Tripos responsibility was to meet a looming NIH deadline for an SBIR grant application. Garland and I agreed that I would propose to build a 3D graphics-based first generation of what today's pharma CADD scientists would recognize as a primitive version of TIBCO's Spotfire. Within that Saturn-like cloud again, each point corresponds to a specific compound and is positioned by three of that compound's physical properties. It happens that one of these points is separated from the others; it would be nice to learn that this oddball represents water simply by clicking on the point, just as today right-clicking on an item can provide more information about that item. However, making this work is a bit trickier in a 3D world than in a 2D world. At the nuts-and-bolts level, clicking reports only the mouse pointer's coordinates; it is up to the software to translate those coordinates into the object to be acted on. In a purely 2D world, no problem—all the relative object coordinates are still whatever they were when the browser first displayed the page. But in a world of interactive 3D graphics, any rotation of the image by the user will have changed the (projected) 2D coordinates of every displayed object. To correctly interpret subsequent mouse clicks, a program must keep track of all those rotations.

Sybyl's 3D display system was already tracking all the changes of atomic coordinates that occurred as a user rotated a molecule. In retrospect it seems obvious, but it then seemed to me a deep insight when I recognized that Sybyl could easily do for my Saturn of data points what it was doing for molecules, simply by representing the data points with a "molecule" that had no bonds—only isolated atoms. Better yet, if you now visualize the data represented by such a point cloud as coming from a spreadsheet, the rows could represent something other than molecules—for instance, cancer patients, with the columns then containing results of various tests and therapies. Maybe, just as had happened with the Saturn of compound properties, the 3D graphing of columns from such a cancer spreadsheet would reveal a previously undiscovered pattern, predicting which patients will respond to which therapies. So, as an experienced NIH grant awardee, Garland recommended a medically expansive title for my SBIR application, "Development of Interactive Statistical Software to Facilitate the Use of State-of-the-Art Methodology in Cancer Clinical Trials," and I, a grant newbie, met the impending deadline for finishing and submitting an SBIR application. It was the first of eight SBIR applications I would submit over the next twenty years, all but one being funded. (However, in today's startup-fertile world, SBIR grants, just like the financial support that eased my way through MIT, are a lot more challenging to get.)

Anyway, I didn't wait for funding to start learning C and the deployments for Tripos code that John McAlister was establishing. He had created two versions of the rewritten Sybyl, ones that shared the same 3D molecular modeling interface to the new VAX–PS 300. One was a functionally equivalent replacement for the Trigraph, dubbed Sybyl 3.0. John took this newborn to some half dozen European sites, ones where a Garland Marshall lecture had previously been well received. Sybyl 3.0 was an immediate hit, and all us Tripos employees began breathing easier. The other Sybyl, the one then undergoing intense development, would extend the applicability of Sybyl's tools to polymers in general and proteins in particular by adding specialized structural descriptors and manipulations. For my project, a third Sybyl version, provisionally named Dabyl, was set up, and I began the programming of the interactive statistical software, mostly from home, alternating local source-code editing with bursts of 1,200-baud phone-line access for code download and testing.

I also began to think about seeking more SBIR funding to renew the development of DYLOMMS. I had never lost faith in its fundamental scientific soundness. Perhaps Svante Wold's partial least squares (PLS) really would overcome the many-more-columns-than-rows challenge, and replacing the Tektronix displays with Tripos's 3D molecular graphics would certainly make 3D-QSAR much easier to practice. But how could I obtain partial least squares? The only published description of PLS used informal mathematical notations, a notation that I have never been at all comfortable with. (And Wold would later confide that even this description was incomplete.)

By August 1984 I had implemented the basic 3D graphics point-picking capabilities and submitted an SBIR Phase II application on the same topic. I demonstrated this proto-Dabyl in Tripos's exposition booth at the national American Chemical Society meeting, where it fascinated Ildiko Frank, an intense and stylish chemical statistician from Hungary who was wandering around the trade show floor. Ildiko told me that her husband, Professor Jerome Friedman of Stanford, a National Academy of Sciences–level statistician, was experimenting with interactive 3D graphics. She was also seeking her own professional outlet, and what was I going to do about contemporary analytics support for Dabyl? Confessing my own inadequacies, I inquired about PLS. Ildiko had worked with Bruce Kowalski, one of the two or three statisticians other than Wold who then understood PLS. Bingo! A few weeks later, Friedman, Frank, Marshall, Wold, and I assembled in a Saint Louis bistro to decide what to do. As I recall, Jerry would specify a dozen types of informative 3D graphs, to be displayable in mutually interactive foursomes as well as individually. With Jerry's advice as needed, Ildiko would program a rich variety of the latest analytics algorithms, including, with Wold's advice, the bleeding-edge PLS. Not, as I would soon recognize, that Ildiko needed much advice! In return, Ildiko, Jerome, and Svante would receive royalties on Dabyl sales.

It was up to Ildiko and me to make it so. One complication for me was that the only programming language that Ildiko would deign to use was scientific FORTRAN. Automatic FORTRAN-to-C translation was not yet available, so I mastered some then-esoteric techniques that made Dabyl's code bilingual. A second complication was a specification that clicking on a point in one graph should be able to highlight one or more logically related points in other graphs, an operation that didn't have a molecular analogy that I could simply copy. Coding these complications was an interesting exercise, intellectually comparable to solving a crossword puzzle. But diagnosing my memory management mistakes, frequent within such newly written C code, was more akin to tracking Bigfoot in a mountain snowstorm. (Diagnostic tools such as Valgrind did not yet exist.) My visible frustrations confirmed John's belief that scientists could not become competent programmers. Nevertheless, in due course an alpha-quality Dabyl emerged.

Meanwhile, I was having doubts about the commercializability of Dabyl. Tripos's staff was innocent of conventional sales or marketing practices. Its only marketing had been Garland's travel and lectures (while wearing his Washington University hat) and exposition booths at chemistry meetings (which Garland eschewed). Sales was simply a former Washington University department secretary answering the Tripos phone and arranging Saint Louis visits for prospects, with, I suppose, Garland himself handling any financial negotiations. All working very well, to be sure. Molecular modeling had reached takeoff, with Tripos as the established market leader, and, in their responses to new technologies, pharma R&D's senior managers often seem to exhibit an avoiding-the-appearance-of-obsolescence paranoia, manifesting itself as a lemming-like follow-the-leader behavior. If the other guys have invested in something and we haven't, won't my bosses start wondering if I'm past it as their R&D manager? But statistical graphics wouldn't have the self-evident relevance to drug discovery that molecular graphics had. It would need to be sold, and how was that to be done? On the other hand, maybe there were other applications and fields where interactive statistical graphics would have more obvious benefits. But when I attended a heavily publicized session on graphics at a national statistics conference, there were only a half dozen other attendees in a hall intended to seat hundreds. Such indifference to graphics among professional statisticians threatened that Dabyl was dangerously ahead of its time. Garland still needed more convincing, though, so I arranged a Dabyl demo by the two of us at Bolt, Beranek, and Newman (BBN), which, as the architect of PROPHET, might be aware of other Dabyl markets and which would have the sales and marketing resources to pursue those opportunities. The BBN demo was a technical success, but no one there could see any commercial potential for Dabyl. Although the idea of a DABYL product was then dropped, its code did eventually generate Tripos revenue as the nucleus of an optional QSAR module for Sybyl.

14 Rebirth of STATS Inc.

Our move to glamour-less Terre Haute disappointed Matt Levine, but Edge 1.000 had become an icon for Pacific Select, and its continuance depended on my continuing participation. Although by now I had implemented all of Edge 1.000's core functionalities, there were scattered gaps in how these functionalities interacted and bugs that occasionally surfaced. So Matt and I continued the same relationship.

One gap was the handling of a team's historical data, and Matt paid someone to type all the season stats for all the current players into one of STATS' three Apples. The associated player IDs, such as 1 for Willie Mays Aikens and 1650 for Rickey Henderson, showed up in the earliest versions of Sean Lahman's well-known baseball database, which he acknowledged when I emailed him about it years later.[1] I'm still curious about the circumstances of this transformation!

Most of my efforts were in trying to add value to Edge 1.000 by creating some additional PDP-10 reports that seemed useful to me, trying to simplify their use, extensively documenting them, and making it more convenient for the operator to pass their content along to team decision-makers. Retrieving information became mostly a two-stage process, the first stage being the isolation of the game, events, or pitch records of interest by a menu-driven dialog that today would be familiar to anyone who works with SQL interfaces, and the second stage being the application of selected reports to those selected records, the results to be downloaded for printing. For 1984 I prepared about twenty-five new reports, mostly split-like tables of situational statistics within which I flagged exceptions—values that notably differed from their expected values. Pacific Select sought additional revenue by billing most of these additions as custom extras. By this time the fifty thousand lines of Edge 1.000 code on the Apple II occupied six floppy disks and invoked more than ten thousand lines of PDP-10 code. Doing almost anything with Edge 1.000 would involve several halts with the injunction to "replace SENDEC with QUERY. Press <space> to continue," or an occasional "put PLAYBALL in your boot disk and press <reset>." In spare moments, I also tinkered with development of a computer baseball game, intended as something like today's Diamond Vision Baseball, although the Apple II was looking more and more inferior to the increasingly numerous IBM PCs and clones. The first Macintosh had also appeared, but it was so memory-constrained that programming required a special Lisa computer, whose use I found impenetrable.

From today's moneyball-colored perspective, it may seem surprising, considering the aura of momentum projected by Edge 1.000's publicity and major customers, that STATS didn't keep acquiring more team customers. But there were financial issues. Totaling operator salary, software support, PDP-10 usage, and long-distance phone calls, Edge 1.000's annual cost to a team was reported to approach a hundred thousand dollars. Not much today, but more than the minimum player salary in 1983, certainly something for a prospective team customer to think about. Some of the overtones in the phone conversations with Pacific Select had started me to wonder whether STATS or Pacific Select itself would still be around next year. Early in 1984, Matt, wanting to fund a new sports video business, offered me complete possession of STATS in return for assuming all its commitments, including debt. But that responsibility was completely unappealing to me. I would continue to support Edge 1.000 and its major league clients only under the current relationship.

The original Edge 1.000 account with the Oakland Athletics was in deep trouble, though I didn't know it. After my 1981 visit, the only Oakland-specific matter I ever heard about was an input-error-filled listing of Rickey Henderson's 1983 stolen bases. Yet that onslaught of Edge 1.000 publications was centered on the A's and how the team's new manager, Steve Boros, was repeatedly quoted as making heavy use of the computer, sometimes with a vehemence that struck even me as extreme. It would not be surprising if, as a sports marketing firm with a product to promote, Pacific Select had purposively stimulated many of these stories. If so, it might be less surprising that I had no interactions with the Athletics' computer activities because I have always been guilty of the scientist's instinct to "tell it like it is." Be that as it may, I first learned that the A's were dropping Edge 1.000 only from a newspaper story, perhaps in the *New York Times*.

Nevertheless, discussions were under way with several additional clubs. And Murray Cook, the Yankees' general manager, was reportedly pleased with a sabermetric-type analysis he had asked me to prepare on possible roster changes. The most interesting of these was whether the 1984 shortstop should be Roy Smalley, certainly the better hitter, or Andre Robertson, the better-regarded fielder. However, in 1983 the frequency of outs resulting from balls hit toward shortstop had been no greater for Robertson than for Smalley. So I recommended that those grounders be individually investigated, while noting that the lineup with Smalley at shortstop and Don Mattingly (not yet Donnie Baseball!) at first would score 30 more runs (generating three more wins) than the expected alternative with Smalley at first. However, Doug Melvin, for one, was scornful of Smalley as either a batter or fielder.

The Yankees even decided that their top minor league team, the Columbus Clippers, should have its own Edge 1.000, an installation I handled myself, as Columbus was a comfortable drive from Terre Haute. Although the Clippers management was very hospitable and themselves somewhat interested, the intent was strictly to benefit the Yankees, and the Columbus Edge 1.000 was not continued for 1985.

Murray Cook's vision, in being one of the earliest general managers to actively seek such a sabermetric analysis, must have been challenged by his position sandwiched between the famously temperamental Steinbrenner and Billy Martin. Cook's interest in Edge 1.000 continued when he moved to the general manager's chair for the Montreal Expos. I was somewhat unsettled during a solo sales call there in pondering the implications in his unexpected hint that a "smart guy" (like me?) could easily become a productive scout. That would have been an odd career move for an MIT PhD!

Meanwhile Pacific Select convinced the Houston Astros to acquire Edge 1.000 for 1984. The two visits that I made there, at the beginning and the end of their 1984 season, were particularly interesting. At the end of April, the Astros' Apple II shipment had arrived, and I was dispatched to put everything together and make sure it all worked. The fun part was watching a game that evening from a folding chair in a buried runway, sitting as close behind home plate as I've ever been, next to Alan Ashby, Houston's regular catcher who had just been put on the disabled list. Unsurprisingly, considering Ashby's successful post-playing career as a broadcaster, for me at least it was a wonderfully relaxed and enjoyable conversation. Two of his comments remain with me. One was how comparatively easy the game looked to him from where we were sitting, whereas my impression of course was how incredibly difficult it seemed. The other was a surprising question—what was the front office's thinking about Mark Bailey, his injury replacement on the roster? Was Bailey an emergency call-up or the new regular? Of course, as technical flunkey for the day I had no idea, but the nature of his question impressed me with the insecurity that haunts the glamor of being a major league player. Ashby's concern was well placed, as Bailey indeed became Houston's regular catcher for 1984 and 1985, but Ashby then recovered his gig for a few more years, quite productively.

The second visit, after the end of the 1984 season, had several surprises. Matt had a good personal relationship with Al Rosen, Houston's general manager, and persuaded him, I was told, that I was smart and worth spending a few days with. Somewhat nervously I complied and began my visit by looking for the computer I had set up with Edge 1.000. "What computer?" Al asked. "Well, the one I installed here in April," I replied. Sensing my confusion, Al summoned his assistant general manager, Andy MacPhail, and asked him about "Houston's computer." The puzzled look on Andy's face confirmed that Houston's Edge 1.000 had somehow been hijacked, and further inquiry revealed that it was actually in the custody of Gene Coleman, an MD who was employed by NASA but had a special relationship with the legendary Houston pitcher Nolan Ryan. Rosen and I then discussed the uses that other clubs had made of Edge 1.000, and he was particularly interested in the story of how the White Sox had benefited by moving in their fences. I agreed to do the same sort of study for him with Houston's 1984 season.

So the next morning I visited Gene Coleman and the Astros' Edge 1.000. On the whole, he seemed to have done a pretty good job with it, having somehow collected pitch details as well as the play-by-play for all of Houston's games. He told me that Nolan Ryan, whom the Houston organization treated as a minor deity, had been the low-profile champion for acquiring Edge 1.000 and that data entry and analysis had been made one of Gene's duties, more in the role of a personal assistant to Ryan than as an Astros employee. But he wasn't sure that the information and insights that Edge 1.000 was generating was worth the cost of its use, including his personal time. We discussed some of the reports he had at hand. I recall one representing how well Astro Phil "Scrap-Iron" Garner hit against different types and locations of pitches. He agreed that the reported information was correct but complained that it was already known.

As I had promised Rosen, I borrowed Gene's Apple to compare the counts of long fly balls hit in the Astrodome by the 1984 Astros and their opponents. The result was that it was Houston's opponents who would most benefit if the fences were pulled in. A predictable finding because the Astrodome had long been the major league's worst stadium for home runs, so the Astros' roster had been stacked with batters who hit more for frequency than for distance. So I had no response to Al Rosen's verbal tantrum when, back at the Astrodome, I reported these findings. It turned out that, simply to generally increase scoring and, hopefully, attendance, Houston had already decided to bring in the fences. Rosen, a home run champion himself in his playing years, feared that the Houston pitchers would be demoralized and "pitch timidly" if they learned of my findings, so perhaps the intensity of his tirade was intended to prevent any such leak from happening. Whatever, it seemed pointless for me to continue my visit.

In November as Houston's management was considering Edge 1.000 renewal, I was forwarded a handwritten letter of complaint from Gene to Pacific Select. The complaints were about "errors," apparent discrepancies between the totals and the splits. Gene wasn't recognizing that if a split was based on a pitch location that had not been recorded for three pitches, then the total pitch count would exceed the total of the split pitch count. The letter also indicated that three of Houston's coaches (Lillis, Walker, and Menke) were supportive and the other coaches noncommittal, but that Rosen was doubtful about its cost-benefit value. A month or so later, I was told that Houston would not be renewing Edge 1.000 because the only thing they had got out of it was to convince Mike Scott to abandon his curve ball.

However, even if that was the lone benefit, it was an important one for the Houston Astros. Scott instead learned to throw the split-fingered fast ball, and two years later his WAR had improved from a career-threatening -1.5 in 1984 to a league-leading +8.2, and he was rewarded with the 1986 Cy Young award, further including psychological dominance and an MVP award in Houston's second postseason appearance. His newfound excellence was ended only by arm trouble after a twenty-win 1989.

Finally (courtesy again of baseball-reference.com), with respect to Rosen's rant, moving the fences indeed doubled the total number of home runs hit at the Astrodome in 1985, from 47 to 94. Despite the implications of the 1984 data, Houston and its opponents divided those home runs evenly, each hitting 47 home runs. Nevertheless, it was a couple of young power hitters, Glenn Davis and Kevin Bass, who more than accounted for this improvement in Houston's home run differential at home.

So at the end of 1984, the White Sox and Yankees were the only Edge 1.000 users, a pairing that would last a few more years. Not so for Pacific Select. As a company whose bread and butter was advice on "putting asses in seats," the pending demise of the United States Football League was a threat to Pacific Select revenues that I kept hearing about. Sometime around the 1985 new year, Matt warned me that without additional funding Pacific Select would soon have to shut down. Could I find backers who would be willing to buy and operate STATS, at a suggested price, as I recall, of $250,000? Libby's sarcastic response is hard to forget, "He's offering you the 'opportunity' to buy yourself!" Not that I knew any such backers. A month or so later, Matt called again, this time with an announcement and a request. Pacific Select was going under. But Matt wanted to preserve his personal reputation within the sports marketing community. Assuming that all of STATS' existing liabilities would thereby be liquidated (including my $15,000 seed loan and around $10,000 owed me in royalties and expense reimbursements), would I take on the entirety of STATS' ongoing commitments to the White Sox and Yankees? I was already the one fulfilling those client commitments, there would be some profit, and there was no prospect of retrieving my $25,000 from Pacific Select. So it wasn't hard for me to consent. There were no complaints from the teams, as they too were fully aware of the realities of how their Edge 1.000 installations were actually being supported.

What next for the business of STATS, which now became only my own half-time proprietorship? I'd never had much interest in nor reason to think about building a business myself. However, primarily as an observer of Pacific Select and Tripos business activities, I did have a conscious if primitive business philosophy: Profits matter mostly because the alternative, losses, will eventually starve a business. The most secure profits are based on superior technologies, whose advantages sell themselves. Otherwise, there's a lot of random luck in business success. Therefore, hanging on while building technology until the lightning of a superior technology strikes seemed the right way to go for me. This philosophy of course contrasts with the grow-or-die mentality that drives most small businesses. An astute reader will also note how well this business philosophy maps onto my own inclinations. As it happened, I was about to become very lucky because three synergistic opportunities materialized.

First, for me an imperative for STATS' continuation was some sort of a collaboration or partnership. A couple of Terre Haute programmers were nationally marketing and operating a first-generation fantasy baseball game, but despite our compatibilities in subject matter and geography, they weren't interested in a partnership with anyone so indifferent to profit maximization. Bill James, already well on his way to iconic status, then came to mind. He had originally been scathing about computers in baseball, particularly in the dugout, but his annual books were now touting something called Project Scoresheet. To break an informal but effective monopoly on baseball statistics, Bill had started asking his readership to send him their scorecards, and their enthusiastic responses now seemed to have self-organized. At least Project Scoresheet volunteers and I might understand one another's motivations.

Some of you may be asking, "Uh, who is Bill James?" The rest of you instead are probably asking, "What's he really like?" With respect to baseball, Bill has been a game-changing blend of Socrates and Voltaire, an eloquent and extraordinarily influential iconoclast. In 2006 *Time* magazine's inclusion of Bill in their list of one hundred "most influential people" who were "transforming our world" seemed amusing overkill. Today I'm not so dismissive because without Bill, sabermetrics, and moneyball, which have had such widespread effects on business cant, the international cultures of team sports, and the aspirations of many youths, the world would be noticeably different. Somewhat at loose ends as a youthful Kansan, Bill had applied his extraordinary creativity and impish facility with words to his baseball obsession, producing a series of baseball ponderings that in a few years metamorphosed from self-published mimeograph to an annual *New York Times* bestseller. Bill championed baseball knowledge obtained by the ethos of science—observe, imagine, analyze, criticize, and unsparingly publicize—to an unreceptive and initially hostile baseball culture (which might sound like a metaphor for how civilization generally advances).

Okay, that's the *who* of Bill James. So what is Bill really like? A reasonable question for a man of such interest to many of you but one that the mere existence of a book titled *How Bill James Changed Our View of Baseball*," filled with grateful encomiums from his closest friends and associates, makes me feel awkward in trying to answer.[2] Yet my experience of Bill is different from that of those friends and associates in at least one way—I can't recall him ever teaching me much of anything. Well, maybe correcting my impression of the player-aging performance curve. But whenever we've—very occasionally—disagreed (clutch hitting and the prospects for players Darren Daulton or Alan

Embree come to mind), subsequent events have supported my opinions. Of course I greatly enjoy his writing, yet it's his complex game
designs that I especially admire. All Bill's designs provided a realistic
and enjoyably rich experience of a baseball season, avoiding any form
of "gameability." He scorns those contenders in historical simulation
games who focus their team building on a single supreme season, and
his game creations withstood the hacks of knowledgeable and competitive STATS employees. My favorite, which STATS briefly ran after my
eviction, treated players as corporations, whose tradeable stock paid
postseason dividends in proportion to their seasonal performances.

Bill the man? It may surprise some of his readers that in person
Bill is observant, unassuming, and unfailingly courteous. Observing
the irritating mix of mindless adulation and unrealistic expectations
that he must gracefully endure as baseball analytics' emblematic icon
has made me more than content with my own relative obscurity. One
example: while on stage at a SABR convention, a questioner rose to
ask Bill what he thought about the possibility of his being elected to
baseball's Hall of Fame. Everyone in the audience knew the answer—in
principle, unquestionably deserved; in practice, highly unlikely. What
would you say in such a situation?

Bill is also rather quiet. Over the decades, my contacts with Bill the
man have had two phases, during STATS and after STATS. At STATS
organizational meetings, he was well prepared with many good ideas
for new business possibilities but had little to say during the relatively
formless discussions of general business strategy. In 1992 after Bill
stayed overnight at my Saint Louis home, we drove together for a five-
hundred-mile round trip to the baseball winter meeting in Louisville,
where Barry Bonds broke my father's heart by abandoning the Pirates
to sign with the Giants. Yet the only exchange I can recall from during
this time together was Bill's sudden question—how good a fielder was
George Davis? (Davis was a very good hitting shortstop at the turn of
the last century, who would be inducted into the Hall of Fame in 1998.
My reply was that I understood his fielding also to be good.) Bill was
silent during a chance encounter there with Phillies president Bill Giles,
whom I assured that in 1993, his last-place Phils would certainly win

more often. (They did, of course, finishing first mainly because their batters drew more walks than any Phillies team ever at that time, and more, than any team since 1955. An oddly unrecognized fact, even by Phillies' articulate stars John Kruk and Curt Schilling when I recently asked them about this during a SABR panel. Kruk described his approach as one of not swinging—until there were two strikes—at pitches that he believed he couldn't hit well.)

These days Bill and I see each other whenever he braves a SABR convention, where I also once enjoyed meeting his charming wife Susie and oldest son Isaac. We invariably agree that we should see more of each other, though any such visits have yet to materialize. To summarize, then, either Bill or Paul Bamberg is the most unquestionable genius I have known well, and their creations of complex and well-balanced games are one shared hallmark.

So—our first encounter. I extracted Bill's Manhattan, Kansas, phone number from information and gave him a cold call, wondering if he would rebuff me as the evil sorcerer behind dugout computers. I later learned that Bill is legendary to his friends for both his comprehensive letters and his terse telephone conversations. However, on this critical occasion he answered my call attentively and told me exactly what I needed to know. There were two key Project Scoresheet activists in Chicago, and I should talk with them about any collaboration possibilities.

Libby usually didn't react much to STATS beyond rolling her eyes and observing that the lawn needed attention, but to my delight she insisted on accompanying me on the four-hour drive to Chicago for two separate discussions. Our first discussion was with a professor of economics metrics at DePaul, Gary Skoog. He seemed to be interviewing me for the privilege of association with Project Scoresheet. He was troubled by my inability to provide satisfactory formulaic underpinnings for the above-described OXS formula that Pete Palmer and I had published ten years earlier. (Why do so many economists place such store in formal mathematical manipulations of often fanciful entities and trends? No wonder that they so seldom agree—either with each other or with what actually happens in our chaotic real world!) Not at all the sort of discussion that Libby and I had been hoping for. However, the second discussion, with John and Sue Dewan in the northern Chicago house where they still live, then felt something like a divine dispensation. John and I immediately understood one another, and Sue and Libby understood their husbands' shared enthusiasms. The potential partnership was obvious. John and Sue were drowning in the thousands of paper scoresheets that project volunteers were submitting. The scoresheets were not much good until they all had been entered in a computer. Suppose Playball technology could somehow replace the paper scoresheets? Making that happen seemed a worthwhile project to me, as usual mostly for its own sake, though Jack Gould, Edge 1.000's White Sox champion, had often complained about how the White Sox database's being limited to its own games constrained Edge 1.000's applicability to his player salary negotiations.

Then came a second game-changing break for me and STATS—Digital Equipment Corporation, the PDP and VAX manufacturer, announced the new MicroVAX. As I wrote to Jack Gould, "Until now, to get reasonable search times for a play-by-play data base, you needed a large mainframe computer. Big computers mean big power consumption, extra air conditioning, high on-site hardware maintenance, and an operating staff and other experts to deal with the resulting complexity. Hence high time-sharing costs. (With the MicroVAX II), all EDGE 1.000 operations can easily be transferred to a $40,000 machine that plugs into a wall and, complete, is smaller than a two-drawer file cabinet." John Dewan, an instinctive early adopter of new technology, had proposed a network of PCs, a concept that trade journals were starting to promote, in a Chicago location, where he and Sue would presumably do much of the programming. But to me that idea sounded unrealistically ahead of its time, so I insisted on the proven VAX hardware, to be located in Saint Louis, where I would do the programming.

That made the third critical ingredient almost self-evident. At this time, all of Tripos's Sybyl development was being done on its lone VAX 750, which like every such mainframe depended on special air conditioning that unfortunately was somewhat unreliable and which was further burdened by the additional projects I was doing for Tripos with the SBIR support from NIH. Suppose STATS could come up with the money for a MicroVAX? Because there was total executable software compatibility among the different VAX models (amazingly to me, and another technology first embodied in the MicroVAX), I could use such a computer for both Tripos and STATS business. Garland agreed that if this were to happen, in return Tripos would provide a business face—phone answering, message handling, and so on—for the still nebulous new STATS.

The White Sox and Yankees readily agreed, once I promised them cost savings, because their time-sharing costs would disappear; there would be someone to handle their STATS phone calls and eventual access to information derived from (almost) all major league games. Of course, there would be a lot of new programming to be done. A big help was a commercially offered data base system for the VAX that was functionally equivalent to the PDP-10's 1022, costing an additional ten thousand dollars. John Dewan had easily convinced me that the Edge 1.000's Apples should be replaced by laptop PC clones, where the existence of a Turbo Pascal language system meant that much of Edge 1.000's sixty thousand lines of code could be preserved. Whatever the details, all this programming, as usual, would be my job.

However, agreements among STATs, its investors, the teams, Tripos, and Project Scoresheet had to be put together first. The real glue had to be personal trust, as there wasn't the time (or the budget) for legal contracts. The MicroVAX was a hot new product in short supply, yet Tripos, as the software champion for E&S and VAX in a very promising market for DEC, could buy one—but only if they reacted rapidly enough. To do so, including the 1022-equivalent software, we would need something close to sixty thousand dollars in cash.

So I incorporated the new STATS as an Indiana sub-chapter S corporation. Sub-chapter S corporations were devised to encourage the formation of small corporations by allowing their shareholders to pass their shares of the corporate operating profits and losses directly onto their personal tax returns. The losses that STATS would surely experience at first would at least reduce the taxable incomes of its investors. The new STATS would have 100 shares, each valued at $1,000. I would retain control with 51 shares, paying in $21,000 and the prior STATS' assets, primarily the White Sox and Yankees agreements, which would be assigned a value of $30,000. John and Sue put in $30,000 for 30 shares. When Bill James agreed to buy 5 shares for $5,000, the troika that would make the new STATS a success had been assembled, and the MicroVAX purchase could proceed.

For STATS, John was to become a quintessential entrepreneur, a masterful hero out of an Ayn Rand novel. His varied visionary skills— technical, marketing, administrative—and unquenchable enthusiasm and dedication were exactly what STATS needed to blossom into the sports statistics leadership position that it still enjoys. Yet his self-effacing wife Sue was of comparable importance, steadfast in her support of John and STATS despite whatever her own preferences may have been, transferring her programming skills from job to STATS even before John did, and spending as many hours laboring in the STATS office as any of us, at least when I was there during the fourteen-hour workdays of spring training countdowns. I have always thought of John and Sue as an entity, with both of them also well-grounded as individuals. And John in particular was not indifferent to life's other offerings, such as the postcollege year he spent in Honduras, attendance at Olympic games, charitable sojourns to Liberia, and uptake of solar energy. John also has some Teddy Roosevelt–like macho impulses—for example taking up parachuting to overcome acrophobia, a story he loved to tell because on his lone jump he had to resort to his backup parachute.

There were two other investors, Tim O'Neill, the marketing manager for Saint Louis's major personal computer store, whose five shares I bought back from him once a lack of mutual fit became obvious. One final share was sold to Kevin Koboldt, Tripos's original employee, who would be a big help to me in getting live telephone communication working on the PC clones. John and I then retreated to our primary responsibilities, his with Project Scoresheet and mine with programming, for Tripos from 9:00 to 5:00 and then for the STATS rewrites until around 11:00 each day.

I was now spending most of my weekdays in Saint Louis, staying at a bed and breakfast in its trendy Central West End. Though I always looked forward to weekends at home with Libby, in Terre Haute it was often not easy to find stuff for the two of us to enjoy together, and during the week, with nothing much for me to share beyond programming and her believing herself forbidden to discuss her own work, I did not phone her as often as she wanted and deserved. My absence also made our Terre Haute house an encumbrance, so we sold it. Libby moved to an apartment, and in that trendy Central West End we bought a loft, originally the central office for the Dorris factory, where automobiles were once built "Up to a standard, not down to a price," while Henry Ford was pursuing a more successful business model. Our weekends together then became almost as frequent in Saint Louis as in Terre Haute. Yet I could never persuade her to consider the straightforward next step of seeking employment in Saint Louis.

During one of those weekend Saint Louis–to–Terre Haute commutes, I detoured through Champaign, Illinois, to take a look at a startup with a new PC-based interactive graphics technology, a field that Tripos tried to keep abreast of. As I vaguely recall, it might have been some guy named Andreessen, who showed me something he may have called a browser. But its graphics performance wasn't nearly good enough to be CADD relevant, and I left wondering if those guys would find anything worthwhile for it to do.

On one of the Saint Louis weekends I had a special treat for Libby. She had always loved airplanes. She often joked about how her love of watching planes at the airport had made her a cheap date in high school. I had learned that a few vintage biplanes were flying out of a small airfield west of Saint Louis and would take individual passengers for an open cockpit experience, optionally including stalls and loops. For Libby that splendid outing yielded two further bonuses. First, she was informed that her monocular vision did not at all preclude her from learning to fly. I was almost as pleased as she was when she began taking lessons because it lifted her spirits, and it was an interest that I gladly shared, reading all her books and taking some introductory lessons myself, though I didn't have the time or, she and I agreed, the temperament, to become a pilot myself. Once she had her license and enough hours of experience, I encouraged her to buy an airplane of her own, so we could fly together on weekends, and she soon found *Bravo!*, a 1956 Cessna 172. She then earned her instrument rating, allowing her to securely fly rather than drive to weekends in Saint Louis. This brings me to the second bonus. When she began taking lessons on those biplanes, there followed a surreptitious courtship, and in the summer of 1991, she left me for her biplane instructor. And then she moved to Saint Louis.

Back to 1985. At that year's winter baseball meetings in San Diego, John, Sue, and I tried our luck at an exposition booth, equipped with some signage by Tim O'Neill. But the only MLB response I recall was a jovial Tommy Lasorda walking by and proclaiming, "I bet your computer says I should have walked Jack Clark," referring to his controversial decision in the 1985 National League Championship Series. And John and Sue were disappointed by my early return to attend a site visit by NIH's reviewers, who were considering whether my latest SBIR application (the one that proposed the future CoMFA) should be funded. Such conflicts for my attention would be more frequent when the competitors were Tripos and new STATS than when they were SK&F and old STATS. However, I would simply concentrate on whatever need seemed the more urgent to me, and I don't recall much pushback. Perhaps there were concerns that if one working environment became uncomfortable to me, my participation, critical for the success of both businesses, might shift entirely to the other.

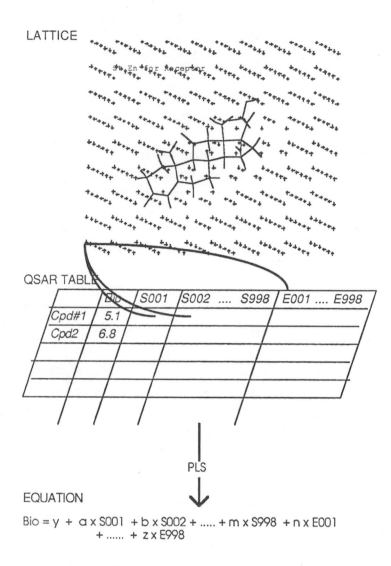

LATTICE

QSAR TABLE

	Bio	S001	S002	....	S998	E001	....	E998
Cpd#1	5.1							
Cpd2	6.8							

PLS

EQUATION

$$Bio = y + a \times S001 + b \times S002 + ... + m \times S998 + n \times E001 + ... + z \times E998$$

Fig. 3. The first published depiction of the comparative molecular field analysis process, from the proceedings of the Istria EuroQSAR conference in 1986. Courtesy of the author.

15 Comparative Molecular Field Analysis

My importance to Tripos resulted from my creation of comparative molecular field analysis, which for the next twenty years ensured Tripos's leadership among maybe a dozen erstwhile competitors, many perhaps better funded or managed. Today, more than thirty years later, its use is still cited many hundreds of times each year, even though it is no longer commercially available.

Since many scientific methodologies are baptized by publication in a major journal, for this memoir and for my own amusement, I'll try to provide an objective assessment of CoMFA's importance by comparing the Google Scholar citation counts for CoMFA's introductory publication (search term: "Cramer CoMFA"),[1] for each of the twenty-eight years through 2015 (when I finished writing the first draft of this memoir), with those for the seminal QSAR paper (search term: "Hansch Fujita")[2] and for the most widely admired method today, docking to a receptor (search term: "Kuntz Dock").[3] Rather to my surprise as well as pleasure, the rate of CoMFA citations had steadily increased until around 2010, to a peak of 350 per year, but with its unavailability this rate is of course declining. Hansch citation rates (1964) are still increasing linearly at a lower rate though over twice as many years, with a 2015 maximum of 241 per year. Docking citations (1982) started off slowly, surpassing 10 per year only in 1990, then growing very rapidly to around 400 per year in 2005, and finally plateauing to 363 per year in 2015. While there's a lot of apples-to-oranges involved here, comparison of these citation rates does seem to support my pride in having created CoMFA.

By 1985 all the pieces that would be needed to make CoMFA a reality had finally become available to me: the original idea of correlating the biological potencies of candidate 3D drug molecules with the fields they exerted at various locations in space; the Dabyl framework, whose coupling of molecular tables with interactive 3D graphics should simplify the initial creation and manipulation of those 3D molecules; and a PLS implementation by Ildiko Frank that hopefully would surmount the "many times more columns than rows" obstacle of using field intensities as QSAR descriptors. So I drew up a SBIR Phase I application for "Correlation of Dynamic Molecular Shape with Activity." Again, I didn't wait for its explicit funding, and long before the end of 1985 I had constructed an assemblage of these pieces, ready for trial.

Validation of a new computational methodology requires at least two inputs, an objective measure of success and an appropriate data set. Ildiko had introduced me to cross-validation, now a universally recognized objective measure of success.[4] One by one, each of the molecules in a data set is omitted, and the new methodology is applied to all the other molecules. Using the resulting model, the biological potency of the omitted molecule is predicted. If the variance among the errors of these pseudo-predictions is lower than some threshold (surely lower than the variance among the input experimental potencies!), the full model, and the methodology that produced that model, have been validated and thereby earn respect. The other crucial input, a choice of the first appropriate data set from the thousands published, took more thought because of that ever-present concern about how each molecule should be positioned within the lattice of field points. To emphasize this key concern by repetition, even identical molecules will have different effects on the same nearby field point if these twins are positioned differently. Yet the potential value of CoMFA to users would be much greater if the structures in its dataset did not have to be very similar. A data set with a nice balance between structural diversity and 3D superimposability, the "CoMFA steroids," the binding affinities of twenty-one structures to corticosteroid binding globulin, was recommended to me by Ioan Motoc, a Romanian postdoc in Garland's academic lab. (At the lone meeting between Ioan and Ildiko, I couldn't resist observing, tongue in cheek, how strange it seemed to an American that a disputed province, vampire-infested Transylvania, could matter so much to anyone. But no one smiled.)

This was the moment of truth for CoMFA. With steroids as the data set and cross-validation as the measure of success, would this new method work? I could think of many reasons why it might not, and indeed its first trials, by a better-forgotten postdoc, generated hopelessly poor cross-validation values. But, despite Einstein's reputed caution, every so often doing the same thing over again and expecting a different result is not insanity. When I repeated his trials myself, hoping only for some diagnostic insight, for whatever reason, the results were more than satisfactory. The variance of the errors from the twenty-one cross-validation potency predictions was not much greater than the variance expected when experimentally measuring such binding affinities. Hallelujah!

Meanwhile my SBIR application for "Correlation of Dynamic Molecular Shape with Activity" was still wending its way through its initial evaluation. Considering how problematic its objective must have seemed, to obtain a useful QSAR from tables having an impossibly high column-to-row ratio, and being unaware that with these steroid results this objective had already been achieved, NIH unusually convened a Saint Louis site visit, by a panel of respected academic scientists. Its scheduling was what had forced me to abandon John and Sue at the baseball meeting, especially because I was worried. My steroid proof of principle was a two-thousand-term linear equation, with a steric and an electrostatic coefficient for each of a thousand lattice points surrounding the steroids. Would they perceive enough credibility and potential value for drug discovery in such a strange and massive statistical model to be worth funding? On the day before the visit, I had an idea. John McAlister had just finished code that would allow Sybyl to display the electron density contours that are the outcome of X-ray crystallography. Couldn't I adapt this code to draw contours around the regions of space where the steric or electrostatic coefficients were largest, the regions that the model was reporting to be most influential for explaining the differences among the steroids' potencies? The drug seeker should then be able to see in three dimensions which structural changes in what locations would be most likely to improve biological activity. On the first day of the reviewers' visit I had only the idea to present, but after a late evening of coding, on the next day I had images to show as well. The grant was awarded, and such images would become a sort of visual trademark within the vast majority of those thousands of CoMFA-related publications.

I introduced CoMFA and the steroid model to Tripos's customers at the next annual user meeting. One of the listeners, Illinois chemistry professor John Katzenellenbogen, was a steroid specialist. He raised his hand to remark that there were now measurements of corticosteroid globulin binding for other compounds. If this CoMFA steroid model really worked, shouldn't it predict these activity values? I agreed that it should, mentally crossing my fingers. Happily, when John sent me ten of these additional structures, the model did succeed in predicting their activities, at least in discriminating the stronger binders from the weaker ones.

The first public description of CoMFA was during the 1986 EuroQSAR conference, at a seaside resort in Istria, then in Yugoslavia but now Croatia. My talk there, the first on the program, was indeed memorable but not so much for its content. Halfway through, the projector screen slowly and ceremoniously rewound itself! Twenty years later, there was an amusing reprisal of this misadventure when the biennial EuroQSAR conference took place on a Mediterranean cruise ship, and my lecture introducing topomer CoMFA coincided with its roughest weather. No, I didn't fall, but the audience must have been distracted by anticipating a rather awkward finish!

Receipt of the SBIR funding in the spring of 1986 allowed Tripos to hire David Patterson, a creative and self-educated statistician and programmer who during the next twenty years would be my closest Tripos collaborator. Dave's appearance and demeanor have somehow always reminded me of a human-scale leprechaun. Dave's career especially flourished after he left Tripos, beginning with a move to Berkeley, where in collaboration with KNIME's future founder Michael Berthold, he obtained an SBIR grant of his own. Today he is director of data insights at AT&T, after a similar role at Walmart Labs, positions that to me at least sound extremely big data relevant!

While CoMFA was emerging from its chrysalis, I had other distractions, and not only from STATS. Back in 1981, while at SK&F, I had been elected chairman of the 1985 QSAR Gordon Conference. (This conference occurs on odd-numbered years, and a term as vice chairman precedes chairmanship.) Unfortunately, the intervening events would conspire to make that chairmanship an embarrassing experience. To begin with, for reasons still unknown to me, at its start perhaps a half dozen misinformed Japanese scientists showed up, unregistered. In the small host town of Plymouth, New Hampshire, finding accommodations for them was a challenge that understandably displeased the central Gordon Conference office. That was poor staging for a bigger issue, my insensitive proposal to better match the conference's scope to its attendees' expanding interests, by renaming it "Computer-Aided Molecular Design." Many of the attendees, true believers in Hansch QSAR and perhaps attributing this proposal to the interests of my new employer, reportedly returned some hostile evaluations to the central office, which responded to all these offenses by threatening to cancel the conference. Fortunately, cooler heads intervened, and eventually—for 2003—the conference was renamed just as I had proposed. However, after having spoken at almost all the previous QSAR Gordon Conferences, I would never again be selected to do so.

Another distraction was that by 1987 Garland had decided to sell Tripos. He had been directing Tripos much as though it were his second academic group, and its vital project, development of the protein version of Sybyl, was going much more slowly than projected. Credible competitors, notably BioSym and Polygen, with funding and advice from the new venture capital community, were already commercializing technologically less ambitious protein-modeling software and building conventional sales and marketing organizations. Garland had tried hiring a manager, but the "drug discovery professional" he chose gave his own perks such a relatively high priority that John McAlister led a successful palace revolt by the Tripos senior staff. There were also rumors that Washington University had demanded that Garland make a choice.

Evans and Sutherland was interested. Its dominance of the molecular graphics hardware market was also being challenged, by cheaper workstations, especially from Silicon Graphics, which featured coarse surface displays and Unix operating systems. Acquisition of Tripos, the leading molecular modeling software vendor, might help E&S to stave off this threat by offering the simplicity of a bundled solution. Only the Tripos purchase price needed much negotiation, eventually converging, it was reported, at around $5 million. Most of the staff was happy with the ownership change, partially because Garland's only profit-sharing initiative, after a particularly good year, had been a gold Krugerrand for everyone. (I contemptuously threw mine into the back of a forgotten desk drawer.)

Tripos's new president was David Luther, a congenial suit and an alumnus of DEC marketing who had been E&S's internal champion for the Tripos purchase. Preferring to stay in E&S's Salt Lake City home office, David delegated most of his managerial responsibilities. John McAlister continued to provide technology leadership, with Tripos's Silicon Graphics developments of course being dropped. Sales and marketing leaderships went to office manager Merrie Ambos and assistant Mary Woodward, respectively, and despite minimal qualifications on paper, these turned out to be excellent choices. John was not enthusiastic about my one-paragraph proposal for a science department to take on customer support and training, software testing, user interface design, and as time permitted a bit of research and publication. But David Luther liked it, especially after the first user meeting under E&S ownership, just before Christmas in Tubingen, Germany, which he, John, and I attended. There the users angrily condemned the bugginess and inconsistent command syntax of an initial release of the protein-modeling version of Sybyl. Happily, though, my closing talk introducing comparative molecular field analysis had seemed to resuscitate their faith in Tripos.

A truly "new science" like CoMFA takes care and patience to achieve credibility. Its methodology must be packaged in an acceptably usable form, and its earliest users must report useful results. My initial packaging of CoMFA, within the optional QSAR module of Sybyl (the former Dabyl), had gone smoothly and effectively. However, John McAlister believed that any code written by a scientist was suspect. He therefore assigned a complete rewrite of this QSAR module to David Patterson and two other programmers, stipulating my complete exclusion. When I nevertheless invaded a project meeting to question an unfortunate limitation on the portability of the QSAR module's output, their sullen indifference drove me away for good. Yet when I eventually could have a look at the result, much of my original code had not been changed.

This exclusion was no more than an irritation than for me, though, because Tripos was now finding other uses for scientists. The new professional Tripos sales force was reporting that, first, prospective customers found "new science" concepts appealing, and second, that such concepts were best presented "beard-to-beard" by a fellow scientist. Current Sybyl users might also have feedback, valuable but needing a scientist for its accurate transmission. So a salesperson-scientist partnership would become the standard retinue whenever Tripos visited a current or prospective customers. Which required more scientists on staff. Who, like me, would then want to participate in the creation and extension of our software products' capabilities. Greg Smith made this practicable by his "skunkworks" creation of a Sybyl Programming Language (SPL), that blended seamlessly, rather as Python does today, with Sybyl's existing command-line operations. I was uneasy when one morning Greg announced both SPL's existence and its inclusion within the latest build of the protein Sybyl. Why risk such a fundamental change to the core of this already mistrusted and delayed release? But Greg's new code was remarkably bug-free, and SPL became a secret sauce that helped Tripos to follow up CoMFA with a stream of new science—innovative computational methodologies that would guide drug discovery, more specifically by emphasizing the drug candidates rather than their targets.

Much of this Tripos-differentiating new science would also be my personal creation. As CoMFA became Tripos's new science centerpiece, I developed a work pattern that lasted the rest of my Tripos career, to intersperse the creation of new products and the extensions of existing products with occasional bursts of travel, much international, expounding on those products' expected benefits. While I personally enjoyed both activities, many colleagues did seem to feel that the marketing flavor of these customer visits diminished my authenticity as a scientist, no matter my forty-odd refereed publications as a Tripos employee. Yet a chiding that I sometimes got for "excessive enthusiasm," especially when speaking at non-Tripos-sponsored events, does seem fair to me.

Among these dozens of business trips, the most interesting were those when something went wrong. For example, a sales guy's scheduling error necessitated a nighttime autobahn drive at 120 miles per hour from Frankfurt to a next-day meeting in Amsterdam, including a post-midnight currency crisis while buying gas at the Dutch border in that pre-euro era. One of my last trips was in a class all its own. To begin with, like many others I was stranded in the UK by the Eyjafjallajökull eruption, precluding a Vancouver conference but instead allowing me, by dint of several baggage car train rides, to reach Italy, my next stop, ahead of schedule. A few extra days of sightseeing there included getting my car stuck in a swimming pool. (On a dark evening, this pool was framed by a blacktop parking lot and covered by a black tarp. What next? Nothing was open except an Italian version of a 7-Eleven, whose proprietor, in response to my language-deficient gestures, roused his auto mechanic brother with tow truck and jack to get me rolling again—and then refused any money.) Mumbai was the last stop of this pilgrimage, where, after arriving at 2 AM, my tuk-tuk rickshaw driver stopped in a deserted Slumdog Millionaire alley to tell me how lucky I was because, although my hotel had burned down, his brother ran a hotel where I could stay. Fortunately, I had an Indian minder to phone, who then talked my driver all the way through the route to my hotel. There was a crass finale—a digestive crisis that forced me off the lecture stand to an Indian Institute of Technology toilet where cleanup perforce ruined a dollar bill. Can any of your business trips top that one?

Some useful improvements to CoMFA resulted from my visits. A brilliant Merck mathematician, Bruce Bush, recognized that CoMFA could be made much faster by replacing cross-validation with some matrix manipulations that he called SAMPLS, and he even most kindly wrote and donated a SAMPLS program that Tripos then distributed to all of CoMFA's users. And, during a Shell visit, I first learned of Y-scrambling, a now widely appreciated safeguard against model overfit. But mostly it turned out that, almost from its first release, CoMFA was a finished methodology, one that did its main job, extracting useful patterns from a set of meaningfully positioned 3D models of arbitrary drug candidates, about as well as could be reasonably expected. With SPL Sybyl's CoMFA code architecture made it possible for any sufficiently motivated user to seek improvements. Yet, dozens of publications reporting systematic variations among its many possible parameter settings have not suggested any changes to the settings' never original default values, although the inclusion of other plausible field types has occasionally yielded improved models.

What most CoMFA users really wanted was "bookends," additional methodologies—during input, for generating meaningfully positioned 3D models—during output, for translating a CoMFA model into specific structural suggestions. I had some ideas, but from a business perspective, trying to create any of them would have certain costs but uncertain returns. So I imitated some Tripos competitors by seeking support from a consortium of customers. A large block of Japanese companies became the consortium's major funders, after a formal Kaiseki-ish dinner in Tokyo presided over by Toshio Fujita, Hansch's coauthor on the seminal QSAR publication, in Japanese so for me incomprehensible. He later told me that, with Japan's hubris and international reputation then peaking, he had urged them to reciprocate in the same spirit of generosity that Americans had shown to Japan after World War II, by participating. Fujita's endorsement of CoMFA was particularly commendable, considering its implicit competition with his own achievements; in contrast, his aging colleague Hansch would eventually tell me that he thought CoMFA "fraudulent."

This consortium funding yielded three new tools. To address the input wish, for more ways to meaningfully position 3D structures, there were DISCO (created by Abbott and licensed to Tripos at the behest of Yvonne Martin, my Abbott contemporary) and field-fit (don't ask—it didn't work).[5] To address the output wish, for suggesting promising structures, Leapfrog, which also provided a direct counter to Ludi, newly offered by our main competitor BioSym. Ludi seemed to Tripos such a serious threat that, in a welcome reversal of previous administrative policies, I was encouraged to create this product myself. Ludi and Leapfrog were the first commercial implementations of so-called de novo CADD methodologies, whereby drug candidate structures are generated "from the beginning" by random structural tinkering, seeking better complementarity to the geometry of a specified biological target. Leapfrog's structural tinkerings were guided by a fashionable new analytics method, genetic engineering. Because Leapfrog was embedded within Sybyl, its structural tinkerings within the biological target were displayed, providing an entertaining and seductive animation for its users. The CoMFA relevance of Leapfrog? I included a process for converting a CoMFA model into the very crude likeness of a biological target, within which Leapfrog could do its thing.

However, once it was finished, I never took much satisfaction from Leapfrog. Its commercial success owed far more to its marketing appeal than to any scientific merit. There's not much of a seminal Leapfrog publication because the lack of access to relevant experimental data prevented any objective assessment of whether its drug candidate suggestions would indeed bind better.[6] And the evolutionary character of its code meant I was stuck with its future maintenance. So it's quite a surprise to discover that Google Scholar now counts 1,140 publications referencing "Leapfrog Sybyl," including fifty in 2015.

Commercial success was the only motivation for another initiative that I took, to apply for a CoMFA patent.[7] To seek such a patent was almost instinctive for me as an experienced industrial scientist, and CoMFA's novelty was incontestable. However, at that time, patents for software (or, more precisely, to meet the legal definition of a patent, "practice of a physical process under guidance from novel software") were not being granted. But one day an interested colleague dropped by with an issued patent that claimed drug discovery software, freshly granted to "3D Pharmaceuticals." Whatever legal wranglings had yielded this patent, it seemed they should constitute precedent for a CoMFA patent. By another bit of good fortune, details now forgotten, Larry

Weinberger became my patent attorney. His biochemical training, informally enthusiastic style, and deep personal interest in new drug discovery methodologies (and his office near my parents' Landenberg home!) would combine to make him my key intellectual partner for the rest of my Tripos career.

There were challenges specific to a CoMFA patent application. A patent is supposed to benefit society by making information public that inventors would otherwise keep secret. But the basic concepts of CoMFA had been made public years ago. No reward for that. However, its key PLS methodology had not yet been formally revealed, so Svante Wold, who had recommended it to me back in 1981, became a co-inventor. The patent application process often becomes a sort of tennis match between applicant and the patent office, and as the CoMFA volley continued, John McAlister, who was at first uncomfortable with software-associated patents and lawyers generally and who by now had become Tripos's key decision-maker, decided to call the match. Nevertheless, Larry found himself committed to the righteousness of the CoMFA patent application, so, without any guarantee of personal compensation, he continued pressing our case to the examiner and ultimately succeeded.

Once issued, the CoMFA patent provided substantial benefits to almost all its participants. Most importantly, for the next seventeen years it assured Tripos of Sybyl license revenues from almost every drug discovery organization. An article of faith, at least among Tripos's frustrated competitors, was that the patent was a major reason for Tripos's relative longevity and stability. John McAlister vigorously encouraged subsequent patent filings, and Larry became one of his most influential and effective advisors. And surely Svante Wold and Ildiko Frank (Tripos's CoMFA would always utilize unchanged her FORTRAN implementation of PLS) were happy with their royalty revenues.

Ironically, though, for me personally the consequences were better described as interesting. At the next QSAR Gordon Conference, a rump discussion on patenting CADD software was mustered. Since the CoMFA patent was the only example, I was seated by myself facing the lecture audience for an hour of reproach, mostly on how software patents would impede scientific progress. Couldn't the many pharma-employed attendees, I silently philosophized to myself, appreciate how dependent their own activities were on their own employers' patents? At least no one there knew that I had personally been the serpent in this Garden of Eden!

My next Tripos project was the design and partial implementation of "Molecular Spreadsheets," essentially an innovative GUI (graphical user interface) for the Sybyl tables that I'd originally created for Dabyl. Continuing advances in pixel graphics technology were persuading many Tripos customers to switch from the E&S VAX configurations to those Unix-based workstations, and E&S now had its own workstation offering and no longer forbade Tripos from participating. The resultant reworking of Sybyl's GUI, necessarily including a CoMFA gateway, provided the opportunity for creating a molecular spreadsheet. At first, to the dismay of other staff, John and I did not agree on how these spreadsheets should behave, with John's injunction to "just make it work exactly like the conventional spreadsheet market leader, Excel," opposing my contention that instead a molecular spreadsheet should directly represent a Sybyl table, with the nature of each cell's contents established by its row-column location. Eventually John acceded, and in much of today's CADD software, such molecular spreadsheets are the central data representations from which all of a user's activities begin.

16 STATS Soars

As Garland and I had agreed, from mid-1986 until early 1988, the STATS office was housed by Tripos at 6548 Clayton Road, a major Saint Louis boulevard, in a converted bungalow also belonging to Garland, whose irregular internal layout reflected its checkered history. My own office, an attic conversion, could barely hold desks for Dave Patterson and me. Calls to the STATS phone were fielded by the Tripos receptionist, which made for considerable excitement when George Steinbrenner's office once called.

An avid White Sox fan as well as a Chicago resident, John Dewan took over that STATS relationship, and I had no more contact with the White Sox. The Yankees continued to be my responsibility, and I visited the stadium offices a couple of times a year. My hotel stays were Yankee comps in the Grand Hyatt, where, on an October 1986 visit, after an evening at the theater with Libby, I turned on the TV to watch that ball infamously spinning through Buckner's legs and, the next day, shared a rainy lobby with some very disgruntled Red Sox players. Former Yankee players seemed to freely come and go through the Yankee offices, and I remember crossing paths with the dignified Roy White, the incorrigible playboy Joe Pepitone, and the surprisingly diminutive Yogi Berra. One visit tangentially involved me in a Steinbrenner tantrum. He was in Tampa and, reportedly angered by an accidental phone call disconnection, ordered the entire staff to work throughout the Memorial Day weekend. The indignant Yankee treasurer locked himself into his office, which became a problem for me when, on departure, I presented my travel expense invoice. My Yankee hosts advised me not to leave if I wanted to be sure of being paid, and eventually a check did appear, thanks, I was told, to a Yankees jack-of-all-trades propitiator, former pitcher Clyde King.

Unfortunately, the Yankees were starting to have cause for serious disappointment with me because in their stadium office the biggest blunder of my entire programming career was emerging. Part of their Edge 1.000 package was Scout, another edition of the player data base I had created for the White Sox. They had been serious about its use, buying a Corvus disk drive that would support access from multiple Apple IIs and charging two employees with entering scouting reports, one being Roy Krasik, now a senior director of baseball operations at MLB headquarters. Roy kept telling me that as more records were entered, the system response was slowing to a crawl, eventually taking an hour for each entry. What was happening? Swallowing my own incredulity, I eventually recognized that the problem was an undocumented quirk in how UCSD Pascal wrote to files. When locating exactly where to write, say, the 1,521th player record, I had assumed its code would simply multiply the fixed player record length by 1,521, but instead it stepped through 1,521 increments of this record length. (Hey, minimizing additions was exactly why the ancient Egyptians invented multiplication!) Once recognized, this flaw could be coded around, and the Yankees shipped their Corvus back to me for this fix. Furthermore, Sue Dewan began work on a SQL-based PC-compatible replacement for Scout. However, whatever mystical aura I had had in Yankee Stadium as a computer wizard was badly tarnished and, hearing a rumor that computer experience was one reason for the Yankees to hire Jim Bowden away from the Reds, I wasn't surprised that the Yankees never wanted their Corvus back. Nevertheless, fellows, if you change your minds, it's still in my Santa Fe attic!

Otherwise, the new STATS would remain a dry hole for its investors until I could finish converting the fifty thousand lines of UCSD Pascal and ten thousand lines of 1022 into their Turbo Pascal and 1032 equivalents. And there was a deadline—the Yankee and White Sox 1987 opening days. So that was my main weekday evening activity (not yet weekends because those were spent in Terre Haute with Libby). I was glad to learn that the PC technology bypassed all the communication woes that had plagued the Apple II's Playball operators. For PCs, there existed Kermit, a free utility software that cleanly transmitted text files between PCs and VAXes. The only thing I needed to add was a simple script that automated the Playball operators' pregame and postgame work flows. On the other hand, the MicroVAX didn't provide nearly enough disk storage to handle multiple seasons of complete play-by-play from Project Scoresheet. So STATS bought another piece of hardware, an EMC disk drive, that, if I correctly recall, cost around ten thousand dollars more, which I provided gratis by means of a loan from my parents.

Project Scoresheet's process and activities were summarized by Bill James.

Here's what has to be done for each game:

1. Somebody has to make sure the game is scored.
2. Somebody has to score the game, write down what happens on every play.
3. A copy of the scoresheet has to be sent to a central location.
4. The account of the game account has to be entered on computer.
5. The account of the game on computer has to be checked for accuracy.
6. The accounts of the all games have to be joined together for analysis.[1]

Project Scoresheet's first payoff was *The Great American Baseball Stat Book*, planned as the first of an annual series.[2] STATS' only direct contribution to this work was the above-mentioned conventional year-by-year career statistics for each player that I'd been updating every winter. Perhaps as a thoughtful courtesy, anticipating my efforts on Scoresheet's behalf, its last fifty-five pages were my linear weights–based evaluations of every team's roster changes between 1985 and 1986 that, as perhaps the first such essay, I am still proud of. Its tables may have been the prototype for my favorite baseball-reference.com table, "Wins above Average by Position" (for any league season, comparing by fielding position, in linear weights fashion, each team's strengths and weaknesses).

Well before the spring of 1987, I had the new STATS software and the migrated PDP-10 data ready for the clubs, reducing their operating financial costs as promised, and, also, for its potential use by Project Scoresheet, potentially reducing its man-hour demands by merging items 2 through 4 and eliminating item 6 from Bill's summary. I didn't anticipate any additional revenue for STATS from my work, not at all a concern because at that moment STATS had almost no ongoing costs to set against the forty thousand dollars of annual income from the teams. That seemed a more than satisfactory return to STATS' investors, considering their sixty thousand dollars total cash investment (not to mention their various psychic incomes), while Libby and I again were sharing more than adequate incomes. (For by now, I was of course being compensated for my SBIR and software product contributions with a conventional Tripos salary.)

John Dewan was eager to dedicate his entire career to baseball, and Project Scoresheet was starting to receive some external notice. Early in 1987 John got a call from Floyd Kephardt, who was operating a sports information service. Kephardt was vague about his market and customers, but in 1987, with fantasy baseball hardly even vestigial, most of them were surely bookmakers. Whoever they were, Kephardt thought there would be a profitable business in serving them with a phone-accessible twenty-four-hour-per-day sports information portal. Kephardt and John agreed on a deal that would generate fifty thousand dollars in revenue for Project Scoresheet, which in turn would pay its scorers twenty dollars per game and pay John enough to allow him to focus entirely on baseball. Since making this happen would also involve STATS' participation, I accompanied John to Kephardt's somewhat scruffy Miami lair. My only question was technologically motivated. Using such a system would involve lots of communication time, especially for the customers, and long-distance phone calls were expensive. Kephardt smiled. Most customers would be making local phone calls, thanks to the growing number of packet-switching outlets.

Except for a few laptop PCs for use by Project Scoresheet, Kephardt reneged on his promised financing and completely stopped communicating after the Black Monday stock market crash that October. Not much of a disappointment to me, as the whole plan seemed hopelessly undercapitalized, even by my modest standards. But packet-switching sounded more than interesting. This should be useful for STATS, if it was something a VAX could work with, and after some searching through the notorious bookcase of VAX manuals, I found assembly code listings that promised to do the job. At the PC end, the only change would be tweaks to the script to divert Playball phone calls to a local packet-switching network phone number, if one existed.

Now many of you will be aware that the internet is itself fundamentally a packet-switching network. Surely the internet existed in 1987? Well, yes, but access to the internet was then strictly noncommercial, mostly limited to defense sites and academic institutions. In 1987 the packet-switching literature seldom even mentioned an "internet."

As the 1987 season was finishing, Project Scoresheet suddenly offered STATS (me!) an exhilarating adventure. NBC asked Project Scoresheet and STATS to provide statistical sound bites for the 1987 NL playoffs, splits just like those I'd begun providing for A's broadcasters in 1981. Despite the years of work that I'd been doing with big league teams, such recognition by a Big Three national network felt "bigger than 'big league'" to me. John Dewan arrived in Saint Louis a few days early, bringing floppies containing pitch-by-pitch records as well as play-by-play for the Cardinals and Giants regular season games. We generated lots of canned splits for all their players and, proudly brandishing our press passes, conveyed the most interesting splits to NBC's production trailer.

Came the fifth inning of game 4. Danny Cox was nursing a 2–1 lead over the Giants and had just thrown his seventieth pitch. The guys in the truck recognized that this was a perfect moment to show an excerpt from a season split for Danny Cox:

Pitches 1–70: .268 batting average
Pitches 71+: .345 batting average

What happened next almost begs belief. On pitch seventy-three, Kevin Mitchell lined a double; on seventy-four Leonard hit a home run; and the next two batters also hit sharply. Vin Scully then added a heretofore unrecognized laurel to his peerless broadcasting crown by becoming probably the first national announcer to emphasize the now pervasive pitch count. His words: "Boy, that seventy-pitch count mark that we talked about has really become prophetic!"

I was of course watching the telecast on a tiny TV that I'd brought to my Tripos office for the occasion. What a pity, I recall thinking, that such an improbably triumphant moment was already past and forgotten. I would never have believed that someday it would be memorialized in a book.[3]

Of more significance, this adventure had also revealed a major flaw. Preparing the NBC splits had been far too slow. For the teams, STATS' databases were essentially five long lists, with each record in each list having a unique ID for linking it to related records in other lists. Loading another game merely involved adding the appropriate records to each list, and when correcting an existing game, the first step was simply to delete every record that had the same game ID. But with this straightforward construction, generating each split, for example, a particular player's batting performance against left-handed pitchers, first required the relevant player and pitchers' events to be selected from the events list, and then the traversal of each of those selected events while totaling hits and at-bats. On the MicroVAX (a memory-constrained computer, compared to its PDP-10 predecessor), whenever several other users were doing the same thing, each execution of this process took many minutes. Furthermore, the NBC database had contained only one season each of two teams' games, but there were twenty-six major league teams and an expectation of many more seasons to follow.

After some thought, I devised a solution. In addition to the five existing lists, a STATS database would now include new lists, containing the current seasonal statistics—the standard batting, pitching, and fielding statistical lines—for every player, both as totals and also for around a dozen of the most requested splits, such as home and road, or left handers and right handers. Updating these seasonal statistic lists would then become an integral step within the process of loading a game. To update these new seasonal split lists, the number of relevant events to be processed would only be the few provided by a new game, rather than the thousands within a complete team season. And all these updates could be done in one pass of much faster C code. Nevertheless, updating these seasonal statistics updates made loading each game into an hour-long process, and any correction to a game that had already been loaded now took two hours because the first step of deleting an erroneous game processed the same seasonal statistics in the same way as adding a new game, while simply applying a minus sign rather than a plus. At the beginning of STATS' daily operations, when our staff and collective experience were both still very thin, I was occasionally awakened by a nighttime call from John or Sue, frustrated because just as a game-loading began, they received a corrected version. I could only do my best to be sympathetic.

I also started hearing from Craig Wright, whose zealous pursuit of objective baseball knowledge had made him the first true sabermetrician to be employed by a major league team, the Texas Rangers, in the 1980s. His experiences, findings, and opinions are detailed in a well-regarded 1989 book, *The Diamond Appraised*, which he was then working on.[4] Craig was putting his firsthand contacts with many major league teams to use by, among other things, trying to interest them in the services of the STATS–Project Scoresheet alliance. Craig told me that the way Playball searches currently worked, expecting the teams to construct their own queries and then select the appropriate reports, was too complicated. Instead he had a list of twenty "canned reports" and workflows that he thought would be appealing, spelling out their contents and formats in exacting detail for my implementation. Craig spent much of that 1987 off-season demonstrating Playball and Scout to various teams, optimistically reporting that the alliance could expect five new team customers by the end of 1988. However, no major league team would ever again be interested in applying STATS' data systems. STATS' original business model was completely dead.

And then, suddenly, and to my complete shock and surprise, STATS' relationship with Project Scoresheet disintegrated. I was vaguely aware that John had quit his day job as an actuary to focus on baseball. But I knew nothing of how strained the relations between John and a dozen-odd other Project Scoresheet honchos had become. Whatever the circumstances, early in 1988 John called in despair to inform me that Project Scoresheet had suddenly and unjustly kicked him out, and he didn't know what to do. As tactfully as possible, I asked him whether it wasn't now obvious that STATS could make better use of the personal commitments that he and Sue had been dedicating to Project Scoresheet? After a few more such phone calls, in a couple of weeks John found himself ready to move on, and STATS had found its true leader. I was delighted!

The STATS office was relocated to a large basement room a few miles from the Dewans' Chicago home, at 7250 North Cicero in Lincolnwood. While the Dewans' full-time commitment to STATS was one obvious reason for this move, the E&S purchase of Tripos was also then under way, with organizational moves and investments that undermined the informal office-for-computer exchange that I had with Garland. So once I had finished the coding just described, the STATS MicroVAX and EMC disk drive were moved to Chicago. As a sort of going-away present, the lone Tripos systems guy built and included an RS-232 cable so that the MicroVAX and I could now communicate via modem. It was a huge relief when the disk drive smoothly booted in Chicago because, considering the absence there of any other VAX-fluent peripherals, restoring the teams' several seasons of pitch-by-pitch data would have been a formidable challenge.

Any substantive future for STATS still depended on the collection of play-by-play records for every future major league game. But those records would no longer be coming from Project Scoresheet! The start of the 1988 season loomed immediately ahead, and although the hardware and software were now ready, the scoring network was nonexistent. Furthermore, I was emphasizing that with the teams still being the only active market for STATS offerings, the timeliness of our information would be critical. STATS' policy must be that every game played today, possibly as many as thirteen, should be loaded into the STATS database by sometime tomorrow, hopefully before noon.

Marvelously, John and Sue had the experience and the fortitude to create a more coherent scoring network. Incredibly, this rebuild took only a month. Opening Day would be April 4. On March 1 John sent a recruitment letter to several hundred of the Project Scoresheet scorers that he and Sue had previously worked with. His goal was the ability to assign each game to two scorers, working from TV, radio, or the ballpark as each scorer preferred. One should have the PC and modem now needed to run Playball, and in return for ten dollars would be expected to send the game immediately on completion. The other would score on paper for five dollars. There would also be a pool of unpaid scorers, who submitted scoresheets for any convenient game. To further encourage participation, diligent pool scorers would have access, essentially exclusively, to the splits for a team of interest. There were struggles to cover some individual games of particular teams, yet in the end John and Sue, with help from STATS' first hire, Carmen Corica, succeeded in obtaining play-by-play data for every major league game in 1988. Looking back, I am embarrassed by my tendency to take for granted their daily triumphs, as I was numbed by pride in my own technological contributions to STATS and my persistent insensitivities to other people's feelings.

I don't remember how all this 1988 activity was paid for. The scorer payments would by themselves have consumed the forty thousand dollars of team income. I vaguely recall a suggestion by Bill James, who soon after the Project Scoresheet meltdown became actively involved with STATS, in particular as its foremost "ideas guy." He thought it should be possible to recruit a publisher for a James-STATS baseball encyclopedia, one willing to provide an advance approaching one hundred thousand dollars. Bill responded to concerns about delivery by explaining that in practice such timelines were extremely flexible. A publisher would actually be buying a kind of option, an assurance of becoming the book's eventual publisher. Such a transaction, if it did occur, would explain how STATS' 1988 expenses were covered. However, when a James-STATS encyclopedia finally did appear in 1997, it was self-published.

In any case, STATS' continued existence required a recurring source of dependable revenue. Were there products that STATS could now offer for sale, and to what customers? One obvious possibility was the same commodity that John and Bill had already been providing to the now rapidly growing multitude of baseball numbers addicts—a book simply containing the conventional yearly statistics. Furthermore, the first desktop publishing program for PCs had just appeared, making it possible for STATS to produce this book itself. Self-publishing might or might not be more profitable, but it would surely allow STATS to control the timing of a publication. We could offer complete player statistics including the 1988 regular season before the 1988 World Series ended, for the first time in baseball history! John found the time and enthusiasm to master the Ventura Publisher software, a printing company was engaged, and STATS' first publication was almost flaw-less (though the book's introduction did include the precautionary caveat that there might be some minor differences between a few of its numbers and the eventual official ones—because scoring changes happen, you know). John and I discussed its pricing, and I advocated a higher two-digit number, believing this would boost STATS' overall prestige and considering that its only competition, *The Official Baseball Guide* from *The Sporting News* wouldn't appear until next year's spring training. As I recall we settled on a price of fifteen dollars and began promoting this new product in advertisements and targeted direct mail. Its sales continued all winter, in numbers more than enough for us to start believing that STATS was going to survive and maybe even modestly prosper.

That was probably the last STATS operating-level decision that I par-ticipated in. As much as I continued to enjoy and value my activities with STATS, it was Tripos where I worked every day and its challenges that got my limited capacity for business-related attention. So, for the rest of my years with STATS, I would have just two roles: formally its board chairman, and in actuality its chief technical officer or chief soft-ware architect, taking direction from John. Major Playball extensions would be needed for every one of the major clients whose business STATS would soon enjoy, and no one else ever touched Playball's code.

The first such major client to approach STATS was *The National Sports Daily*. In case you're wondering, *The National* was the brainchild of a Mexican media mogul who believed that U.S. sports fans would, like those in Europe and Latin America, embrace a sports-centric daily newspaper. Baseball's six months of daily activity would of course provide much of the content, and, perhaps as a fellow revolutionary, STATS had caught their attention. John and I traveled to New York for a face-to-face with their new editor-in-chief, the nationally renowned Frank Deford. On leaving, we both believed from his polite and encouraging responses that we could and would meet all their needs for daily baseball statistics. But a few months later we learned that *The National* had instead chosen the establishment—Elias, purveyor of baseball statistics to the National League (the American League and most minor league statistics then came from Howe).

Well, since that didn't work out, was there some product beyond books that STATS could offer to that growing swarm of stats-oriented fans? Fantasy baseball was starting to get a lot of attention. Yet for some reason, at first neither John nor I got it. Yeah, such fantasy games should provide customers for our automatically updated stats, but operating fantasy leagues ourselves seemed a small-change activity, not a serious enough arena for STATS to engage in. Nevertheless, our lone employee, Carmen Corica, a passionate fantasy player, recognized the opportunity, and John found himself yielding to Carmen's enthusiasm. Bill also saw the opportunity in fantasy baseball, had some well-conceived ideas for a more sophisticated fantasy game, and perhaps Bill appreciated this opportunity to share the fruits of his creativity with his followers (and his STATS partners) without having to write book after book (I am supposing, as Bill and I never discussed this point; indeed, though it seems strange in retrospect, I have never asked anyone about the financial arrangements among Bill, John, and STATS).

But somebody would have to do some writing of code, and—you guessed it—that would mostly be me. As usual I began by working weekday evenings in Saint Louis. The fundamental operation, updating the current scores of the fantasy game players' rosters from newly loaded games, was trivial to program. However, for no reason that I can now recall, generating a league of Opening Day rosters from the contestants' draft lists was one of the few projects I've ever done where I had to completely discard my first coding efforts. With Opening Day approaching and lots of other coding tasks yet for me to address, most urgently of all, safeguarding the legitimacies of preseason fantasy rosters as contestants released, drafted, and traded their players, I had to start working full-time on finishing the game, and that time would be most effectively spent in Chicago with everyone else. So off I went for a couple of weeks, sleeping on an aged convertible sofa in John and Sue's basement, and the three of us worked twelve-plus hours, day after day, getting everything ready. Such a few weeks of intense on-site programming before Opening Day, as a third member of the Dewan household, became a practice I would repeat every year until the strike in 1994. I can't recall ever hearing complaints about these absences from anyone at Tripos. And, considering how notorious is the late delivery of programming projects, taking some pride in having never been late for Opening Day seems reasonable.

Next, Bill had an even better opportunity for STATS based on his personal relationship with John Walsh of ESPN, who among his other accomplishments there had created Sports Center. ESPN was about to become Major League Baseball's first cable provider since 1983, committing to the telecast of 175 games, six per week. Bill convinced Walsh that STATS' unique databases, queried interactively as an evening's games progressed, might add something distinctive and worthwhile to ESPN's baseball production. So, playing hooky from one of those New Hampshire Gordon Conferences, I picked up Bill and John Dewan at the Hartford airport, to meet in Bristol with John Walsh and some other ESPN honchos and make our pitch. A few weeks later, on September 9, I was back in Bristol for a live tryout as actual games were being broadcast. Dickie Thon hit a game-tying three-run home run in the ninth inning, and I had ready a few relevant tidbits, along with a quick search for all the similarly dramatic home runs that had occurred in 1989. Everything must have clicked because John soon told me that STATS was signing a contract to provide its services to ESPN. An unquestionably big league customer, our first!

To make this work, a STATS employee would have to work late every night in Bristol, which accounted for a completely unexpected call that fall from Paul Bamberg's wife, Cherry. One of Paul's favorite student-disciples, David Pinto, wanted to work for STATS, but he had growing family responsibilities. I enthusiastically tried to reassure Cherry that a STATS employment would be secure because I had already met Dave and knew that he would be an ideal candidate. The circumstances of our previous meetings make for an interesting story on their own. A few years earlier, despite Paul's outstanding teaching record, the Harvard physics department had effected economies that included his salary, and, somewhat as I was also doing, in 1982 Paul took on a second career, joining a speech recognition startup named Dragon essentially as its chief technical officer. For the next few years, whenever I would visit, Paul would ask his latest speech recognizer to distinguish my enunciations of such words as "ball" and "strike" but without any success or even any sign of progress. I was too polite to express my doubts. On one Bamberg visit, during a lawn croquet party (how Anglophilic!) I also met Dave Pinto, a computer science student whose joint interests in baseball and the Harvard Band had caught Paul's attention. The next time I met Dave, he had become a Dragon employee, and he was demonstrating to me an extraordinary leap in the performance of Dragon technology, accurately writing out continuous speech in the form of a pseudodictation by a pathologist performing an autopsy.

Just to complete this Dragon sidebar, in another few years I began seeing Dragon speech recognition kits on Best Buy shelves, with Paul's daughter Lisa as the fetching young woman on the box cover. However, Dragon's technological accomplishments did not generate consistent profitability, and, as cash was running out, in 1999 Goldman Sachs was engaged to find a buyer for Dragon. Unfortunately, that buyer had fraudulently exaggerated its own financial circumstances, and the merged entity quickly folded. So another visit included my witnessing of the Bambergs' signatures on a formal complaint, suing Goldman Sachs for its negligent performance of services. Alas, considering Goldman Sachs's extensive experience in this type of situation, it is not surprising that the resulting legal machinations have yet to converge. Anyway, Dave Pinto took STATS' offer, and his years of nightly toil as STATS' man on the scene at Bristol continued long after my own eviction.

Despite the ESPN contract, STATS scorers were still unwelcome in every baseball game's information hub—the press box—so the accuracy of STATS' raw data, particularly its details, was still vulnerable to the whims of announcers and cameramen. "Was that a wild pitch or a passed ball?" Or, yes, there was a base hit and a run scored, but with the scorer's broadcaster's team now down by 10 runs, surely the broadcaster's listeners are more interested in hearing the story about that Hall of Famer than in the pitch sequence leading to the base hit. And, "say, isn't that Jones now in right field? When did he come in?" In the press box, any happening that's box-score relevant and not self-evident will be announced. But in the 1980s, baseball's hallowed press box culture only sanctioned newspapers. A computer information service seeks press box access to help support a cable TV newbie? Well, sorry, but our last open seat went to that guy from the college newspaper. Maybe next century? But STATS scorers wouldn't be excluded from press boxes for much longer.

The lever that opened those doors was *USA Today*, which, already being itself something of a daily sports paper, surely saw *The National* as a potential threat to circulation. Its longtime baseball editor Paul White had already designed an "extended box score." Could these STATS guys protect *USA Today*'s competitive posture by making Paul White's design a reality? Thinking how delightful it was to be the only arms dealer during an armaments race, I flew to *USA Today*'s Washington office to meet with White, who systematically unveiled the paper's requirements. STATS was already routinely generating most of the box score extensions he sought but only as numerical values. Instead, he would require STATS to supply the extended box score text itself, in ready-to-print form, including the traditional agate codes to properly format that text. He also wanted, in sentence form, the play-by-play for those half innings in which runs were scored. All this seemed to be content that I could readily program. The bigger programming challenges would be logistical. A daily such as *USA Today* needs to be printed and delivered in time for East Coast breakfasts, hopefully even including complete accounts of the previous night's West Coast games. Until now STATS' central computers (we had invested in a second MicroVAX) had been the only conduit for STATS' information. But passing *USA Today's* box scores through the central computers would be a serious bottleneck, and an extra burden on those central computers, during the same time period that was most critical for STATS' other activities. So *USA Today* would instead need to get its box scores directly from the STATS scorers, as Playball's first postgame activity.

The execution of a *USA Today* contract would present an even bigger logistical challenge for Sue and John. *USA Today* was undeniably a newspaper, so its sponsorship should have provided STATS with the opportunity to demand press box access for its scorers. Nevertheless, hospitalities varied among the twenty-six major league teams, with STATS' immediate neighbors, the Cubs, being the most resistant, STATS perhaps being a victim of the prophet-in-one's-home-country trope. Yet access was only one small part of the overall challenge. John and Sue had to recruit a few computer-competent scorers in each city who could frequently and reliably commit themselves to all the hours needed to get to the park, and well ahead of the game starting time, to make sure of a working phone jack and to retype excerpts from the home team's game notes, another *USA Today* requirement. A much more demanding commitment by a prospective STATS scorer, who until now needed only to plant himself and his computer in front of a home TV, shortly before game time.

The Playball code enhancements went smoothly. I incorporated a small improvement to White's extended box score format prescription, a one-space indentation of the records for substitute players, to distinguish them from the nine starters but was told that White rejected it. However, John's suggestion of a "hold" statistic was accepted, after a few tweaks to refine its definition. As usual I was in Lincolnwood for the last few weeks before Opening Day 1990, frantically creating a workflow that could be reliably executed by our recruit scorers in the unfamiliar and unforgiving press box environment while adapting Playball's operations, for the first time, to merge with those of a computer system that STATS did not control. *USA Today*'s computer system had a prescribed naming for the dozens of nightly files from STATS scorers, including any postgame retransmissions, so that their ready-to-print contents flowed seamlessly into the right openings on the printed pages. Floppy disks with the final Playball revisions were overnighted to reach scorers early on Opening Day. When box scores then started to show up at *USA Today*, I triumphantly speculated that there must be a lot of skeptics there paying off losing bets!

Not that Playball's creations of *USA Today* box scores yet correctly handled all the vagaries of actual baseball games, and during the first few weeks of the season, I bought and studied as many editions of *USA Today* as possible. It was a novel means of debugging a program, and it reinforced my egotistical feelings of the power that my unilateral control over Playball's capabilities gave me. Driving home from a jazz gig late one night, I listened to Cardinals announcer Mike Shannon praise Ozzie Smith's groundout advancing a runner with "You won't see that in the box score." I could and should fix that, I thought, and the next distribution of Playball quietly added this category to *USA Today*'s latest box score. A fun story, yet the bottom line is that at *USA Today*'s insistence, relayed to me by an irritated John Dewan, the new category was quickly eradicated.

In 1991 Playball became essentially the only source of major league box scores when STATS also signed up Associated Press, which supplies the box scores in most daily newspapers. After *USA Today*, for me this project was almost a vacation—just lines of the same familiar numbers, each now labeled by one of Associated Press's player codes. And what an ego trip—the code I had over the years created singlehandedly might now be producing more daily lines of text than anyone else's code anywhere in the world (assuming the code that generated daily stock price listings was not the work of a single individual).

17 Cheerlessness and Lyme Disease

However, though coincidentally, I was about to find that my pride was going before a fall. A Hawaii vacation that John and Sue shared with Libby and me did not, as I had hoped, soothe Libby's growing impatience with my STATS distractions. Instead, my pinch hitter (in case of emergency) pilot training had been interrupted by being called back to Chicago for something. That was probably the last straw because in June of 1991 when I asked what was bothering her, I learned of her biplane instructor romance. Libby had never wanted to be married and now cared much more for someone else with whom she could perhaps be happier. For both of us, divorce was undebatable. For me, this divorce became the opening event in seventeen years of cheerlessness, though a cheerlessness I didn't fully sense until it ended because it was more wasting than catastrophic.

Cheerlessness is not fun to write about and seems unlikely to make enjoyable reading. Furthermore, post-1991 computer technology does not seem quite so charmingly anachronistic, and today's big data no longer seemed such a futuristic fancy. Finally, in early 1996 STATS expelled me, and the memoir-worthiness of my own life tailed off. These are some of the reasons why there seems a lot less worth describing about the last twenty-five years. But the biggest reason is the conflict between candor and courtesy. Some of those closest to me, though no doubt believing that their actions were completely justified, caused me acute or relentless distress, yet Gandhi's observation that "an eye for an eye will only make the whole world blind" fits both these situations and also my personal inclinations. Still, this is a memoir—obligating me to report feelings, and the relevant facts, as best as I remember them. If there was a common theme among these years, it was an assortment of hubris. Not my own hubris, though—instead the three most important people in my life each pursued their own visions, with effects on me that were mostly unfortunate.

My second divorce did not feel nearly as emotionally traumatic as the first. Been there, done that, knew what to expect. Nevertheless, some weeks after the decision, I began experiencing strange muscular spasms and aches so intense and debilitating that nothing I tried would let me sleep for more than an hour or so. I would spend much of each night soaking in a warm bathtub. The physicians all agreed. "Divorce does that sort of thing, but not to worry, sleep deficiency is self-limiting. Here's some muscle relaxants that will help." But the pills didn't help, the symptoms slowly worsened, and I didn't believe they were psychosomatic, as I hadn't felt much emotional turmoil before they began. Doing some pre-Google reading on my own, I somewhere discovered something called Lyme disease. I'd recently been to the East Coast for one of those rural family reunions and had indeed noted a remarkable circular inflammation where something had bit me. Seemed worth investigating to me, but at that time no one in Saint Louis had ever encountered Lyme, and of course any patient's self-diagnosis of an exotic illness is automatically suspect. I couldn't persuade anyone to prescribe the tetracyclines that were already Lyme's established treatment or even to do any testing.

Good health is about as fundamental as a need can be, and I was feeling more ill than I would ever feel in my entire life. So another pending Gordon Conference arguably became the greatest piece of luck in my fortunate life, when as usual the conference was preceded by a weekend with the Bambergs. In Massachusetts Lyme was already a recognized fact of medical life, and when I told Paul and Cherry something of what I was experiencing, Paul insisted on taking Sunday to drive us many miles through Boston traffic congestion to one of a few public health locations where Lyme testing was being done, leveraging his credentials as a Massachusetts resident on my behalf. Back in Saint Louis a few weeks later, when the test results reported me positive for Lyme, the tetracycline prescription was forthcoming, and I became one of the luckier Lyme victims who seems to have experienced a complete cure. It is hard to express too much appreciation for Paul's thoughtful actions, which may well have made the rest of my life livable.

Nevertheless, there could be some cognitive bias in one response to this experience, "Yes, Dick, but you had met someone," thereby relieving my presumably psychosomatic symptoms. True but irrelevant. This time I didn't feel much impetus to seek a third wife. The demands from both STATS and Tripos were keeping me extremely busy. The 1991 equivalent of Zoosk (not Be Naughty!)—placing a personal advertisement in the hip Saint Louis weekly—would be my only initiative.

When I got around to leafing through the batches of replies during those sleepless nights, one stood out. From a PhD biochemist, a postdoc in the Washington University Medical School, a loyal Cubs fan (and my ad had said nothing about baseball), and very eloquently written, by Kathe Andrews. So we had lunch, then a few dates, and, though I was seventeen years older, Kathe seemed to find me very attractive. She was the single mother of a five-year-old boy, Alex Chrisope, each week splitting custody with his father, and a devotee of animals, particularly dogs, and horses as a semiprofessional. More on the horses later! She was about to be hired by the central campus of Washington University as a biology instructor, where her gift for teaching would soon find her picture featured in the student guide. Kathe was and is serious and energetic, ruthlessly dedicated when pursuing a goal, yet easily and vigorously offended and distracted by slights, imagined or anticipated as well as real, and somewhat given to flamboyant self-expression.

What should I do? Marriage had agreed with me, and Kathe seemed about as good a candidate for the wife number three role that she sought as I was likely to find, as I wasn't inclined to put much effort into looking, particularly within Saint Louis, where apart from Washington University the dominant female ethos was still traditional and somewhat subservient. So I learned to ride at the stable of a matriarch for whom Kathe had become a protégée because they shared an attachment to saddlebred horses (the nineteenth century's equivalent to a Porsche, favored by Civil War generals, whose other aficionados include Don Mattingly and William Shatner). We met one another's families, with hers charming me more than mine charmed her. In March 1992 we married in the matriarch's country home and settled into a classical University City neighborhood. For the first couple of years our lives together went smoothly, much as I had hoped and expected.

18 The Rise and Fall of TRPS

This saga began in 1994, when E&S spun out Tripos to become a tiny NASDAQ-traded company, with John McAlister its president. Every morning would now begin with a peek at the latest TRPS stock price—hypnotic! Yet as a tiny publicly traded company, both that TRPS price and even Tripos's continuing independence, considering the liquidity of its $10 million bequest from E&S, depended on its prospects for dramatic revenue growth. Surely our drug design software business could not promise such growth. What else could we do? Something that would be a natural extension of our existing resources and expertise?

In fact, just such a technological opportunity had just presented itself. Robotics was making possible the simultaneous testing of many different compounds by cyclically and repetitively depositing an individual compound into its own tiny compartment within a tray and performing a single assay procedure on the entire tray. Especially at the start of a discovery project when nothing active is known, it seemed self-evident that practicing such high-throughput screening (HTS) would yield many more and better lead candidates. However, just as growing a real tree demands many times more fallen acorns or pine cones, HTS would make sense only if there were lots of compounds to screen—a thousandfold more. The market demand for more compounds, dramatic and presumably robust. Therefore, why shouldn't Tripos, with its established leadership in methodologies for compound design, go the next step and also become the preferred supplier of the compounds that it designs?

But doesn't the design of compounds intended for random ignorant screening seem an oxymoron? To fully understand everything that followed, the following conceptual background may be helpful.

First, please consider the fundamental axiom of medicinal chemistry—similar compounds are more likely to have similar biological properties. This axiom even has an existence proof, and an objective one. If biological activity were randomly distributed among chemical structures, then it would be futile and pointless to synthesize specific structures. Medicinal chemistry itself would not exist.

But, then, how can the similarity between two compounds be determined? In practice, the answer to this question has always been mostly subjective—the intuitive opinions of individual medicinal chemists. The rest of the TRPS story—both the company's and mine—was conceptually centered on a quest—successful—for an objective measure of compound similarity, one that, for the company, would be commercially appealing, and especially for me, would be scientifically acceptable.

More background. The most fundamental business constraint would be the cost of compound synthesis, and robotics could also be used to produce the floods of compounds that the market should demand. However, although robotics could, in like manner to HTS, make many different compounds in a single cycle, there is a fundamental limit on what each such cycle can make. The efficiency of laboratory robotics results from applying an identical procedure to each of the little compartments in a tray. While such uniformity is highly desirable for biological testing, the goal of synthesizing molecules for screening is diversity.[1] To get as much diversity as possible under this constraint of performing an identical synthetic operation on many compartments, a robotic synthetic reaction almost always forms a bond between two preexisting molecules. For convenient reference, let's abbreviate this process as A + B => A - B, where A and B are types of molecules having complementary reactivities, such that any A can form a bond with any B. If 100 A's and 100 B's are available, then 100 × 100 (10,000) structurally distinct A-B molecules are possible. More dramatically, many structures can form bonds to both A's and B's. Let's call these AB's. If 100 AB's are also available, then 100 × 100 × 100 (a million) different

A-BA-B structures are possible (in two synthetic steps to form the two bonds). The bonanza expected from the pairing of these apparently limitless horizons for combinatorial chemistry and HTS was exciting pharma researchers everywhere.

However, only a few hundred structures, pairings of an A with a B, could practicably be chosen, per library, for actual synthesis and sale. Which ones? According to that fundamental axiom of medicinal chemistry, with chemical similarity implying biological similarity, for purposes of random ignorant screening, the chosen A structures and the chosen B structures should be as *dissimilar* as possible. Put differently, once it is known that a specific structure is *not* active, then its most similar nearby structures become less likely to reveal activity than those farther away.

Which then resurfaces that big scientific question—what measurement of chemical dissimilarity would best predict biological dissimilarity? There was (and still is) a de facto 2D standard—Tanimoto fingerprints—which as earlier mentioned I had pioneered, but I still believed that some sort of 3D shape-based similarity approach should work better. The spin-out had anointed me as Tripos's chief scientific officer and vice president of science, and I had already created products Legion and Selector, with which our software customers could create and manipulate conceptual combinatorial libraries.[2] So I was agreeable when John McAlister assigned me the task—hands-on—of devising something better, something novel that would differentiate the library subsets that Tripos might offer from its burgeoning competitors. Furthermore, the market, and I as a scientist, would be satisfied only with a something whose superiority for predicting biological similarity could be objectively supported.

In retrospect, John's expectation and my confidence that I might uncover such a novel something seem almost fanciful. Nevertheless, that is what happened, and rather quickly. To hopefully bypass the perennial complication for 3D shape comparisons, the squirming and wiggling of actual molecules, I proposed topomers, a canonical standardization of molecular shape.[3] At least as insightfully, David Patterson then devised neighborhood behavior, a method for objectively comparing the capabilities of various chemically based measures of similarity to predict biological similarity.[4]

To visualize how a topomer shape is generated, imagine one of these A's or B's as a tree-like structure, one made with Tinkertoy pieces so that its sparse branches can twist freely.[5] Start by overlaying its intended root bond onto some arbitrary fixed line. Proceeding stepwise from this rooted tree, fix the twist of each Tinkertoy rod so as to push the remainder of the structure as far away from the root as possible. When you come to a branch, resolve its ambiguity by positioning the biggest remainder as far away as possible, and push the next biggest remainder to the right (where "right" is defined locally, with respect to the direction of the preceding Tinkertoy bond). Rings are a special sort of branch, so as you approach a ring network, twist the Tinkertoy rod that connects that network to push the bigger side of the ring to the same local right. If, during this process, things bump into one another, don't worry about it; just keep going. Although there are a lot more details that are peculiar to molecular structures, like aromaticity, unsaturation, stereochemistry, ring flips, and the definitions of "big," these are the general ideas. Then, to define a similarity between two such topomer shapes, you should estimate their volume difference, the total of the volumes occupied by one of the pair but not the other. The smaller this volume difference, the more similar the structures, and—hopefully!—the more likely that the two shapes will bind to biological targets in the same way. When a few topomer shapes were inspected as a 3D overlay, this hope did appear to be a reasonable possibility, especially after later including differences in locations of hydrogen-bonding atoms with this volume difference.

However, both Tripos and I now needed to validate this visual impression with an objective methodology and to compare the effectiveness of topomer similarity in predicting biological similarity with the effectiveness of other similarity predictors, especially those Tanimoto fingerprints. Dave Patterson mastered this challenge by coming up with neighborhood behavior. His idea is based on a conventional X-Y graph. But the points on his graph represent compound pairings, not individual compounds. Specifically, the X coordinate of a point is the chemical difference between a pair of compounds, as measured by topomer shape difference, Tanimoto fingerprints, or anything else worth trying, and the Y coordinate is the biological difference between the two compounds, the difference between their experimentally measured potencies. Now, please consider how these points should distribute themselves. If two structures are chemically not very similar (generating a data point anywhere toward the right side of this graph), they may or may not happen to be biologically similar. But whenever the two structures are chemically similar but biologically dissimilar (indicated by a data point toward the upper left corner of this graph), then this measure of chemical similarity has failed. Therefore, for a good descriptor, there should be a strong tendency for these points to fall below an imaginary diagonal line. The steeper such a diagonal line, the weaker its underlying chemical similarity descriptor as a predictor of biological similarity. The steepness of this slope also provides a calibration for its descriptor, suggesting how chemically dissimilar two compounds must be to achieve some chosen probability of biological similarity. When Patterson and I applied the neighborhood behavior test to around a dozen random compound sets whose biological potencies had been published, topomer similarity was, as hoped, found to be significantly more powerful and robust than Tanimoto fingerprints for predicting biological similarity.

Tripos now had a coherent, convincing, and distinctive rationale for designing superior screening libraries, libraries that, per compound, spanned larger and sparser regions of chemistry space and were therefore more likely to contain lead structures to any arbitrary biological target. For their synthesis, Tripos had already formed an alliance with PanLabs, a respected Seattle-based company whose existing contract service business, seeking novel biological activity by partially purifying natural products extracted from soils and jungles, was threatened by pharma's newfound fascination with combinatorial screening libraries. PanLabs convinced Tripos that it could redirect its experience and facilities to synthesize the screening libraries that Tripos designed. Tripos would then be responsible for marketing and selling these vials of compounds as Optiverse screening libraries. With the capable and conscientious support of Farad Soltanshahi, Dave and I wrote Chem-Space, software to direct Optiverse library production, which balanced our topomer dissimilarity and Tanimoto fingerprint dissimilarity goals against other library design constraints, such as biological compatibility, synthesizability, and costs.[6]

Optiverse libraries were an immediate commercial success, a compelling new product concept for a booming new market. Yet they were too successful by half. Somehow it never really occurred to me or to almost anyone else at Tripos that in contrast to the dependable make-and-copy process of software production, with chemical compounds there might be issues of product quality. So Tripos trusted without verifying the quality of PanLabs' compounds. True, in these early days of combinatorial enthusiasm, a chemically pure product was not demanded for HTS. Indeed, the presence of multiple structures—additional chances that something would tickle the assay, with only the very infrequent hits then needing to be purified—was almost desirable. However, PanLabs' chemistry experience had been limited to the mild conditions of natural product purification. Chemical synthesis uses much harsher reagents, which if still present in the library vials as traces could generate false positives when that library was screened, by poisoning the biological target. Customers who then purified such apparent hits only to learn that their biological response was caused by a biologically corrosive impurity rather than the structure on the label understandably became angry at Tripos and its management. Soon there were a lot of irate customers. Should we have limited Tripos's offerings to software, something we had learned how to provide reliably?

No. For John the screening library business was a glass half-full, not half-empty. The potential market size for Tripos-designed compounds had proved to be at least an order of magnitude larger than that for its CADD software. But a reliable source for those compounds was needed, especially as PanLabs now had to be sold. So a worldwide search for another supplier began. Bruising cleanup negotiations among Tripos, PanLabs' new owner, and disgruntled Optiverse customers surely encouraged John in preferring a future source that he could buy, and therefore control, rather than another synthetic partner. (The lone investigator that Tripos sent to explore partnering possibilities in China, where most of this work is now done, came back suffering from food poisoning.) Tripos couldn't afford to buy any of the few existing synthetic facilities that were large enough to feed the market profitably. But instead, with the guidance of a small but established and trusted compound provider, perhaps Tripos could grow its own world-class compound synthesis facility.

John's eventual choice was Receptor Research, a rural garage laboratory atop the rugged Atlantic shoreline of Cornwall, the southwestern tip of England, and staffed by a former Glaxo chemist, Tony Cooper, and his wife. On my first visit there, the three of us had to take turns plugging our laptops in to the only available outlet. Yet the tiny libraries that Receptor Research had been producing had the highest quality recommendations from its customers. And Tony, in his understated British way, was quite enthusiastic about helping Tripos to scale up his practices, making full use of the automated compound purification technologies that were also starting to appear. But there was a catch. That facility would have to be situated in the same village of Bude, Cornwall, where the Coopers were living and working.

Not such a bad idea, John thought, for he was totally charmed by these surroundings. Bude, reportedly the English location farthest away from the railway network, was something of a British time capsule. Not only would it have been perfect for filming an Agatha Christie village murder mystery, it could have done almost as well by Jane Austen. For example, I usually stayed in a former coach hotel, heavy on rose bushes and staircases but light on thermal insulation, where everyone who was anyone in Bude would convene each Wednesday evening for curry or fish and chips in its pub. The hotel overlooked a canal with manually operated wooden locks and a narrow harbor centered by a reportedly Napoleonic-era fort and capped by a massive stone jetty that protected its fishing boats and tourist beach from the ravages of Atlantic storms.

However, traveling to Bude ordinarily required plane, train, and automobile, the last twenty miles on one-and-a-half-lane roads framed by vine-covered stone walls and frequented by aggressive drivers indifferent to their own high fatality rates. The roads did traverse a delightfully varied landscape, an impressionistic rural panorama dotted with abandoned mines and ruined foundries, a mecca for tradition-minded British vacationers and retirees, though not so much in winter, when the Atlantic gales were much colder, windier, wetter, and altogether oppressive.

Anyway, Cornwall had attractions beyond aesthetic charm for Tripos expansion. The nearby presence of Maybridge, a long-established supplier of compounds for screening or synthesis, in an abandoned slate mine near Tintagel, King Arthur's legendary hangout, might make it easier to recruit more chemists to this isolated locale. Best of all, Cornwall is both economically depressed and Prince Charles's duchy. If Tripos could promise to create high-quality employment opportunities in Cornwall, there could be grants from the British government that would enable a rapid expansion.

Indeed, for many years Tripos Receptor Research would prosper and grow, just as projected, under the leaderships of Peter Hecht, an engaging Austrian who had originally earned John's confidence while a postdoc with me in Saint Louis, and Mark Allen, a proper British chemist who loved laboratory automation but seemed a bit doubtful about CADD, Conservatives, and Americans in general. There were two waves of laboratory expansion, the first being a move from the garage to a row of "porta-labs," whose deliveries down those Cornwall roads must have been harrowing, and the second a move to Tripos Discovery Research (TDR) Laboratory, a masterpiece of a combinatorial library factory that housed two hundred chemists and beguiled visitors with the cows in the surrounding pastures and a top-floor view of the Atlantic. As hoped, its $15 million construction cost was subsidized by $9 million in British grants, and its July 2004 ceremonial opening was graced by Prince Andrew's appearance via helicopter. John McAlister was further honored by tea with the queen at Buckingham Palace. Greg Smith spent a year in Bude with his family to develop a world-class informatics system that would automate and monitor all TDR operations. TDR Laboratory's ultimate synthetic prowess was best exemplified by the delivery of 400,000 different compounds, each with its own certification of purity, to the Pfizer laboratory where Viagra had been discovered. (Some 600,000 syntheses were begun, but, quite as expected considering the vagaries of chemical synthesis and purification, many attempts fail.)

During these half dozen years, my only responsibility for Tripos was to provide Bude with more and better versions of ChemSpace, used on-site by two or three CADD specialists. Every month or so, I would visit Bude for a few days of discussion, flying overnight to a London airport, then driving myself across southern England, usually arriving in time for evening dinner. I'd often carry a cornet because it turned out that many of the best British trad jazz musicians and their fans had retired to Cornwall and accepted sit-ins at their rural pub jams.

Of course, TDR's active business focus was still screening libraries (rebranded as LeadQuest). But John's vision for TDR went much further. Shouldn't a world-class combinatorial synthesis laboratory also be an attractive partner for improving on lead structures as well as for discovering them? Might there then follow partnerships that would hint of a true Eldorado for Tripos—a small royalty on a new drug—eventually? Something with which to tantalize Tripos investors—today?

So I was encouraged to come up with a series of extensions to the topomer idea that might broaden TDR's conceptual appeal to drug discoverers. The first, an obvious inversion of its rationale for screening library design and another embodiment of medicinal chemistry's fundamental axiom, had already been implemented though not yet validated, as follows. A likely place to look for improvements on a newly discovered lead structure would be among structures that are topomerically similar to that lead. To enable lead-hopping (i.e., directing synthesis to a different lead series or library, perhaps because the original lead is too difficult to work with or is patented by a different company), I had improvised, as dbtop, a program that was not limited to the topomer similarities among A's and B's but instead proposed a minimal topomer dissimilarity between any arbitrary pair of complete structures.[7] By the prospective testing of some compounds already on TDR's shelves that were topomerically similar enough some to newly published lead structures, the TDR CADD scientists provided some experimental support for dbtop's effectiveness as a predictor of biological similarity.[8]

What about combining topomers and CoMFA, trying out these canonical topomeric shapes as those pesky suitably aligned inputs for CoMFA? This idea was embarrassingly slow in occurring to me, surfacing only when the TDR CADD group lamented that a TDR customer couldn't afford the conventional CoMFA study that its project findings prescribed. But it was then an almost out-of-the-box idea for me to implement. For its validation, I grabbed fifteen random CoMFA papers, each evidently requiring enough effort to merit publication, and applied topomer CoMFA to their input data sets. Ten minutes later, I had fifteen CoMFA models whose statistical qualities were almost as good as those that had been published. Moreover, the topomer CoMFA models were completely objective in their construction, whereas the published models were necessarily based on more or less subjective structural alignments by the publication's authors.[9]

My climactic topomer extension was AllChem, supported by another SBIR grant from NIH, which proffered a practical approach for identifying a few of the most promising drug-like structures from among the 10^{20} that seemed most synthetically accessible.[10] So just how big is 10^{20}? There's an estimate that in total all the world's beaches and deserts contain 7.5×10^{18} grains of sand. With a few of the planets and moons and other space junk being completely sandy, maybe 10^{20} is around the numbers of grains of sand in the solar system? Anyway, it's a lot, and, yes, you should be a bit skeptical. So here's how this searching worked. The two key ideas have already been mentioned: first, that most drug-like compounds are at least conceptually composed of side chains attached to scaffold structures, and second, the fundamental axiom again, that topomer similarity is a good way to identify structures that are biologically similar, and hopefully superior, to some lead structure of interest. Most—like 99.9999..99 percent—of the side chains and scaffolds whose combinations composed those 10^{20} structures are by themselves too topomerically dissimilar, from any of the side chains or the scaffolds extractable from that lead structure, to be a part of any complete structure that includes that scaffold or structure, thereby directly and rather quickly eliminating $(100 - 99.9999..99)^3$ (assuming an A-BA-B construction) of those 10^{20} structures.

Okay, such searching is possible. But why bother? And where did the 10^{20} structures—or more exactly, their side chain and scaffold components—come from? Why those particular 10^{20} structures, and why so many? TDR's operational ChemSpace libraries represented a "mere" 10^9 structures, and rather simplistic ones, those that could be assembled from the 10^3 A and B side chains affordably available from commercial suppliers and the few A-B scaffolds that the TDR chemists had already had occasion to acquire or synthesize. Unfortunately, chemistry space is so super-astronomically immense that these libraries were unlikely to contain anything that would be appealingly similar to a discovery partner's arbitrary drug-like structure of interest. However, a more relevant and interesting assortment of side chain and scaffold structures would be obtainable by adding steps to their synthesis, much as I had already helped to program a computer to do, thirty years previously. So the side chain and scaffold constituents of this AllChem database encompassed all the 10^7 structures that conceptually could be made by applying a sequence of no more than four among a hundred of the most familiar synthetic operations to any of a few hundred commercially accessible starting compounds. My fantasy was that TDR's synthetic chemists, being the right experts to evaluate such AllChem-proposed synthetic sequences, would themselves directly seek and evaluate AllChem's suggestions, though unfortunately somewhat disintermediating the CADD specialist.

However, life is what happens when you've had other plans! By this point in 2005, almost all TDR's revenue and profits were coming from that mammoth screening library contract with Pfizer, which for Tripos generated most of its peak annual revenues, $60 million, and valuation, $350 million. Fulfilling this contract had focused TDR's attentions on compound production rather than design. A TDR CADD colleague complained to me that the TDR chemists had even effectively sabotaged another topomer validation experiment, jointly agreed upon with Pfizer, by substituting easier compounds to make for the ones designed for the experiment. And it did seem a bit ominous when TDR did not invite me to attend their last Pfizer review. (Nonetheless I crashed this gathering, and my pitch was included in their presentation.) From

TDR's point of view, design had become an irrelevant complication because TDR felt so sure of being the most successful among Pfizer's four library suppliers that it expected to receive a much larger follow-on contract. Therefore, Pfizer's actual decision was a catastrophic body blow, one that as it happened was delivered by phone in the middle of a stunned Tripos management meeting. None of Pfizer's current library contracts were to be renewed. Instead, all their future screening library purchases would be from a Chinese firm whose selling price per compound was lower than TDR's production cost per compound, despite all TDR's automation and informatics.

Initial hopes that screening library demands from other pharmaceutical companies would keep TDR's compound factory humming were soon disappointed. The high-throughput screening strategy for drug discovery—the expectation that testing many more random compounds would produce more and better drug candidates—had not been all that productive. A newer philosophy, something of a Hegelian antithesis to HTS called fragment-based lead discovery, was taking hold, and involved screening a few hundred fragments, mostly the same commercially available side chains and scaffolds themselves, for weak affinity that would be improved upon by then combining or expanding on the promising fragments. Still, AllChem's extraordinary capabilities for shape similarity searching within such a huge chemistry space might also be uniquely valuable when pursuing such fragment-based leads.

Unfortunately, Tripos management instead had an existential crisis to struggle with. The imminent termination of the Pfizer contract would leave only enough other work to support around thirty chemists rather than two hundred. The British government grants were intended to stimulate Cornwall's economy, and so had been conditional on TDR's employment commitments. If TDR couldn't keep those high-tech chemists working and spending in Cornwall, the queen wanted her money back. Disastrous, for of course Tripos had already spent all that money in building TDR and could reimburse the Crown only by selling TDR's assets—and TDR, being a geographically remote facility equipped to supply a collapsing market now dominated by low-cost

Chinese producers, didn't prove to be very attractive to anyone else. There was a year or so of thrashing, but in the end Tripos's software business was sold to Vector Capital, an equity capital firm, TDR's Bude showplace was vacated and remains so, and the public TRPS was liquidated, with shares that once fetched more than $30.00 netting $0.75 after all debts were paid.

Painful as all this was for most Tripos employees, especially those in Bude, where the layoffs and relocations surely deflated home values, for me personally the outcomes, at least the nonfinancial ones, were positive. My new boss, Jim Hopkins, in association with Vector Capital, had chosen Tripos as the basis of a plan to assemble and eventually sell a portfolio of leading drug discovery informatics vendors, today known as Certara. His low-key Jimmy Stewart–like manner quickly endeared him to all the rather enervated Tripos survivors. Jim would treat me particularly well, perhaps in part because he too had been a musician turned computer geek before becoming an investment banker. He'd had notable success in all of his careers, for example doing well enough as a guitar player to lead the backup band for an Everly Brothers revival and to purchase those house-and-car family basics.

For Jim the creation of Certara was intended to be something of a career coda, with Tripos as its nucleus. Instead Tripos would be by far Jim's most disappointing Certara acquisition. Hypnotized by the screening library business, Tripos management had paid little attention to the rapidly changing demands of a no longer expanding but still competitive CADD marketplace. A decade of treating Sybyl as a cash cow to help feed the compound business, adding only a few heavily promoted but insufficiently validated new methodologies, had eroded its credibility. Dbtop (as "topsim") and topomer CoMFA could now be incorporated into Sybyl but by then were too overripe as novelties to help much. After several attempts to repackage Sybyl (one of which I briefly led), Tripos's annual revenues had fallen by 80 percent, and the Tripos label disappeared from the Certara literature. Finally, at the end of 2014 my own position was eliminated, and in 2015 Sybyl itself, necessarily including CoMFA, was taken off the market.

19 Repudiated by STATS

STATS of course continues, though my own involvement was painfully severed at the beginning of 1996. Until then, STATS programming at John Dewan's direction continued to occupy most of my evenings and took me to Chicago for the week or so before baseball's Opening Day. John, with Sue's quietly dependable support, was doing a brilliant job building revenue, profits, and an effective organization, leveraging the software architecture that I had created and mostly coded to meet the explosive demand for richer statistics as numbers-loving baseball fans discovered fantasy baseball, Bill James, and the personal computer. Soon only about a third of STATS revenue was coming from the *USA Today*, ESPN, and Associated Press contracts that I had been directly involved with. The rest was from consumer products—Bill's fantasy game designs, including a historically based winter game; a half dozen annual books, some containing prose as well as statistics; downloadable statistical reports and notes, updated nightly; and statistical support for other vendors' baseball products, such as games, bubble gum cards, and other sabermetric startups. John initiated most of these consumer offerings and handled all sales to other vendors himself. Soon there were eighteen employees and another larger VAX to power all these deliveries. From 1987 through 1992, STATS revenues doubled year-on-year to $1.5 million in 1992, achieving 144th place in *Inc. Magazine*'s growth-rate rankings of small privately held companies.

Whereas John seemed almost mesmerized by his remarkable accomplishments, often speculatively likening this initial growth rate of STATS to that of Microsoft, for me STATS was still mostly a pleasant diversion from my Tripos responsibilities. Thus he and I were not entirely on the same page about three strategies that John had for continuing STATS' growth. The first, getting into other sports, appealed to me, especially as building their Playball counterparts would be my task, allowing me to continue to enjoyably earn twenty dollars an hour for programming on STATS projects that could be done remotely, disentangled from STATS' daily office activities. The second, going live by providing play-by-play updates to STATS' databases as each game proceeded, didn't sound like much of a market to me, with dial-up and keyboard then the only means of consumer access (while the World Wide Web had just gone public, browsers were still three years away, and to me John seemed overly enamored of AOL and a now forgotten proto–smart phone, Newton). But I was willing to undertake the rather challenging enhancements that Playball would need. Finally, John wanted to accept one of the investment offers that STATS was beginning to receive, to accelerate the hardware and staffing increases that the other sports and the many more live customers he expected would require. To me, this was unattractive. John, Bill, and I had always enjoyed working together, and we did so smoothly because whatever we were each seeking from STATS was mutually compatible if not always identical. Would that still be true with a fourth investor? Nevertheless, with John's commitment and contributions to STATS far deeper than mine, and his business judgments probably sounder, I didn't express my concerns with much conviction.

STATS' initial "other sports," the ones for which I tried to build the Playball-like functionalities (play-by-play data capture and storage capabilities), were football and hockey. Football was easy. The NFL was already distributing basic play-by-play for every game, containing just enough detail to compile their standard player stats, though it did take the occasional insertion of some pseudo-plays to make the sums of their player yardages match their team yardages. STATS also collected videos of every NFL game, and from these a STATS staffer would add new statistical details to the NFL's skeleton, for example introducing yards after the catch into a pass receiver's statistics. Somewhat idealistically, I did regret that for cost reasons John wouldn't consider tracking football's incessant player substitutions.

But in fairness, tracking player substitutions, which is a mandate for hockey, presented a technical problem that I never solved. The new challenge in creating a hockey Playball was that hockey is mostly continuous flow, rather than the play-by-play sequence of discrete events that make up a baseball or football games. Furthermore, with hockey's established plus-minus statistic requiring that every player substitution be accurately game-time-stamped, the purely keyboard inputs I had depended on for baseball and football play-by-play wouldn't do. I tried to develop a new Faceoff architecture for hockey entry, envisioning two simultaneous operators, one using a mouse to control the PC's in-game timer and create empty player substitution records, into which the other operator, at the keyboard, would as time permitted insert the player identities. Struggling with an early version of Visual C++ to provide the more sophisticated access to peripheral devices that this Faceoff scheme required, I produced a prototype. The National Hockey League did favor John and me a presentation at their central office in Manhattan, with commissioner Gary Bettman even stepping into the room. My contribution was the demonstration of a not-very-flashy Faceoff prototype. However, nothing came of that visit, rather to my personal relief, as this Faceoff prototype suffered from the memory management errors notorious among C++ programmers, a challenge that I wasn't confident of resolving.

And STATS' more immediate priority, going live with Playball to continuously transmit the pitch-by-pitch events back to STATS central, was already presenting me with a stiff challenge. Although STATS was now using the internet for its communications, any internet access still required a dial-up telephone call. Playball's existing processes for game data transmission were entirely file-centric, with the scorer's initial "playball" command starting an MS/DOS shell that followed Playball game entry by invoking Kermit, a separate program, for each transmission of results to *USA Today* or STATS central. To instead transmit the result of each pitch, one by one, to the STATS central computer, the Turbo Pascal Playball program would have to maintain a continuous phone connection without distracting the scorer from his fundamental responsibility of accurate game entry. Yet phone connections were often erratic, especially in press boxes. A dropped call required detection, redial, and catchup, all to be performed by Playball as automatically as possible and at the very least without crashing the program. With today's universally available 3G and 4G router-based technologies, these sorts of application requirements are effortless to satisfy, simply by linking an internet-savvy utility into the programming project. And if something special is required, lots of example programs can be found on the internet. But in the early 1990s, I had to stumble across and then try to solve these problems myself while writing code that bridged a formidable gap between some 8088 assembly code provided by Kevin Koboldt and Playball's main data entry loop. Its development was very slow because performing even a first test of the latest modification required much of an evening's work. These tedious struggles haunted my last years of off-season evening programming for STATS. Especially frustrating for everyone once a version was put into use were the occasional press box failures, which were invariably irreproducible and therefore impossible to diagnose and remedy. But making it work as well as possible was on me; no one else had ever touched a line of Playball code.

Meanwhile, in 1993 John had some really big news. For something called the World Wide Web, Microsoft cofounder Paul Allen (more exactly, his Starwave startup) had begun developing IT environments intended as chassises for major enterprises to use in deploying themselves within such an exciting new environment. With Starwave's number one customer being STATS' client ESPN, Allen and Starwave were interested in making an investment in STATS. At least, I thought, Allen, as a programming prodigy and incredibly successful entrepreneur, then becoming an owner of sports teams and an avid amateur musician, might be the rare investor whose interests and motivations would be compatible with those of STATS' existing triumvirate. John insisted on a face-to-face meeting with Paul Allen himself, which after a little hesitation was granted to the two of us. The somewhat Hobbit-like impression he made on me was reinforced by his polite responses to my mention of how my work had helped Harvard obtain the computer that he and Bill Gates had famously used to code the original Microsoft

BASIC and to John once again likening STATS' initial growth to Microsoft's. After some months of negotiation with Starwave, the STATS board (John, Sue, me) all agreed early in 1994 to accept an investment of eight hundred thousand dollars in return for a roughly 40 percent STATS holding, a board seat, and free sports data for Starwave.

Unfortunately, for me this agreement would have two very melancholy consequences, one corrosive and somewhat foreseen, and the other acute and completely unexpected, that would keep feeding on one another until STATS and I parted company. The acute and unexpected shock was the agreement's effects on Kathe. Until then, the place of horses in her life had seemed to me that of an avocation, a serious one to be sure, playing a similar if much more important part in her life as jazz did in mine. She had long been a skilled semiprofessional, a few months ago parlaying her meager horse-based compensations into a first horse of her own, and each summer hanging out for a week at the saddlebred horse world show in Louisville. As part of closing the Starwave deal, we'd received an unexpected forty thousand dollars from STATS, my share of its accumulated retained earnings, with which I'd proposed some home improvements. Instead, at the next Louisville show, Kathe used it all to buy three mediocre saddlebred horses who now needed care.

Never before or since would anything any wife did surprise or alarm me more. Yet if Kathe had apologized for what she surely recognized seemed to me a major betrayal, I would soon have forgiven and forgot. Instead she muttered something about how I should surely understand that it was something of a traditional expectation that, blessed with unexpected surplus funds, a wife might feel free to indulge herself with some surreptitious spending. I didn't challenge that canard, which no doubt contributed to the onset of a deterioration in the rest of our marriage. Instead, both my nature and nurture are to avoid emotional confrontations, especially as unpleasant as anything that Kathe took as a slight would become. So my unhappiness found its only expression as a passive silent sullenness. And that sort of depressing cycle—an unexpected transgression involving major spending or animal purchases, to be revealed to me with little or no apology only when it was unavoidable and irreversible and to which I would respond with only a stolid emotional withdrawal—would become a sadly familiar script during the last fifteen years of our marriage.

You are probably wondering why I nevertheless stayed this course. Mainly, with many other things not going that well either, I doubted that ending the marriage would make me happier. Her misbehaviors had little effect on my work, which was always what mattered most to me, and her spending binges never deprived me of any of my small wants. Furthermore, unlike the situations with my earlier wives, Kathe was not eager to end our marriage, and with my STATS ownership and her accumulating horse-related assets, such issues as property division would present unusually trying complications. Our marriage had obvious financial benefit for her, and if she were opposed, her emotional outbursts and her indifference to my feelings were serious concerns. For she has the gifted teacher's or salesperson's ability to make those around her feel her pain, an effect to which for some reason I was particularly susceptible. I also felt constraints of moral responsibility that further rationalized my inaction—toward Alex's future and toward the upholding of marriage vows, particularly the "in sickness and in health" clause, when, five years into our marriage, Kathe revealed that she had bipolar disorder but had stopped taking medication to provide her the energy she needed for work in a stable. Better to let sleeping dogs lie and quietly carry on.

The other corrosive and somewhat foreseen consequence of the Allen/Starwave investment was the STATS board composition. STATS' new board member was Tom Phillips, in midcareer as a rising manager of a succession of publishing-related enterprises. His MBA ethos contrasted with the personal passions that motivated John, Sue, and me, and it wasn't very long before I started getting distress calls from John. Starwave was making STATS' business goals secondary to those of Starwave by accepting sports statistical input from other sources. That contradicted John's pre-investment expectation of a STATS exclusivity, though I shrugged off his wish that he and I should straighten matters out by appealing directly to Paul Allen. There were also calls from Phillips that were more in the flavor of a feeling out but that made me aware of how awkward my position, as chairman of a four-person board with two of its members married, might become.

And when in August 1994 the baseball strike broke out, my discomfort became an oppression. On the one hand, the Allen and Starwave investment had provided cash in the bank, which with judicious economies in staffing should keep STATS afloat for some time. Phillips and I agreed on the wisdom of applying this textbook business strategy to STATS. On the other hand, John and Sue, who maintained that the strike could end any day, would experience "judicious staffing economies" as the actuality of firing loyal, hardworking, and lightly paid employees. The strike ground on, and John and Sue were in the driver's seat. Repeated attempts that John and I made to change one another's opinions eroded the trust in each other's judgment and character that John and I had always enjoyed.

Meanwhile, there was serious trouble for Kathe. Her employment as an untenured instructor at Washington University was limited to seven years by the professors' union. Yet the biology department valued her current work so highly that it had, or so she believed, blocked her attempt to transfer to an uncapped administrative post. Why shouldn't she instead embark on an altogether different career, something related to her deepest passion, horses? I had no objection to her resignation—not much of a risk in burning a bridge that was already scheduled for destruction! But she soon found, once positioned within the horse culture as an employee rather than a colleague or a customer, that what she knew wasn't as valuable as whom she knew and how she knew them. To obtain the professional stability and respect that we both hoped for her, it seemed she would have to become the proprietor of her own horse business. And the only business she could imagine, a horse farm, needed some upfront investment funds.

As the strike dragged on into 1995 and STATS' thin off-season income streams trickled away, STATS' financial reserves withered. When in February, as I recall, STATS learned that its *USA Today* contract would be going to a different vendor, John finally budged, calling a Chicago meeting to propose that, to secure its future existence, STATS should be sold. To me his proposal came as a welcome relief, for over the last year my STATS dream had become a nightmare, one from which I couldn't awaken. And my share of the sale proceeds could become Kathe's horse farm.

Events moved quickly. On April 2 the strike ended, and both Gannett (*USA Today*'s publisher) and ESPN responded vigorously to the opportunity to buy STATS. But now there was a different STATS board conflict. Starwave wanted to sell—no better outcome for a professional investor than a quick and profitable flip, especially if the winning bid were to come from ESPN, Starwave's major customer. But John and Sue thought differently. STATS was the center of their life, and with the strike settled, STATS' survival no longer depended on its sale. The ultimate decision then rested with me, and there was a lot to think about. Did I want to keep trying to cope with management stresses and conflicts in both STATS and Tripos—two growing and evolving companies? Shouldn't enabling my wife's dream take precedence over my partners' preference for independence? As board chairman was it justifiable for me to ignore Starwave's preference? With the Starwave-provided funds having been expended on survival rather than growth and *USA Today*'s defection warning of stronger competition, how likely were STATS' growth and profitability to continue? The recent turmoil had awakened me both to the financial value that my STATS avocation had created and to its vulnerability. Shouldn't I pull out while I was ahead? As the bids arrived, I became increasingly indifferent to John's pleas to support his arguably self-serving wish to reverse his own decision.

Then came a further complication. With financing in sight, Kathe was looking for a horse farm, which, considering its prospective marketplace and my commute, could not be far from Saint Louis. She thought that we would have to buy a small farm property and build the horse stables and a riding arena ourselves, magnifying the risks unavoidable in every business startup. But suddenly a perfect property popped onto the market—suitable stable, arena, house, all immediately ready for use—as an estate sale priced to move. Certainly affordable, if and when a STATS sale closed. But wasn't the property likely to have been sold by then? Therefore, to raise the funds *now*, I made the following unorthodox proposal to the other STATS shareholders: I was willing to sell them shares now at a price much lower than the bids that were starting to come in, under the condition that if STATS was sold within the next year, they would pay me much of the expected increase in the value of those shares. There were more than enough takers! I've forgotten who bought what for how much, beyond a vague recollection of receiving around $600,000. Whatever, it was enough for Kathe to go ahead, buy the horse farm, and launch her business but still leave me with enough STATS shares to make my vote decisive in accepting a bid.

There were no hitches in the board's agreement to ESPN's winning letter of intent, an offer of $7 million for STATS. However, that offer was substantially whittled by ESPN's due diligence (the process during which a prospective buyer investigates the realities underlying the financial representations that the seller had provided), which painfully contrasted with a healthy resurgence in STATS' businesses. Could it be that ESPN assumed that, whatever the final figure, my unorthodox stock sales to fund the horse farm would ensure my decisive agreement to any sale? Nevertheless, Kathe now had her horse farm, and simply maximizing my net worth has never had much appeal for me. And I was missing the previous camaraderie of STATS. Therefore, I listened to John's renewed appeal as he began emphasizing that I should consider the wishes of STATS employees as well as his own. What then, I asked, about Starwave? They would probably want out if the sale fell through, and as board chairman I had to consider their interests. As I remember his response, John assured me he knew of individual buyers for STATS stock. The upshot was, when the STATS board convened with the ESPN team by phone as usual to pass judgment on ESPN's final offer, as the last to speak, I stunned and silenced everyone, even myself a bit, with a "No."

I have never regretted that decision. Phillips just snorted derisively in our postmortem call when I told him of John's mysterious buyers. But I do feel badly about how coldly, even angrily, I received John's call later that evening, fervently thanking me for my decision. The intervening hours happened to be unpleasant, with Kathe's ire at my decision and the day's other incidents reinforcing a growing realization that for me the horse farm venture was to be more a hell than a heaven. My attempts to please everyone had left me feeling a complete fool. So I scornfully responded to John that I was fed up with my recent STATS experiences and would probably be selling most of my remaining stock to his buyers.

Not that a different attitude would have made any substantive difference, probably. John's mysterious buyers never materialized, which left me feeling more mistrustful than ever. Far more importantly, I was soon to discover that John had completely misjudged the feelings of his employees. They had expected that the sale to ESPN would bring them corporate security and benefits, maybe better pay, and a few of them started calling to tell me so. Worst of all, several were unhappy with John's decisions and leadership, and there were those who felt they would do better, given a chance. All of this was effectively confirmed to me by a strange phone call from John, who tremulously told me how he was loath to leave his office because he was feeling such hostility from the cubicles. Many of you probably are wondering why I didn't respond to this obvious call for support by getting on a plane, but John no longer seemed my friend, and that idea never occurred to me. Instead I started making some calls to a few other employees whose objectivity I trusted. They confirmed everything I had been hearing. Furthermore, the situation was getting worse—with John's previously unchallenged leadership shaky, the whole organization was paralyzed and crumbling amid mutual accusations and recriminations. Who other than me could or would make any changes? What, if anything, should be done? What could I possibly do from hundreds of miles away?

At that moment, all the other pieces of my life—the horse farm customers arrogant and too few, my marriage more a standoff than a partnership, and a temporarily humiliating reassignment of my Tripos duties—were almost as depressing. In order to sleep I had begun drinking more and more heavily, until finally one night Kathe came in from a late night at the barn to find me passed out on the floor. But at last I decided on something that I should and could do about STATS. I called Dick Glover, the ESPN dealmaker, to tell him that if ESPN were to make another bid for STATS, it would now be accepted. Quite shortly there was another bid, a much lower one, and one also strongly contingent on John's continued participation. Starwave resurfaced, and something of a Keystone comedy conspiracy began to unreel, though beyond a few cursory phone calls, I don't recall and was probably never informed of much that followed. Everyone but me of course had a lawyer, John's counsel affordably also being STATS' counsel. (Most of my own experiences with lawyers other than Larry have been expensive, ineffective, and mercifully brief. Perhaps a cultural incompatibility.) There was one call including Sue and lawyer in which John warned me that if I persisted, his enmity would be total and enduring. But it had already been many months since STATS had requested any constructive activity from me. In any case, what my role might be wouldn't matter if STATS didn't survive.

When everyone else's lawyers had finished their discussions early in 1996, the results were ugly but decisive. The new ESPN bid was rejected, with Starwave perhaps having changed its vote. The Starwave board seat had disappeared. Several senior STATS managers were fired, and there was an office memo warning employees that henceforth anyone who spoke with me would also be fired. More importantly, though, it seemed through the fog that John and Sue had emphatically reasserted their command and leadership. As STATS returned to prosperity, it seemed at least possible that my personally disloyal actions had catalyzed these positive developments, and I cheerfully assented to Sue's chilly request to turn over all my STATS-related code.

Such a contrast of Cramer cheerfulness with Dewan chill would characterize all my future interactions with STATS, still required for two reasons. One was my continuance as board chairman. Probably under the advice of counsel, every six months or so, I was sent a financial summary and an invitation to participate in a stilted and carefully circumscribed phone conference. For example, I can't recall any discussion of the enterprise-threatening lawsuit that the NBA famously filed against STATS and Motorola for collaboratively "rebroadcasting" the forbidden "descriptions and accounts" of an NBA game. (STATS eventually prevailed but only on appeal, so I guess I'm just as happy not to have been exposed to this lengthy trauma.) Finding myself in Chicago for one of these board phone calls, on a whim I instead dropped by the STATS offices, maybe an hour early. After a quick call, the receptionist ushered me through the whispering cubicles to a secluded office, where a Kabuki-like board meeting quickly started and ended. By the time the lawyer arrived for the now superfluous phone call, I had already been shown out of the STATS office. So, as had been threatened, the Dewan enmity indeed endured.

The other continuing matter was my shares. STATS was still the S corporation that I had refounded, and its original tax advantages had become tax liabilities for me because an S-corp's profits become taxable personal income to its shareholders. STATS of course distributed checks to pay these tax increases, but taxation differences between Illinois and Missouri effectively left me with a substantial negative dividend on my STATS holdings. Since there seemed no possibility that John and Sue, now in total control, would ever sell all of STATS, I accepted an offer that John obtained from an outside investor to pay a modest price for most of my shares and yield my board chairmanship. When early in 1999 there was an unexpected offer from some ten STATS employees to buy my remaining shares, nothing seemed to have changed, so I sold the last 10 percent. However, late that year, Kevin Koboldt dropped by my Tripos office to, he thought, share in celebration of our anticipated payouts from STATS' sale to Rupert Murdoch's News Corporation (then Fox's owner), for $45 million. Many times more than STATS was intrinsically worth, but that was the peak of the e-business boom, and unlike most e-businesses, STATS was established and authentically profitable. Since that valuation was maybe twenty times what I had just received for my shares, his congratulations quickly became condolences. My first and also my current feeling about this surprise is something like "sour grapes," in that I received about as much I fairly deserved, an amount I construct by considering STATS' actual enterprise value and the relative magnitude of my own contributions. However, at that time, Kathe's costly activities, and, some might say, justice, prompted me to complain. The buyers of the last 10 percent probably knew of three 1998 bids for STATS, whose existence was only revealed to me years later, within *The Numbers Game* book, and I was assured that it was not only morally questionable but a federal crime if a seller in my position had not been suitably informed.[1] The lawyer who handled this for me expected that John would respond to my pro forma law suit with a settlement offer and insisted that we must also treat every individual purchaser as a defendant. When instead the response of John's counsel was fiercely combative, my lawyer unwittingly delayed further action until the federal statute of limitations for this offense had expired.

What pained me far more for the six years (and it felt a lot longer!) after my eviction from STATS was how to STATS I seemed to have become a historical nonperson, like one of those Egyptian pharaohs whose cartouches have been chiseled from their obelisks by a successor. But I started attending SABR meetings again, at first mainly to participate in (and win a couple of!) the trivia contests. At the Boston SABR meeting in 2002, two events raised my spirits. One was the appearance of OPS on the Fenway Park scoreboard—a former fantasy had become a reality! Pete Palmer couldn't understand my excitement—by now this was old stuff for him. But he said that another meeting attendee was this *New York Times* reporter writing a book, who'd probably want to talk with me if Pete suggested that he do so. Some guy named Michael Lewis.

20 Tidying Up

Friends beset by some annoying but probably transient problem are not all that comforted in hearing me say, "This too will pass, and someday it will make a great story." But so it has often proved to be, even for my seventeen-year cheerlessness. These days I am as happy, by almost any definition of that word, as I've ever been in my life. Two major events helped in making it so. The first, just before Al Gore was not elected president, was a move to Santa Fe. The second, just before Barack Obama was first elected president, was Kathe's recognition that the two of us should separate.

What first brought me to Santa Fe was an invitation for Kathe and me to a star party hosted by Dave Weininger, who had installed an observatory-quality nineteen-inch telescope in his backyard. Such a sophisticated DIY project was one of many from Dave, whose extraordinarily versatile engineering talents and relentlessly 1970s-cool guru style had made him an icon in the small CADD world that we both inhabited. Dave had created SMILES, a molecular shorthand by which the complexities of chemical structure can be completely and concisely represented as ASCII text.[1] He then made SMILES the core of a chemical database software API, one whose accessibility destabilized MDL's market domination, much as PCs had once destabilized VAXes and IBM 360s, through its integration into many of the computerized instruments that now dominate chemistry laboratories. For its distribution, Dave and a business partner had formed Daylight, whose location had followed Dave's romantic partner's medical apprenticeship from Los Angeles to Santa Fe by way of a New Orleans houseboat. Daylight was now buying him a lot of toys! An accomplished aviator, Dave did environmental penance for the sin of his fuel-guzzling RAF trainer with one of Santa Fe's first solar energy installations. An accomplished contemporary jazz bassist, he imported a Bosendorfer piano when he took up the instrument, which awed many of Santa Fe's other talented musicians. Dave also continued to do more than play with his toys, experimentally measuring, with an apparatus he built, the directionality of sound perception and developing a new method of brewing chocolate beans that he reportedly sold to Nestlé.

That weekend Kathe and I also enjoyed some of the cultural diversity that was making Santa Fe so appealing to a growing congregation of eccentric and energetic technologists, many having interests similar to mine, with a new book on *The Info Mesa* even promising to explain "how [its] entrepreneurial scientists are using complexity theory and powerful, experimental computer programs to . . . convert vast diverse data, whether chemical or biological or computational, into useful information."[2] Everyone at Dave's star party seemed to be in Santa Fe not because they happened to be but because they wanted to be. I felt that I too would fit in here, better than anywhere else I'd ever resided or visited. And that's how it has turned out.

This enticing move was also unreasonably easy to execute. Kathe was even more enthusiastic than me about a move—by now almost anywhere away from Saint Louis was appealing to her, and Santa Fe had its own vigorous horse culture. A prosperous real estate investor saw potential for a profitable return in the location of the horse farm, which as a business enterprise by then was not even a shell. Tripos was accommodating because moving another thousand miles from the Bude laboratory for which I was working would hardly matter. And there was a mutual recognition, though unspoken, that if Santa Fe was where I really wanted to be, there were other plausible employers, and not only Daylight, because like many successful gurus Dave had attracted acolytes who had formed their own Santa Fe startups. There was even a reason for Tripos to encourage this move—Kathe would be leaving too. To supplement her horse business struggles, she had become a Tripos employee, adding a lot of commercial experience to her strong scientific credentials as she ricocheted from position to position but meanwhile exasperating almost everyone, particularly her various managers. Relocation would resolve this husband-wife conundrum, and Kathe immediately found a laboratory-based position at Phase 1 Toxicology, a Santa Fe biotech venture (into which, coincidentally, at my patent counselor Larry's suggestion, Tripos had previously and profitably been a seed investor). Less than four months after the star party, Kathe and I had moved to the first of two successive Santa Fe McMansions. That's how I describe our local suburbia—dramatically sited rambling adobe houses, each within its own five acres where anything growing is good, enclosing a drip-irrigated manicured courtyard. Radiant heat and no central air—hey, it's dry here, no insects, and at 7,200 feet, ceiling fans provide adequate cooling.

But the move was not, for Kathe, happily ever after. Maybe half a dozen times she repeated a new script. Each episode would begin with a promising new technology position, increasingly senior, often for a firm centered somewhere else, like Chicago or London. But then, after around a year, she would develop some indignation toward her boss or her general situation, for some lack in respect or opportunities or compensation, which would of course soon be followed by termination or resignation. Between these episodes there would mostly be black despair, with me its only audience, for the months until a next position materialized. Horses were something of a solace, with the proceeds from the horse farm, the STATS stock sale, and, with my parents' passing, an inheritance, now allowing her to assume the respected role of "horse woman" (economic supporter) rather than the subordinate professional, and she embraced both halves of New Mexico's horse-and-guns culture. Her saddlebred addiction also continued, and she even achieved one of many horse women's dreams of triumph, selecting and buying a colt that with Kentucky training became a world champion mare and that with artificial breeding then produced its own valuable colt. It was still of course a notably expensive hobby overall, but many such upscale sporting forays are not nearly as successful. I have always been impressed with Kathe's skills, energy, and many accomplishments, if not so much with her behavior and companionship.

The financial consequences of Kathe's horse addictions would also bring about the second enlightenment for me: Kathe's effective decision to separate. One of the post-Bude economies by Tripos had been to stop paying for my Santa Fe office space; I would instead work from home. I was glad to do so because there were unused rooms, and for me any commuting has been a boring waste of time. Kathe, though, who was deep in another frustrating episode of unemployment, was not so glad, and before long she insisted that if I were at home during the day, she needed to be elsewhere. And then the financial crash of 2008 suddenly revealed to me, in the form of margin calls, that to pay her surprisingly high (for me) ongoing expenses, instead of selling shares, Kathe had been borrowing against their value, even applying this negative leverage to all of our holdings once the Tripos stock had lost its value. I ignored the margin calls, anticipating the continuing market declines and the futility of throwing good after bad, so most of our (well, really, *my*) savings irretrievably vanished.

Some hard decisions and actions were now unavoidable. Physical separation mattered to Kathe, and now financial separation seemed imperative to me. To achieve both these ends, I would move out, and furthermore, I would deposit my salary, the continuance of which I felt confident about as long as any Tripos-related business entity persisted, into my own bank account. There were no futile arguments over the usual fifty-fifty split of our remaining financial assets, and as I felt myself perforce stuck with the hefty mortgage payments, Kathe would also have a free place to live for a few years. I carted my computers, clothes, and a few books to a furnished rental casita in a nearby backyard.

In many memoirs, these events would constitute a calamitous tragedy, one that casts the writer into a wretched and lonely depression, not to emerge for months or even years. But as I started poking my own head out of its transitional emotionless shell, I found my spirits rising. Living with Kathe had constrained my activities in many ways and dampened my spirits, but I had been telling myself, "no problem, as long as my work is not affected." Yet now I was completely free to live my nonwork life exactly as I cared to, surrounded by the eclectic options and atmosphere of Santa Fe and fortunately still without any hindrances of health or finance. So today, the baseball-science-jazz trinity that still anchors my life has branched into cohousing, calorie restriction, Kindle-flavored mountain hiking, climate politics, and exotic travel.

Let's start with baseball and some STATS sequelae. Michael Lewis was not (yet!) an iconic name, but my conversations with this unassuming and obviously intelligent *New York Times* guy were enjoyable, and the A's were taking him seriously, so maybe there would actually be a book. He asked and listened—for example, as overlooked as on-base average was, I didn't agree with the A's telling him that it was ten times as important as batting average. And then I remembered his name as the author of other books I had enjoyed reading, *Liar's Poker* and *The Next New Thing*. Our follow-up telephone and email conversations became discussions rather than interviews. When *Moneyball* was published, and then appropriately acclaimed, I was jubilant (though doubtful about some preposterous rumors of a *Moneyball* movie). Whatever the circumstances that had made me a STATS nonperson, *Moneyball* had released me from their spell. Eventually I was also interviewed by Alan Schwarz, who was working on *The Numbers Game*. He ended our talk by regretting that his STATS chapters were already finished. Be that as it may, the minor flaws I perceive in what either author wrote about my baseball activities are omissions or simplifications, ones that arguably increase the justification for this memoir.

John Dewan and I next crossed paths at the 2011 SABR meeting. He greeted me as jovially as if nothing had ever gone wrong. Surprising, I thought, but that works for me. I had long been ready to forgive John and Sue, especially on realizing that any related financial disappointments, whatever their intention might have been, were by now actually making me happier, by having facilitated the end of my unhappy marriage. Otherwise, we had shared a fantastic adventure and today should enjoy those memories together, while simply ignoring the unfortunate sequelae. So over a lunch tête-à-tête I explained how I now felt, to John's apparent acceptance. Since then, I've appreciated the company of John and Sue at maybe a half dozen SABR gatherings, often sitting or eating together, and I hope that the candor of this memoir will not change anything.

One final STATS-related adventure involved a resuscitation of the A's Apple and Playball. It started with a phone call from Farad Sayeed, a lawyer helping to represent Fox Sports as the defendant in an alleged infringement of a baseball information patent. I remembered the inventors' name, Barstow, as STATS customers for whom I'd made some minor Playball enhancements sometime in the early 1990s when this patent had also been filed. But their patent's claims mapped, almost one to one, onto a description of Playball's original operations from back in 1981. Helping the Fox defense by testifying to these facts as an expert (i.e., neutral) witness sounded like profitable fun. Furthermore, despite the irritated derision of two wives, I'd dragged a carton containing one of the Apple IIs and a miscellany of floppy disks through a half dozen moves. Show-and-tell evidence, using a computer that had almost disappeared by the time the Barstows filed their patent application, would be difficult to argue away. There were a lot of challenges in making Apple Playball run again—thirty-year-old hardware, floppies, and memories. But my live demo of an Apple II running Playball brought nostalgic responses from almost everyone in the courtroom—no less than those, I imagined, that would be felt if a Model T Ford had been driven through the doors. Although my status as expert witness barred me from viewing most of the trial, it was flattering to be told that my testimony had been the most dramatic moment of Fox's successful defense.

For the last dozen years, most of my baseball activities have supported Retrosheet, which to me is the most extraordinary sabermetric phenomenon of them all. In 1989 Dave Smith, a recently retired professor of microbiology and also the former campus ombudsman at the University of Delaware (about five miles from that farm where I grew up!), dismayed by the disintegration of Project Scoresheet, launched a seemingly quixotic project to collect, computerize, and make publicly available the play-by-play records of every Major League Baseball game ever played—and to do so as a strictly volunteer effort. Believe it or not, by any reasonable criterion this foolhardy endeavor has completely succeeded. For example, no matter how old you are, if you know some odd fact about, say, the first game you ever saw, you can recover and read its entire play-by-play account. For example, Retrosheet corrected my vivid memory from one of the earliest games I ever saw, of Del Ennis dropping a left-field fly ball in front of my Connie Mack Stadium bleacher seat just before winning the game with a home run. Wrong, though—in that game Del actually played right field. And you can very likely do the same sort of thing for your father's or grandfather's first game; I'm currently helping to wind up the 1938 season. Baseball-reference.com, as usual, offers the most convenient way to browse and search this treasure.

Most of Project Retrosheet's play-by-play sources are the scorebooks of teams and individual newspaper reporters, augmented pre-TV by afternoon newspapers. Play-by-play for games that lack a scorecard is recreated or derived, as completely as possible and often conclusively, in a sort of baseball sudoku, by fleshing out the box score's implications with bits of information culled from as many newspaper accounts as Dave's interlibrary loan privileges can assemble. I particularly enjoy doing these reconstructions, some so tightly constrained by their box score as to be extremely challenging. This work also gives me a welcome sense of accomplishment, by creating once and for all the most complete primary records possible, within an organizational context that ensures their permanence and public accessibility. Over the years, I've derived perhaps a thousand such play-by-plays, which should be about 5 percent of the total.

Retrosheet is as much a human relations accomplishment as a technical accomplishment. Dave is unfailingly capable, gracious, grateful—and whimsical—in managing and coordinating his Retrosheet coterie. He even put aside his busy schedule for a few days when I received a lifetime computers in chemistry achievement award from the American Chemical Society to contribute a lecture on why and how baseball appeals to scientists such as the two of us. Some of the audience confided that Dave's talk was their favorite of the day. Not a surprise, considering that Dave's talks usually receive the judges' highest marks at the national SABR convention, where he and I also anchor a competitive trivia contest team. No longer are we trivia champions, though—the neurons still fire accurately but not as quickly as they once did! A second age-related handicap, one that many other trivia contestants also report, is that recent events, those we have lived through as adults, never seem to have been mentally catalogued as well as the earlier ones. I'm still a tough competitor on everything that happened before, say, 1969, but that's some fifty years ago!

I am generally treated kindly at national SABR meetings, at least as well as I feel I deserve, and not simply as an honored has-been but also as a minor member of the inner circle. SABR too has developed and matured to become an exceptionally well-administered organization and a respected inhabitant of MLB's professional circles, with its experienced leaders tuned to many of the changes underway in and around Major League Baseball and often responding vigorously with their own timely and creative initiatives.

All of this contrasts with the current state, muddled and somewhat frustrating, of my drug discovery activities. In short, my latest approach to the long-standing challenge of productively aligning 3D molecules, template CoMFA, could potentially become one of the most useful CADD methods yet devised,[3] by combining an extraordinarily superior ease of use with wide applicability and surprisingly including somewhat more ability (well, more accurately, less inability) to perform off-target predictions of unanticipated good biological effects (like those of Viagra) and bad ones (like Vioxx).[4] The latest template CoMFA results were encouraging and surprising enough to merit publication in *PLOS One*, the most prestigious journal in which I had ever published.[5]

Good news—but the bad news is that my efforts to make this capability available to anyone else seem to have fizzled out, though not for any lack of effort on my part. When I was dismissed by Certara, anticipating the ends for Sybyl and CoMFA, I completely recreated template CoMFA as CoMFAble, a pair of command-line tools, one doing the topomer-based template alignments, the other CoMFA itself. Using this program architecture, template CoMFA can now either be run directly or be included within a larger system. On the other hand, although the relevant patents have all expired and although I created all the underlying knowhow in the first place, Certara believes that it has an intellectual property claim on these programs. CoMFAble also depends on some basic molecule manipulation software kindly provided to me by Open Eye, one of today's leading CADD software vendors, who also happens to be a Santa Fe neighbor. I had supposed Open Eye might be interested in commercially distributing template CoMFA, but not so. Nor has anyone else been interested, perhaps understandably considering both this murky intellectual property situation and also a concern about the high and prolonged support costs whenever a fundamentally novel methodology is being introduced. Nevertheless, Open Eye and I have agreed to open source these CoM-FAble programs on its website, so at least the technologies are having a possibility of survival.[6] Should I announce their availability to the CADD community? I'm conflicted, as I have neither the resources nor the inclination to provide any sort of support. Anyway these misfortunes do not justify any personal regrets, inasmuch as I had previously been very fortunate in the vigorous commercial backing that CoMFA itself had received when its unfamiliar rationale and workflows had needed such nurturing.

Then will I do any more science? In principle there's a possibility, with the many directions that template CoMFA and its further tweaking could explore, and computing being an easy activity to continue in isolation. Yet in practice what would be the value for anyone in my performing and publishing more refinements and example applications, using what seems likely to have become a scientific road not taken? And my interest in doing science seems to be suffering from my disconnection from the scientific community, while my other activities are as satisfying as ever, and there are new interests—like writing this memoir! So it's a question of incentives and priorities. At this moment, one intriguing possibility is a collaboration with a West Coast startup, which for me would be a recapitulation because their business plan is based on selling compound libraries. However, their compound offerings would themselves be novel; macrocycles, intermediate in size between the familiar structures synthesized by medicinal chemists and the biologics that are getting more attention today. Bigger structures imply that the chemical space (or potential structural variety) that might be explored for biological activity is much bigger, while the customary Tanimoto fingerprints are poorly suited for characterizing these types of structures. Combining the topomer technologies with other recent findings that better distinguish those macrocycle structures that are most likely to reach a biological target, seems a promising approach for exploring this space. We'll see.

Then what about the music? In Saint Louis, the little playing that I'd been doing was as trumpet in Rich Dammkoehler's band. When deciding to move to a city as small as Santa Fe, I had resigned myself to the complete loss of any Dixieland opportunities. Even a trade paper listing of a weekly Santa Fe Dixieland event seemed highly suspect, likely a fossil, as no such weekly gigs still existed even in New Orleans or New York. Wrong again, and most happily: since my first week here I've played trombone with the Santa Fe Chiles. These days it's once a month on the first Saturday afternoon, in good weather, at The Cowgirl, with the most accomplished group of musicians with whom I've ever played regularly, some having résumés that included a Carnegie Hall appearance and gigs with Ray Charles, Maynard Ferguson, Max Kaminski, and Buddy DiFranco. To imagine our current sound, think more of the small swing bands of the 1930s, like Django Reinhardt or Fats Waller, than of a New Orleans street parade.

What about the newer stuff—what's cohousing? I describe my community as a special sort of condo, whose inhabitants are expected to pay attention to one another and with a physical layout that makes conversation easy and inevitable. There's also a common house where many of us share a weekly meal. After eight years of domestic isolation in two Santa Fe McMansions, mostly ignorant of any neighbor's name or face, the cohousing concept appealed to me, suggesting a community spirit like the one I grew up in yet that would allow me to live exactly as I cared to, furthering my preference for doing stuff rather than owning stuff. Googling "Santa Fe cohousing" was so productive that, just a week later, after a couple of visits to Sand River Cohousing, I made a deposit on a small unit, one featuring a glare-proof potential "computer cave." A good call, because among the fifteen neighborhoods I've lived in since my first marriage, my seven years in Sand River Cohousing have been far and away the most satisfying.[7] Also a fortunate call because there has happened to be a lot of complementarity among the interests and skills of our "over 55" inhabitants, and, perhaps because of our vast female majority, a low-conflict atmosphere, which I especially appreciated during a recent dual tenure as president and treasurer. We Sand River residents have led an interesting diversity of lives—for example, four of a random six seated at one recent weekly meal had lived and worked in different parts of Africa.

Okay, what's calorie restriction (CR)? Hopefully, CR is providing me with some additional years of very healthy life by my eating less than a "normal" healthy amount. At least CR works this way for all the animals it's been tried on, including chimpanzees, with the *some* and *less* values being as much as 30 percent. The cause may be that the stress of CR on cells selectively kills the less healthy ones, the ones that are more likely to have toxic effects on the human organism. I began this curious practice sometime in 2004, while investigating ways to avoid the Alzheimer's that my mother died from. (Although she herself seldom seemed unhappy, the demands of providing her with caregiving were a lengthy and relentless stress on my siblings that I hope not to inflict on anyone else.) So far, my health markers, some from participation in a few clinical studies of CR practitioners at Washington University, are all excellent, except for a dip in bone mass that seems now to have ended.[8] And except for a few scattered days during travel, I have not been sick in bed for at least a decade. A caveat, though: my libido has vanished, indeed rather as though it had never existed, which for most people would not be the blessing that it is for me, after three marital misadventures.

Otherwise, what does CR feel like to practice? Moderate hunger quickly became a normal feeling, and also a virtuous feeling, perhaps much as I suppose piety feels to a monk. At the same time, I anticipate and savor my meals far more than before. I offset the sparseness of quantity in each meal with a variety of tastes—often one bite per meal of many different foods. So counting calories would be impractical as well as tedious. Instead I obsessively monitor my weight, which has been within a 113-to-118-pound range for 99-plus percent of my 4,000 observations (previously I weighed 160 pounds). I suppose my daily intake to be about 1,300 calories. So far, any effect that CR has had on my physical fitness seems to have been positive. My daily hikes expanded to a daily average that is now longer than three miles, with almost a mile of total climb per week, most of the latter on mountain trails, where tripping and perhaps tumbling on the loose rock also became less frequent, despite another eccentric practice of mine; except on steeper downslopes, I intermittently read from a small Kindle in the palm of one hand with the Next Page key under its thumb (and walking stick in the other hand). Strangely, this Next Page key has disappeared from the latest handheld Kindles, replaced by one of those sloppy Web 2.0 swipes that requires two hands. "New and improved" can be an oxymoron! Anyhow, as you may be thinking that the "oxymoron" label can also be applied to CR, I will consider it as a personal success if and only if, whenever its magic finally fails, my mental capabilities have remained functional.

To a physical chemist like me, global warming is the certain outcome of relying on fossil fuels, quite as inevitable as sunrise or the tides. (Climate change is to weather as the ocean's tide is to its waves.) Any carbon taken from the ground wants to become carbon dioxide, which then via the greenhouse effect will capture more of the sun's radiation. The already unpleasant effects of this accelerating temperature increase are getting worse, and more rapidly than climate scientists have been expecting. Sufficient and practicable policy responses are proving hard to craft. Yet there is one proposal that to me seems uniquely likely to be both effective and politically palatable. If you're as curious about this proposal as you should be, please check out www.citizensclimatelobby .org. A responsibility that I feel, to spend hours each week trying to help move forward so important a proposal, is amplified by living in the state capital of New Mexico. There are only a few New Mexicans for our admirable senators and congressman to represent, so we members of CCL's Santa Fe chapter have been able to develop constructive personal interactions with them. Also, I am plaguing scientists' email addresses with www.citizensclimatelobby.org suggestions, citing a favorable editorial by *Nature*. Hopefully these activities will help to minimize the destructive impact of climate change on future generations.

Though traveling is not central to my life, it's my travels, past or planned, that people usually ask me about, probably because travel is much easier to relate to than other activities that matter more to me. Yet those other activities cost so little that I do spend more on travel than everything else together. I'm a sightseer and museum visitor rather than a fun-in-the-sun-and-surf guy. I've devoured most of Europe and tasted China, Japan, and India, mostly while tacking personal travel onto business trips. Since my last marriage ended, I've restored a two-trips-per-year pattern that Libby and I once had, mostly to bucket-list destinations like Machu Picchu, the Taj Mahal, or the Pyramids. My sister Sally has often traveled with me, as one appreciative remembrance of that transformative baseball program she once sent me. But with the basics like England and Italy still on her bucket list, these days I am traveling by myself, increasing my country count with places like Kazakhstan, Brunei, Algeria, and Ethiopia.

What's next for this ambivalent retiree? With this memoir finished, my current activities, as enjoyable or responsible as they may individually be, have been threatening to leave me feeling a distressing lack of purpose. To be a contented retiree, I clearly need a project, and to my delight I have just found one. Dave Smith had indefinitely postponed any extension of Retrosheet to the nineteenth century. So, with the online availability today of so many newspaper archives, I am myself now building Retrosheet-compatible play-by-plays for the 1899 season. They will be "most probable" versions only, because there were few scorer-oracles or even press boxes in most nineteenth century ballparks, so the primary sources often differ. And there are delightful surprises, the biggest for me being a controversial new balk rule for 1899, which as well as advancing the base runners put the batter on first base.

21 In My Humble Opinion

If, forty years ago, anyone had asked me whether analytics would have more influence on baseball or on drug discovery, it should be no surprise that drug discovery would have been my choice. But that's not at all the way things have turned out. The fundamental reason is clear—using analytics to make predictions and guide decision-making has turned out to be far more productive for baseball than for drug discovery. But why was this not foreseeable? Yes, biological systems are far more complex than baseball games—but that has always been obvious, and it also seemed obvious that the huge benefits that analytics might bring to drug discovery would attract huge investments. But instead, a very important and completely unexpected source of baseball analytics materialized, the activities of baseball nonprofessionals, outsiders who, behaving very much as a healthily self-critical scientific community, are responsible for many of the continuing conceptual advances in the practice of baseball. Also unexpectedly, by now many of the professionals and amateur analysts are listening to one another, collaboratively seeking new insights from baseball's annual feedback cycles, which contrast with the secretive decade-long feedback cycles of drug discovery.

Like all analysts, these baseball professionals and nonprofessionals depend on more and better data for their work, and, seeing how analytics has—again surprisingly—fueled baseball interest among the target youth market, Major League Baseball has become a technological leader in capturing and making public all its potentially relevant information. Today, every on-field movement is tracked—the trajectory of every pitch, the velocity and launch angle of every batted ball, the reactions of every fielder and base runner. The application of analytics to the megabytes of data now being accumulated from every single game is having major effects on how the game is being played. Here are two provocative and less obvious examples. The first is pitch framing. It turns out that major league catchers consistently vary in their abilities to influence an umpire to miscall balls and strikes. Although the proportion of such catcher-induced miscalls is always slight, the differences among pitch framing skills that do occur affect team wins and losses at least as strongly as does the variability among those catchers' batting skills. The second is pitch tracking. It has always been obvious that pitched balls that are faster or curve further are harder to hit. However, another previously inconspicuous way that pitches can become harder to hit is for their types to be indistinguishable for more of their trajectory to the catcher—to follow the same track.

Surely the searches for "second-order effects," from all the potential combinations among pitch quality, framing, tracking, ball-strike count, and so forth, will engross sabermetricians, both professional and amateur, for a long time. Nevertheless, it is also true that random variation—luck—won't stop accounting for half of the differences among the performances of baseball teams. A skeptic might wonder about diminishing returns—yet my impression is that analytics approaches have become irreversibly embedded throughout major league operations, recently spreading into physical therapy, and, of course, sales and marketing decisions. Much of today's baseball fandom would regard an analytics-less baseball team at least as critically as an investor would regard a seat-of-the-pants investment advisor.

But why is the analytics of drug discovery so lagging? My impression is that the disappointingly low effectiveness of current CADD methodologies has plunged the entire CADD community—innovators, providers, practitioners, users—into a morose lethargy. Despite humanity's need for better means of discovering therapies, the number of fundamentally new CADD insights or methodologies within the last two decades can be counted on one hand. Quite a sharp contrast with the continuing ferment of baseball analytics! The biggest obstacle to any renewal of CADD innovation—in another vivid and perhaps revealing comparison to baseball analytics—is the meager access that would-be CADD innovators can have to its raw material—biological data. The quantity of biological data behind intellectual property walls may exceed that publicly available by a millionfold.

Nevertheless, improving the effectiveness of drug discovery is surely worth more attention, so I am closing with some notions—hardly challenges, merely musings, though perhaps heretical, around three of drug discovery's conventional wisdoms.

The first conventional wisdom is an extreme caution toward testing in humans, the ethics of which has always seemed arguable to me because the human sufferings that persist invisibly whenever a promising new medicine was too risky or too costly to be pursued, don't seem to be a part of that ethical equation. Until a substance is first tested in humans, its actual therapeutic value is little more than a wishful hope, so surprising results are the norm, usually disappointing ones, although there have also been Viagra and chlorpromazine (the first antipsychotic). Yet, for example, if pharmacokinetic data (absorption, transportation, metabolism, excretion) were to be measured in humans for many more structures, then by applying big data analytics to the results, we might at least make better predictions of which one, among some promising structures, is most likely to reach its intended target. Or what about much earlier efficacy screening in humans, even during discovery? Yes, there are health risks from exposure to a new structure, but with what frequency and intensity? Google couldn't tell me, but it is interesting that organic chemists were once routinely expected to taste every new substance (a practice that revealed LSD). As long as there is informed consent, shouldn't the person who might be tested, rather than a clinician with an organizational reputation to safeguard, be the best judge of whether to participate based on the rewards and risks as she sees them? Yes, there would be abuses if human testing were made easier—but how many more? Doesn't fortune still favor the brave?

The second is a current emphasis, within discovery, on fashionable biologics, usually produced by specially engineered bacteria, rather than traditional small molecules, usually produced by chemists. A "biologic" is simply a special variation of the substances that all living systems are constantly making in great variety—proteins and DNAs and RNAs. The new drugs that are demanding such a notoriously high price per dose are mostly biologics. At least some of this high price arises from the unavoidably much higher cost of turning a biologic into a usable drug compared to the cost for a small molecule. A specific bacterial producer must be engineered, and the resulting biologic must be cleanly separated from the many thousands of very similar bacterial proteins or DNAs or RNAs. The enormous uncertainty about whether these two steps are performed equivalently, or at least as effectively, by another supplier is why "biosimilars" are so controversial. Furthermore, reliable means must be found to protect the biologic from being dismembered before reaching its intended target. In particular, stomachs do this dismembering so very well that biologics are almost never administered orally. Finally, once within a human body, to the immune system, a biologic is just another suspicious stranger, quite likely to produce an allergic response. Traditional small molecules have almost none of these problems. Yes, there are serious diseases for which only biologic treatments have been discovered. But can society afford such unavoidable high prices per dose if large numbers of patients are to be treated? Or, conversely, can such high costs of discovery be afforded for diseases that affect only small numbers of patients? Doesn't the growing controversy that surrounds all drug pricing exacerbate these concerns?

Finally, the CADD geeks' implicit and explicit models of how things work at the molecular, drug-meets-target level are too static. To re-emphasize, at the molecular level everything is constantly wiggling and squirming, colliding with everything else, which implies that, for a drug to effectively interact with one desired target among the tens of thousands of target possibilities, not only must their shapes be complementary, but the rebounds between the interacting drug and target, still bumping into one another, must be minimal in their effects. Put differently, therefore, shouldn't the wigglings and squirmings of drug and target be particularly in sync, or, translated into the language of physics, shouldn't their individual internal vibrational frequencies be especially harmonic? This possibility gets little explicit attention from experts in molecular dynamics, the CADD technology that explicitly considers the nonstatic natures of molecules, with one reason perhaps being that an approximation fundamental to molecular dynamics calculations, parameter transferability, is incompatible with any computational exploration of small variations among relative harmonic frequencies. Yet there is a bit of experimental evidence for this hypothesis in a report that replacing hydrogen with deuterium in a small molecule changes its odor (smell is simply a special instance, probably the most primordial, of drug-meets-target).[1] Might an expert in molecular dynamics calculations put this conjecture to the test by doing thought experiments, comparisons of simulations using isotopically differently parameterized structures?

22 Summing Up

Different people take pleasure or pride or comfort in different activities. A particular activity can become so absorbing to someone that she organizes her life around it. Or an activity can become so respected and widespread that many people find security or approval from its practice, regardless of whether it personally appeals to them. To offer a specific example, building net worth is one of the most commonplace goals today. However, for most people, building net worth, especially that of their employer, is not absorbing in itself but only as a means to some other activity. (Actually, to me building net worth also seems a sort of universal game, one that is more or less intensely and publicly played and scored by almost everyone, which therefore motivates extra effort and results, and one that is certainly less harmful than its historical predecessor, maximizing glory, valor, or honor.)

These thoughts are here as background for why I believe myself to have been so extraordinarily lucky. For almost a half century, one type of activity has been of paramount importance to me—self-expression, creating useful new stuff, mainly by my own efforts. So many factors might have made this activity impossible. Perhaps my favorite medium, computers, might not have become so powerful and accessible. Perhaps, on the one hand, my chosen fields of computer application, baseball and CADD, could not have provided me with a satisfactory income, or, on the other hand, perhaps these fields might have already matured when I entered them, making them resistant to the many innovations that I have had the delights of performing myself. Building new systems has been a lot more satisfying to me than extending and maintaining them, and there have been few historical moments when so much of this sort of activity has been possible. Finally, satisfaction in one's current role can be an entrapment, especially for someone as relatively unambitious and risk averse as I have been, but on several occasions circumstances kicked me out of my nest—not always improving my immediate situation, but generating more adventures to look back on today!

What about other familiar life-centering goals—pursuing wealth, fame, power, or possessions, cultivating domesticity or friendships, devotion to a cause? I've flirted with many of these activities in enough depth to be certain that, for me, "creating new stuff" is far more satisfying. So another way that I have been lucky is that there were never any situations where some responsibility forced me to abandon self-expression. Instead, some circumstances reinforced my own preferred activity.

In many lives there have been moments when some unforeseeable event changed everything. In retrospect, it is hard for me to imagine that any imaginary replay of my life would have completely omitted computers, chemistry, or baseball. But three airline mischances were for me, and for many others, the apocryphal butterfly wing flaps starting a hurricane. At the 1979 Hawaii meeting, there was the interminable wait at baggage reclaim where my relationship with Garland began, then the airline strike that surfaced opportunity for both of us, leveraging the beginnings of Tripos and the creations of Sybyl and CoMFA. And if not for a January 1981 flight cancellation that kept me in San Francisco to impulsively telephone Matt Levine, STATS would never have existed.

The gigantic scale and scope of today's big data activities have long passed by my individual capabilities and pioneering activities. However, my life has been remarkably interesting and productive so far, and I'm at least hoping for its long continuance!

Appendix

Bamberg Mathematical Analysis of Baseball

While batting average remains the time-honored yardstick of a baseball hitter's performance, in today's age of big data, On-base Plus Slugging has surged to become a major competitor. For three reasons: OPS is better—a much more accurate indicator of the teams and players who have tallied more runs and won more games. OPS is comfortable—a simple, intuitive combination of numbers that are already familiar to many fans. OPS is reliable—validated by dozens of statistically based studies that have not yielded anything much better.

However, OPS is not the first such better, comfortable, and reliable measure of batting performance to have been reported. To the best of my knowledge and judgment, that distinction belongs to a high school science project, one of forty finalists in the national Science Talent Search for 1959, but which until very recently was otherwise completely buried. I have reproduced the report describing this forgotten research project here.

"Mathematical Analysis of Batting Performance in the Game of Baseball" by Paul Gustav Bamberg Jr.

ABSTRACT

Data accumulated by playing a commercially available baseball game, in which each player is represented by a carbon disc made from his batting record, was used to devise a new method of evaluating batting records and to prove its accuracy and its superiority to other methods. Other applications of mathematics to baseball were also investigated, and the common method of arranging a batting order was proved mathematically sound.

METHODS OF OBTAINING DATA

Since baseball is a game played by people, the number of variables is very large. For example, some players are noted for hitting better on crucial situations than at other times. Also, a player's past performance does not necessarily indicate his future performance. In order to permit a mathematical approach to the game, a simplified version was used, which is available commercially (All-Star Baseball—Cadaco Ellis). This simplified version stresses batting, the game being designed so that pitching and fielding remain constant. Each player is represented by a disc with the center cut out so that it can be placed under a spinning pointer.

KEY	
1	Home Run
2	Ground out
3	Fly out
4	Fly out
5	Triple
6	Ground out
7	Single
8	Fly out
9	Walk
10	Strike out
11	Double
12	Ground out
13	Single
14	Fly out

The periphery is divided into fourteen spaces, each of which represents a certain batting performance. As examples: In fig. 4, space 1 corresponds to a home run, space 2 corresponds to a ground out, etc. In table 1 (page 000) the size of the spaces is proportional to the performance at bat of that particular player. For instance, if a hypothetical player came to the plate 360 times and made a home run 14 times, fourteen degrees of the circle would be coded to represent a home run. If he made a three-base hit eight times, this would be represented by eight degrees of the circle. Each time a player comes to bat is represented by one spin of the pointer, and his performance is determined by where the pointer stops.

The original game was expanded by making players using baseball record books until about 250 players had been created. In all, about 500 games have been played.

The players were divided into twenty-six teams, each of which consists of two pitchers and one player at each other position. The teams were chosen so that they could all be expected to score the same number of runs over a long period of time, according to the method of evaluation which I shall describe later. Because there were three persons, the teams were grouped into three leagues, the American, National, and International, consisting of from six to nine teams each. In each "season," every team in a league played every other team three or four times. The length of a season ranged from twenty to twenty-four games for each team.

For each game played, a scoresheet was kept (fig. 5). At the end of each season, each player's records on the scoresheets were totaled and entered in a "life-time record book" (fig. 6).

Campanella , Roy

Seas.	T	AB	H	BA	TB	SP	1	2	3	H	RBI	W	R	SB	CS	SO	TV
1N	P;	82	23	.281	36	.439	17	2	1	3	18	22	18	0	0	-	.385
2T	St	79	27	.342	45	.570	19	2	2	4	23	8	17	0	0	-	.460
3N	A	92	26	.283	44	.478	17	4	1	4	16	9	11	0	0	11	.341
		253	76	.300	125	.494	53	8	4	11	57	39	46	0	0	11	.419
Expected - 315		93	.294	172	526	55	15	5	18								430

C_4	0	0	0	1	0	1	0	3	3	8
R	0	0	0	4	0	2	0	0	0	6

		AB	1	2	3	H	RBI	W	R
	Avila	⊥⊥⊥	l						)
	Davis	l/ll	ll					(	l/l
K	Ennis	⊥⊥⊥	l						
	Mathews	ll ll	l	l		l	ll)l l		) l
K	Robinson	ll)				l	ll	l	)
	Hodges	llll	l	)			l		)
	Nieman	lll'	\				)		
	Bartell	l\l'							
K	Gomez	(ll							
	Tobin	l							
K	Higgins	l l	l			l	)l/	(	
	Smith	⊥⊥⊥	)l						l
	Kluszewski	⊥⊥⊥		l			)		)
	Banks	⊥⊥⊥	l			l	(l)		)l
	Keller	l\ll						l	l
K	Clift	ll\(							
K	Goodman	(ll			)			\	
K	Bailey	l lll	(						
	Porterfield	l/lll	l					(	

The conventional method of appraising a player's batting skill is the batting average. This is obtained by dividing the number of hits made by the number of times at bat. But this is unsatisfactory as a measure of overall skill, for it is independent of the types of hits made. For example, one player might make three singles every ten times at bat; another player might make 3 home runs. Although each of these players would have the same batting average, the one who hit all home runs would be the more valuable to his team.

The slugging percentage is another figure used to appraise a player's batting skill. It is obtained by diving the number of times at bat by the number of total bases (one for a single, two for a double, etc.) But this figure is unrealistic because, for example, a double is not worth as much as two singles.

Still another measure of a player's batting skill is the number of runs produced; that is, the sum of the number of runs scored and the number of runs batted in, minus the number of home runs (this last correction is necessary because, for example, a home run with the bases empty would otherwise be counted as 2 runs produced.) But this method, also, is unsatisfactory because factors such as the skill of other players on the team and position in the batting order, as well as batting skill, affect the number of runs produced.

I have devised a new and more accurate figure for appraisal of batting skill which I call "total value." I obtain this figure by adding the number of hits, walks, and total bases and dividing by twice the sum of the number of times and the number of walks. This figure, I have found, gives a very accurate indication of a player's batting skill. Also, the number of "total value points," i.e., hits plus walks plus total bases, is very nearly proportional to the number of runs produced.

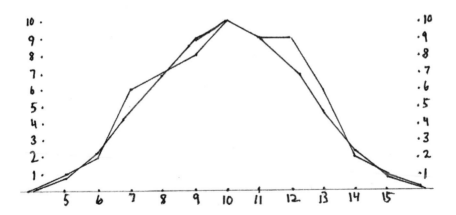

RESULTS OBTAINED FROM EVALUATION OF DATA

Figure 7 is a graphical representation of the number of times a certain number of games out of twenty was won. This is compared with the distribution that is predicted by probability theory if it is assumed that all the teams are equal and therefore each team has one chance in two of winning any given game. The close correlation between the two lines suggests that if a large enough number of games were played, the actual distribution of games won would be the same as that predicted by probability theory. Therefor all the teams must be of equal batting skill. Since they all also have equal total values, it follows that total value is an accurate method of evaluation of batting skill. The fact that the teams are not equal as measured by batting average or slugging percentage indicates that these figures are not as accurate as total value.

Another example also helps show that total value alone gives an accurate indication of the percentage of its games a team will win. Two teams were chosen whose total value was equal to that of the other teams; but one of these teams had a very high team batting average and low team slugging percentage and the other had a low team batting average and high team slugging percentage. It was found that each of these teams won almost exactly half of its games.

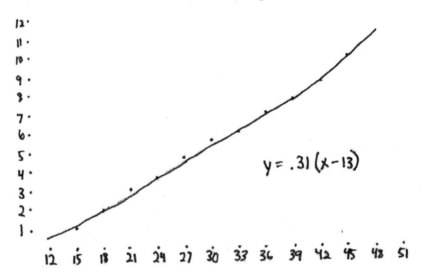

$$y = .31 \, (x - 13)$$

Figure 8 represents the equation derived to show the relation between the number of total value points made by a team in a nine-inning game and the number of runs scored. The median number of runs was determined for each group of three total value points to obtain the points on the graph. For example, the median number of runs per game scored by teams that made 32, 33, or 34 value points was six.

The equation is accurate for values of x from 15 to 42. The standard deviation from the mean number of runs was 1.4 when y=2 and 2.1 when y=7.

The same relationship was also calculated for a full season of 20 or 21 games. It was found that the formula y=.315*(x-13n), where n is the number of games played, x is the number of total value points, and y is the number of runs scored, was the most accurate relationship. The standard deviation of the ratio y/(x-13n) was only +/-.0245.

Table 1 is a comparison of the relationships of hits, total bases, and total value points to runs produced. The figures for the individual players represent the results of three seasons' play. The four players were chosen because they represent four extreme types of players. It can be seen that the number of total value points is more closely related to the number of runs produced than either of the other two sets of figures is.

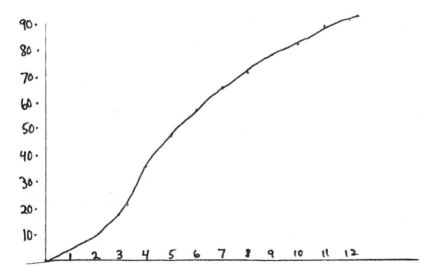

I have also made investigations of other mathematical relationships in baseball. Figure 9 shows the results of one of these graphically. X is the average number of runs scored in a game; y the expected percentage of games won assuming average opposition. It can be seen that the slope of the curve is greatest when y = 40 or 50 per cent. This indicates that an increase in the number of runs scored won in the case of a team that wins about half its games than in the case of a team that wins a very large or very small percentage of its games.

Table 1

Name	RP	H	Pct.	TB	Pct	TVP	Pct
Harvey Kuenn	74	114	0.65	138	.536	263	.335
Joe Medwick	122	113	1.07	179	.681	314	.389
Babe Ruth	132	88	1.50	182	.725	324	.408
Ferris Fain	99	83	1.19	121	.820	278	.359
Mean			1.10		.691		.378
Standard Deviation			.304		.104		.022

Table 2

Pos.	H&W	RS	Pct	TB	RBI	Pct	TVP	RP	Pct
1	760	329	.432	697	142	.204	1457	471	.323
2	697	298	.427	723	186	.257	1420	484	.341
3	743	300	.406	822	321	.390	1566	621	.396
4	705	319	.452	819	349	.426	1524	668	.438
5	664	274	.413	803	337	.421	1467	611	.416
6	572	219	.383	688	275	.400	1260	494	.394
7	517	188	.363	648	272	.418	1165	460	.395
8	448	146	.326	572	237	.414	1020	383	.375

Table 2 shows the effect of the position of a player in the batting order upon the relation between total value and runs produced. The figures were obtained by combining the season totals of 15 first batters, fifteen second batters, etc. . . . In the first column is the position in the batting order. The second column shows the number of times the players reached base, and the third column shows the number of time they scored. The fourth column equals the number of runs scored divided by the number of times on base. Columns 4, 5, and 6 give the same information for total bases, runs batted in, and runs batted in divided by total bases. Column 7 gives the number of total value points and column 8 the sum of the number of runs scored and runs batted in. Column 9 shows he number of runs produced per total value point.

The information contained in this table is useful in arranging a team's batting order. The pitcher always bats ninth, because, as a rule, pitchers are weak hitters and, therefore, are put where they will have to bat the least number of times. Since the fourth batter produces the most runs per total value point, he should be the player with the highest total value. The next two best players should bat in the third and fifth positions, with the one known to get on base more often batting third. The first and second players should have a high ratio of hits plus walks to total bases; the last three batters should have a high ratio of total bases to hits plus walks. This mathematically derived method is the same as the one now used by most managers.

PLANS FOR FUTURE WORK

At the moment the total value concept is bearing quite well. The next step will be an elucidation of the relationship between a pitcher's earned-run average and his won-lost percentage, using techniques similar to the ones described above. Ultimately I hope to introduce the variable of pitching into my game, so that real baseball would be simulated almost perfectly; but, since I have aspirations of becoming a scientist rather than a big league baseball manager, the project will probably die a natural death unless I can influence some of the younger participants in the game to take over.

Sources of Material: *Who's Who in Baseball*, years 1931, 1939, 1949, and 1957. These were consulted only for the statistical information used in the construction of the players.

Notes

Introduction

1. Lewis, *Moneyball*.
2. Schwarz, *Numbers Game*.
3. Thorn and Palmer, *Hidden Game of Baseball*.

2. Baseball and Science Surface

1. Turkin and Thompson, *Official Encyclopedia of Major League Baseball*.

3. College

1. Goldfarb, Mosher, and Patterson, "Online System for Integrated Text Processing."
2. Goldfarb, "SGML."
3. Goldfarb and Prescod, *Charles F. Goldfarb's XML Handbook*.

4. Graduate School and the Computer

1. Cramer, "Mechanism of Nucleophilic Displacement."
2. Lawrence, *Duke Ellington*.
3. Cook, *Percentage Baseball*.

5. Industrial Synthetic Chemist

1. Stanley M. Bloom and Richard D. Cramer, "Novel Photographic Compositions," U.S. Patent 3,615,440 (1971).
2. Corey and Wipke, "Computer-Assisted Design."

6. Harvard's Research Computer

1. Corey, Cramer, and Howe, "Computer-Assisted Synthetic Analysis."

7. Computer-Aided Drug Discovery

1. Free and Wilson, "Mathematical Contribution."

2. Cramer, Redl, and Berkoff, "Substructural Analysis."
3. Cramer et al., "Application of Quantitative Structure-Activity Relationships."

8. Sabermetrics' Infancy

1. Thorn and Palmer, *Total Baseball*.
2. Cramer and Palmer, "Batter's Run Average."
3. Palmer, "On Base Averages."
4. Mills and Mills, *Player Win Averages*.
5. Cramer, "Average Batting Skill."
6. Basco and Davies. "Many Flavors of DIPS."

9. Scientific Recognition

1. Cramer, "'Hydrophobic Interactions.'"
2. Cramer, "BC(DEF) Parameters."
3. Hopfinger, "A QSAR Investigation."
4. Wise et al., "Progress in Three-Dimensional Drug Design."

14. Rebirth of STATS Inc.

1. SeanLahman.com: Baseball, Data, and Storytelling, seanlahman.com.
2. Pierce, *How Bill James Changed Our View*.

15. Comparative Field Analysis

1. Cramer, Patterson, and Bunce, "Comparative Molecular Field Analysis."
2. Hansch and Fujita, "ρ-∂-π Analysis."
3. Ewing, et al., "DOCK 4.0."
4. Cramer et al., "Crossvalidation."
5. Martin et al., "Fast New Approach."
6. Cramer, "Design and Preliminary Results."
7. Richard D. Cramer and Svante B. Wold, "Comparative Molecular Field Analysis," U.S. patent 5,025,388.

16. STATS Soars

1. James, *Bill James Baseball Abstract*, 31.
2. James, Dewan, and Project Scoresheet, *Great American Baseball Stat Book*.
3. Schwarz, *Numbers Game*, 173–74.
4. Wright and House, *Diamond Appraised*.

18. The Rise and Fall of TRPS

1. Cramer et al., "Virtual Libraries."

2. Clark and Cramer, "Taming the Combinatorial Centipede."

3. Cramer et al., "Bioisosterism."

4. Patterson et al., "Neighborhood Behavior."

5. Jilek and Cramer, "Topomers."

6. Cramer et al., "Virtual Libraries."

7. Andrews and Cramer, "Toward General Methods."

8. Cramer et al., "'Lead-Hopping.'"

9. Cramer, "Topomer CoMFA."

10. Cramer et al., "AllChem."

19. *Repudiated by* STATS

1. Schwarz, *Numbers Game*, 193.

20. *Tidying Up*

1. Weininger, "SMILES."

2. Regis, *Info Mesa*.

3. Cramer and Wendt, "Template CoMFA."

4. Cramer, "Template CoMFA Applied to 116 Biological Targets."

5. Cramer, "Template CoMFA Generates Single 3D-QSAR Models."

6. CoMFA template, GitHub, 2016, https://github.com/OpenEye-Contrib/Template_CoMFA.git.

7. Sand River Cohousing, accessed September 25, 2018, www.sandriver.org.

8. Holloszy and Fontana, "Calorie Restriction in Humans."

21. *In My Humble Opinion*

1. Turin, *Secret of Scent*.

Bibliography

Andrews, Katherine M., and Richard D. Cramer. "Toward General Methods of Targeted Library Design: Topomer Shape Similarity Searching with Diverse Structures as Queries." *Journal of Medicinal Chemistry* 43, no. 9 (2000): 1723–40.

Basco, D., and M. Davies. "The Many Flavors of DIPS: A History and an Overview." *Baseball Research Journal* (Fall 2010). Available at https://sabr.org /content/baseball-research-journal-archives.

The Baseball Encyclopedia: The Complete and Definitive Record of Major League Baseball. New York: Macmillan, 1969.

Clark, Robert D., and Richard D. Cramer. "Taming the Combinatorial Centipede." *CHEMTECH* 27 (1997): 24–30.

Cook, Earnshaw. *Percentage Baseball.* Cambridge MA: MIT Press, 1966.

Corey, E. J., and W. Todd Wipke. "Computer-Assisted Design of Complex Organic Syntheses." *Science* 166, no. 3902 (October 1969): 178–92.

Corey, Elias J., Richard D. Cramer, and W. Jeffrey Howe. "Computer-Assisted Synthetic Analysis for Complex Molecules: Methods and Procedures for Machine Generation of Synthetic Intermediates." *Journal of the American Chemical Society* 94, no. 2 (1972): 440–59.

Cramer, Richard D. "Average Batting Skill through Major League History." *Baseball Research Journal* 9 (1980). Available at https://sabr.org/content /baseball-research-journal-archives.

———. "BC(DEF) Parameters, 1: The Intrinsic Dimensionality of Intramolecular Interactions in the Liquid State." *Journal of the American Chemical Society* 102, no. 6 (1980): 1837–49.

———. "Design and Preliminary Results of Leapfrog, a Second Generation De Novo Drug Discovery Tool." *Journal of Molecular Graphics* 11 (1993): 271–82.

———. "Do Clutch Hitters Exist?" *Baseball Research Journal* 6 (1977). Available at https://sabr.org/content/baseball-research-journal-archives.

————. "'Hydrophobic Interactions' and Solvation Energies: Discrepancies between Theory and Experimental Data." *Journal of the American Chemical Society* 99, no. 16 (1977): 5408–12.

————. "The Mechanism of Nucleophilic Displacement for the Triphenyloxonium Cation." PhD dissertation. Massachusetts Institute of Technology, 1967.

————. "Template CoMFA Applied to 116 Biological Targets." *Journal of Chemical Information and Modeling* 54, no. 7 (July 2014): 2147–56.

————. "Template CoMFA Generates Single 3D-QSAR Models that, for Twelve of Twelve Biological Targets, Predict All ChEMBL-Tabulated Affinities." *PLOS One*, June 12, 2015. doi: https://doi.org/10.1371/journal.pone.0129307.

————. "Topomer CoMFA: A Design Methodology for Rapid Lead Optimization." *Journal of Medicinal Chemistry* 46, no. 3 (2003): 374–89.

Cramer, Richard D., Jeffrey D. Bunce, David E. Patterson, and Ildiko E. Frank. "Crossvalidation, Bootstrapping, and Partial Least Squares Compared with Multiple Regression in Conventional QSAR Studies." *Quantitative Structur.- Activity Relationships* 7 (1988): 18–25.

Cramer, Richard D., Robert D. Clark, David E. Patterson, and Allan M. Ferguson. "Bioisosterism as a Molecular Diversity Descriptor: Steric Fields of Single Topomeric Conformers." *Journal of Medicinal Chemistry* 39, no. 16 (1996): 3060–69.

Cramer, Richard D., Robert J. Jilek, Stefan Guessregen, Stefanie. J. Clark, Bernd Wendt, and Robert D. Clark. "'Lead-Hopping': Validation of Topomer Similarity as a Superior Predictor of Similar Biological Activities." *Journal of Medicinal Chemistry* 47, no. 27 (2004): 6777–91.

Cramer, Richard D., and Pete Palmer. "The Batter's Run Average (B.R.A.)." *Baseball Research Journal* 3 (1974). Available at https://sabr.org/content/baseball -research-journal-archives.

Cramer, Richard D., David E. Patterson, and Jeffrey D. Bunce. "Comparative Molecular Field Analysis (CoMFA), 1: Effect of Shape on Binding of Steroids to Carrier Proteins." *Journal of the American Chemical Society* 110, no. 18 (1988): 5959–67.

Cramer, Richard D., David E. Patterson, Robert D. Clark, Farad M. Soltanshahi, and Michael S. Lawless. "Virtual Libraries: A New Approach to Decision Making in Molecular Discovery Research." *Journal of Chemical Information and Computer Science* 38, no. 6 (1998): 1010–23.

Cramer, Richard D., George Redl, and Charles E. Berkoff. "Substructural Analysis: A Novel Approach to the Problem of Drug Design." *Journal of Medicinal Chemistry* 17, no. 5 (1974): 533–35.

Cramer, Richard D., Kenneth M. Snader, Chester R. Willis, Larry W. Chakrin, Jean Thomas, and Blaine M. Sutton. "Application of Quantitative Structure-

Activity Relationships in the Development of the Antiallergic Pyranenamines." *Journal of Medicinal Chemistry* 22, no. 6 (June 1979): 714–25.

Cramer, Richard D., Farad M. Soltanshahi, Robert J. Jilek, and Brian Campbell. "AllChem: Generating and Searching 10E20 Synthetically Accessible Structures." *Journal of Computer-Aided Molecular Design* 21, no. 6 (2007): 341–50.

Cramer, Richard D., and Bernd Wendt. "Template CoMFA: The 3D-QSAR Grail?" *Journal of. Chemical Information and Computer Science* 54, no. 2 (2014): 660–71.

Ehrlich, Paul R. *The Population Bomb*. Cutchogue NY: Buccaneer Books, 1971.

Ewing, Todd J. A., Shingo Makino, A. Geoffrey Skillman, and Irwin D. Kuntz. "DOCK 4.0: Search Strategies for Automated Molecular Docking of Flexible Molecule Databases." *Journal of Computer-Aided Molecular Design* 15, no. 5 (2001): 411–28.

Free, Spencer M., and James W. Wilson. "A Mathematical Contribution to Structure-Activity Studies." *Journal of Medicinal Chemistry* 7, no. 4 (July 1964): 395–99.

Goldfarb, Charles F. "SGML: The Reason Why and the First Published Hint." *Journal of the American Society for Information Science* 48, no. 7 (July 1997). Available at http://sgmlsource.com/history/jasis.htm.

Goldfarb, Charles F., Edward J. Mosher, and Theodore I. Patterson. "An Online System for Integrated Text Processing." *American Society of Information Science* 7 (October 15, 1970). Available at http://sgmlsource.com/history/jasis .htm (2018).

Goldfarb, Charles F., and Paul Prescod. *Charles F. Goldfarb's XML Handbook*. 5th ed. Upper Saddle River NJ: Prentice-Hall, 2003.

Hansch, Corwin, and Toshio Fujita. "ρ-∂-π Analysis: A Method for the Correlation of Biological Activity and Chemical Structure." *Journal of the American Chemical Society* 86, no. 8 (1964): 1616–26.

Holloszy, John O., and Luigi Fontana. "Calorie Restriction in Humans." *Experimental Gerontology* 42, no. 8 (August 2007): 709–12.

Hopfinger, A. J. "A QSAR Investigation of Dihydrofolate Reductase Inhibition by Baker Triaines Based on Molecular Shape Analysis." *Journal of the American Chemical Society* 102, no. 24 (1980): 7196–7206.

Humphreys, Michael A. *Wizardry: Baseball's All-Time Greatest Fielders Revealed*. New York: Oxford University Press, 2011.

James, Bill. *The Bill James Baseball Abstract 1985*. New York: Ballantine Books, 1986.

James, Bill, John Dewan, and Project Scoresheet. *The Great American Baseball Stat Book*. New York: Ballantine Books, 1986.

Jilek, Robert J., and Richard D. Cramer. "Topomers: A Validated Protocol for their Self-Consistent Generation." *Journal of Chemical Information and Computer Science* 44, no.4 (2008): 1221–27.

Lawrence, Austin H. *Duke Ellington and His World: A Biography.* New York, Routledge, 2002.

Lewis, Michael. *Moneyball: The Art of Winning an Unfair Game.* New York: W. W. Norton, 2003.

Martin, Yvonne C., Mark G. Bures, Elizabeth A. Danaher, Jerry DeLazzer, Isabella Lico, Patricia A. Pavlik. "A Fast New Approach to Pharmacophore Mapping and Its Application to Dopaminergic and Benzodiazepine Agonists." *Journal of Computer-Aided Molecular Design* 7, no. 1 (1993): 83–102.

Meadows, Donella H. *The Limits to Growth: A Report for the Club of Rome's Project on the Predicament of Mankind.* New American Library, 1972.

Mills, Eldon G., and Harlan D. Mills. *Player Win Averages: A Computer Guide to Winning Baseball Players.* Cranbury NJ: A. S. Barnes, 1970.

Palmer, Pete. "On Base Averages for Players." *Baseball Research Journal* 2 (1973).

Patterson, David E., Richard D. Cramer, Allan M. Ferguson, Robert D. Clark, and Laurence E. Weinberger. "Neighborhood Behavior: A Useful Concept for Validation of Molecular Diversity Descriptors." *Journal of Medicinal Chemistry* 39, no. 16 (1996): 3049–59.

Pierce, Gregory F. A., ed. *How Bill James Changed Our View of Baseball.* Skokie IL: ACTA, 2007.

Regis, Edward. *The Info Mesa: Science, Business, and New Age Alchemy on the Santa Fe Plateau.* New York: W. W. Norton, 2003.

Schwarz, Alan. *The Numbers Game: Baseball's Lifelong Fascination with Statistics.* New York: St. Martin's, 2004.

Thorn, John, and Pete Palmer. *The Hidden Game of Baseball: A Revolutionary Approach to Baseball and Its Statistics.* Garden City NY: Doubleday, 1984.

———, eds. *Total Baseball.* New York: Warner Books, 1989.

Turin, Luca. *The Secret of Scent: Adventures in Perfume and the Science of Smell.* New York: Harper Perennial, 2007.

Turkin, Hy, and S. C. Thompson. *The Official Encyclopedia of Major League Baseball.* New York: A. S. Barnes, 1951.

Weininger, David. "SMILES: A Chemical Language and Information System, 1: Introduction to Methodology and Encoding Rules." *Journal of Chemical Information and Computer Science* 28, no. 1 (February 1988): 31–36.

Wise, Margaret, Richard D. Cramer, Dennis Smith, and I. Exman. "Progress in Three-Dimensional Drug Design: The Use of Real Time Colour Graphics and Computer Postulation of Bioactive Molecules in DYLOMMS." In *Quantitative Approaches to Drug Design,* edited by John C. Dearden, 145–46. Amsterdam: Elsevier, 1983.

Wright, Craig R., and Tom House. *The Diamond Appraised.* New York: Simon and Schuster, 1989.

Index